美国社区报实操指南

无以复加的当地化

Community Journalism Relentlessly Local

（美）赵克（Jock Lauterer） 陈凯 著

南方日报出版社
NANFANG DAILY PRESS
中国·广州

图书在版编目（CIP）数据

美国社区报实操指南 ：无以复加的当地化 / (美)赵克，陈凯著. — 广州 ：南方日报出版社，2014.6
ISBN 978-7-5491-1060-5

Ⅰ. ①美… Ⅱ. ①赵… ②陈… Ⅲ. ①社区－新闻报道－美国－指南 Ⅳ. ①G219.712-62

中国版本图书馆 CIP 数据核字(2014)第 097743 号

MEIGUO SHEQU BAO SHICAO ZHINAN

美国社区报实操指南：无以复加的当地化　[美]赵克　陈凯　著

出版发行：南方日报出版社
地　　址：广州市广州大道中 289 号
电　　话：（020）83000503
经　　销：全国新华书店
印　　刷：广州市怡升印刷有限公司
开　　本：787 mm×1092 mm　1/16
印　　张：18
字　　数：325 千字
版　　次：2014 年 6 月第 1 版
印　　次：2014 年 6 月第 1 次印刷
定　　价：45.00 元

投稿热线：（020）83000503　读者热线：（020）83000502

网址：http://www.nfdailypress.com/index.html

目录

Contents

自序一

当一个国家的人对于“社区”一词的定义与美国人的理解截然不同时，他该如何开始阅读一本关于“社区新闻”的书？更何况这个国家连“新闻”一词都有众多不同的内涵？

对美国人而言，“社区”是一个积极的、具有包容性的、易于理解的词，它被用以形容一个物理空间、族裔化地方或意识形态场域（地域或网络上）。在这里，人们为促进共同生活的改善而和睦聚居。如果冲突、问题或议题在这里出现时，社区成员都知道：妥协是交往的核心，是社区前行的推动力。

对美国人而言，开国宪法使“新闻”一词变得神圣而不可侵犯。想象一下：他们要白手起家成立一个新国家！所以美国开国元勋聚在一起，一致认同“新闻”（即报纸）对于一个新共和政体的运转和维持是如此重要，以至于需要制定一部不可撤销的法律，规定政府从今往后永不能干涉报纸！

因此，在美国，“社区新闻”这个词汇被用以形容一种重要而独特的新闻形式，其目的不仅是告知新闻，而且更是为民众服务。而“服务社区”这一点是非常重要的。

事实上，如果对美国社区报的愿景存在一种共识，那么它会是如下内容：“优秀的社区媒体有助于优秀社区的建立、培养和维护。”

FOREWORD

How does one begin a book about Community Journalism for a nation whose definition of the word "community" is so different from the American meaning? And for whom even the word "journalism", has vastly different connotations?

To Americans, the word "Community" is a positive, inclusive, accessible term describing a physical, ethnic or ideological place (geographic or on the Web) where people agree to gather in peace and harmony for their mutual betterment. And where, when conflict, problems or issues arise within that community, that the members realize that compromise is the soul of diplomacy, the way forward.

To Americans, the word "Journalism" is a word enshrined in our founding Constitution. Just imagine: a start-up that happens to be a new nation! And that the creators of that start-up nation sit down together and decide that "the press" (newspapers) is so important to the functioning and maintenance of that new republic that they write an irrevocable law that says that government must henceforth never tamper with newspapers!

Thus, the term "community journalism" is used in the U.S. to describe an important and distinct form of journalism, whose purpose is not just to tell the news but also to serve. And this is very important: To serve the community.

In fact, if here was a commonly agreed upon Vision Statement for U.S. community newspapers, it would be this: "Great community media help build, nurture and sustain great communities."

自序二

敬爱的中国读者：

在我的国家，初出茅庐的记者接受的教育是——写每一个故事时，必须写明五个基本问题：

谁（Who）？什么事（What）？哪里（Where）？什么时候（When）？为什么（Why）？有时候也要回答怎么样（How）。

也许这5个“W”翻译成中文后并不能达意，不过还是让我们试试看。

谁：

先说你，再说我。

这书是为你们——中国新闻学的学生和学者、试图更好地理解美国社区新闻的专业记者，以及那些有兴趣借鉴我们“最佳实践”经验的人——而准备的。

我曾在北京、上海、重庆、合肥和郑州的讨论会上见过“你们”；当我访问新成立的社区周报《郑州晚报•登封金版》时，我见过你们。所以，我知道我在为谁写。

听你们说，你们都想知道如何做好社区新闻。在这点上，我可能有用武之地。

如果你正在阅读这些文字，你肯定和我一样关注新闻事业，可能听说过社区新闻，并为“全球化思维，本土化报道”的理念而激动不已。我也如此。在我的工作岁月中，我一直在身体力行这一理念。

我是位美国学者，教了20多年的社区新闻，曾经拥有并经营自己的社区新闻报长达15年，写过关于社区新闻的教科书，现在它出到第三版，20年来在全美范围内被当成经典教材。

但这并不意味着我在中国就是专家，否则就太狂妄了。正如美国学者费正清在《中国新史》一书中所写道：

“我们的图书馆里堆放着不少撰写者大发其对中国无所不知之论，却对自己无知之程度茫然的作品。殊不知，我等知晓得越多，愚昧无知的边缘也就越大。”

什么：

为了让这本书发挥作用，它应该像一位亲切的、值得信赖的、年长的朋友；像一个可以为你雪中送炭的人；像那些当你寻求灵感，当你准备从他人的经验中学习新东西的时候，能及时为你提供帮助的人；像那些走在你前方的人；像一位仁慈但不加道德评判的导师。

我希望本书能体现社区报的精髓：为读者服务，让生活更美好；当你热情报道本地新闻时，能提升你对本地报道内在价值的理解和欣赏；能让你在这漫长的事业征途中保持一份高涨的情绪。

正如老子所言：“千里之行，始于足下。”

所以，让我们无所畏惧地迈出第一步。

哪里：

美国有句习语：“将经历的点串起来。”它的意思是，把那些看似遥远实则相关的事实紧密地联系起来。两位学者因为共同的专业目的，已在北京和教堂山两地间构建起连接纽带，形成了合作伙伴关系，成立了一个工作组。我们在各自的地区开展有关社区新闻的研究越多，就会发现我们之间的联结越紧密。美国的社区新闻报道已有很长历史，其专业水准达到相当高度，对于社区新闻发展尚未成熟的中国来说，可能可以当作一个标尺。

什么时候：

中国新一届领导人的上任标志着中国对前瞻性思考做好了准备，中国媒体行业也渐渐意识到社区新闻给社会和市场带来的契机。我们认为现在是地方媒体大力发展的好时机，应当抓住这一历史机遇。如美国总统所说：“是的，我们可以！（Yes，we can！）”在美国，当许多大都市日报在2008年经济大萧条时期遭遇重创时，小报纸——特别是高度地方化周报——比那些大城市的难兄难弟们的表现好得多。社区报不仅挺过了这些艰难时期，在许多情况下，它们更在繁荣地发展。凭借其在经济危机中的抗风险能力，以及对新社交媒体环境的灵活适应，社区报重新获得了全美新闻界的尊重和重视。

最后的结论是：社区报提供给当地读者在别处无法获得的服务和内容——那

就是：经验丰富、内容真实、值得信赖的社区报无以复加地对与人们生活息息相关的事件进行报道。作为重要的社区机构，社区报与公民保持零距离，注重报道准确性并敢于承担责任。

为什么：

为什么中国需要社区报？中国确实需要啊！13亿人口，约占了世界人口总数的20%，中国需要社区媒体。至少，以我们的愚见是如此。

我从美国前国务卿亨利•基辛格和玛德琳•奥尔布赖特两位深入研究中国问题的智者身上汲取到灵感。

“中国有自己的发展方式，”奥尔布赖特说道，“……大到无法被忽视，太压抑以至于很难接受（新事物），难以被影响，而且非常非常自傲。”

每个中国学者都应该读读基辛格博士于2011年推出的《论中国》一书。他总结出：“中美……需要对方……因为两者都太大而难以被控制，太过特别而难以被转变，以及太需要对方而难以采取孤立态度……尽管这样，能实现共同的目标吗……谈到哪里为止？”

在这里，我要提醒的是，其实我们有一个“共同目标”，即我们都在寻求构建一个和谐社会……实现这一目标要靠普通百姓接受教育后积极投身社会建设。为了和谐社会的到来，人民必须成为“公民”。也就是说，人民回报社区的责任感需要被唤醒，只有大家都不求任何回报地为社区付出，一个健康的社会才能到来。随着中国人接受自己的“公民”角色，至关重要的是普通民众会逐步意识到自己对社会应该具有影响力，其前提是被告知实情。我们相信，一个强大的本地媒体是通过构建共识完成“社区建设”任务的核心力量。一个知情的社会可以在不受干扰、没有烦恼的情况下，做出明智和善良的抉择。当人们醉心于自己的角色，积极参与到村庄、城镇、都市、公寓住所等所在地的公共事务中时，他们会体会到自身价值，从而收获社会资本，就像有钱一样富有。一位深入介入公共事务的本地公民在家人和同事之外往往拥有丰富的人脉关系，扩展个人“社会资本”需要信息充分流动的社会的支撑，这正是当地媒体和社区新闻的用武之地。中国社会更加和谐，世界也将更加和睦。这样一个大图景，难道不够令人激动吗？

怎么样：

这本书旨在为你的旅行之路提供向导，或成为你沿途的参考，或是当一个能为他人提供帮助的朋友。可能下面这个比喻更为形象：如同在中国圆形宴会桌前，一道又一道的菜在你面前转过，作为用餐者，尽可以挑选自己喜欢的菜肴，不动自己不感兴趣的。厨师无法做到让你尝遍所有菜肴，我们也是。我们不曾想过书里提及的每样东西都能让你高兴，然而，我们仍热切希望，我们的智慧盛宴能给你带来食物和灵魂上的满足。

至于“甜点”，是由一位来自美国的拥有三重身份——报刊所有者、编辑兼发行人——的独立报人所准备。

当我请我亲爱的朋友肯•里普利帮忙写点特别的东西来介绍这本书时，他上了这么一道“菜”。

好好享用吧！

PREFACE

Dear Esteemed Chinese Reader,

In my country, fledgling journalists are taught that for every story they write, they must answer five basic questions.

Who? What? Where? When? Why? And sometimes How?

Those "Five W's" may not translate very well into Chinese, but let us try!

WHO:

You first; then me.

This book has been created for you — the Chinese journalism students and scholars, the Chinese professional journalists seeking to better understand community journalism in the American context and for those who may be interested in borrowing our "best practices."

I met "you" at workshops in Beijing, Shanghai, Chongqing, Hefei, and Zhengzhou; I met you when I visited the start-up weekly community newspaper, the *Deng Feng Golden Edition*. So I know for whom I am writing.

And the thing I heard you saying was: you all wanted to know how to make a success out of community journalism. Maybe I can be of use.

If you are reading this, then you must care about journalism as I do. Perhaps you've heard about community journalism and are excited about the notion/concept of "thinking globally, reporting locally". Me too. I've done this all my working life.

I am an American scholar who has taught community journalism for over 20 years, owned and run by own community newspapers for 15 years, and wrote the community journalism textbook, now in its third edition, which has served as the American classic text on the subject for almost 20 years.

But all that in no way makes me an expert on China. That would be presumptuous. For as American scholar John King Fairbank writes in *China: a New History*.

"Our libraries are littered with the pronouncements of writers who knew all about China but could not see how much they did not know. The expansion of our knowledge has expanded the circumference of our ignorance."

WHAT:

For this book to be useful, it should be like a dear trusted elder friend, someone who you can turn to in times of need, when you seek inspiration, and when you are ready to learn something new from another's experience-someone who has gone before you, a benevolent mentor who offers help without judgment.

So I intend for this book to serve, much as community newspapers should serve, to make life better, to elevate your understanding of and appreciation for the inherent values of intensely local reporting, and to keep your spirits from failing over the course of your long march.

As Lao Tzu said, "A journey of a thousand miles begins under one's feet."

So let us take that first step, fearlessly.

WHERE:

In the U.S., we have an expression: "Connect the dots." It means making a significant correlation between seemingly distant but related facts. We scholars have formed a partnership, a working group with the bond of mutual professional purpose that "connect the dots" between Beijing and Chapel Hill. The more we conduct research on community journalism in our respective physical areas, the more we find that we are connected. Community journalism, which is well established historically and professionally, might serve as an example for China, where community journalism is not so mature.

WHEN:

With a new president signaling China's readiness for forward thinking, and with the Chinese media industry awakening to the social and market possibilities of community journalism, think that now is the right time for local media to blossom, to seize this moment in history. In the words of the American president: "Yes, we can!" For in the U.S., where big city metro dailies suffered mightily at the hands of the 2008 Great Recession, smaller papers — particularly all-local weeklies — weathered the Great Recession far better than their big-city cousins. And in spite of these tough times, community papers aren't just surviving-in many cases they're thriving. Their ability to survive the economic tempest, along with their nimble adaptation to the new social media scene, has gained community newspapers new national respect and attention.

Here is the bottom line: Community newspapers provide a service and content local readers can find no where else: relentlessly local reporting on matters immediately relevant to their lives — coming from a tried and true and trusted community institution that is accessible, accurate and accountable.

WHY:

Why China? Why China indeed! With 1.3 billion people and nearly 20 percent of the world's population, China needs community media. At least in our humble opinion.

I draw inspiration from the wisdom of former U.S. Secretaries of State Henry Kissinger and Madeleine Albright, both of whom studied China extensively.

"China is in its own category," Albright says, "…too big to ignore, too repressive to embrace, difficult to influence, and very very proud."

Dr. Kissinger, whose 2011 book, *On China* should be required reading for every China scholar, concludes, "The U.S. and China… need each other… because both are too large to be dominated, too special to be transformed, and too necessary to each other to afford isolation…Beyond that, are common purposes attainable…? And to what end? "

Here's a "common purpose" I propose we all agree upon. That we all seek a harmonious society…and that reaching that goal is dependent upon ordinary people becoming educated, and then embracing their role of constructive engagement. For that to occur, people must become "citizens". That is, people must awaken to their own responsibility to give back to a healthy society, to "pay it forward". As the Chinese people embrace their role as citizens, we propose that it is crucial that ordinary people realize their own impact and importance in society. To be informed is to be effective. We believe that a strong local media is central to this task of "community building" through consensus building. An informed society can make wise and compassionate choices without disturbance or upset. When people "buy in" to their roles as active participants in the maintenance of their places (villages, towns, cities, apartment towers) then they feel of worth, and thus gain social capital, not unlike being rich with money. An engaged local citizen is rich with relationships outside his or her family and place of work. Such "social capital" requires an informed society. That's where the local media, and community journalism comes in. And the more harmonious China's society is, the more harmonious the world is. How's that for the big picture?

HOW:

So this book aims to serve as a guide along the road you will travel, a source along the way, one friend reaching out to help another. Perhaps a more useful metaphor is that of the circular Chinese banquet table, upon which multiple dishes arrive, one after another, over time, rotating past you on the round dinner table. You, the diner, pick what you like, and ignore what you do not prefer. The cook does not make you eat it all; and neither do we propose that everything between these pages will delight you. Yet it is our fervent hope that our intellectual feast will give you sustenance and satisfy your soul.

For "dessert" we have the following "dish", prepared by an independent owner-editor-publisher from the U.S..

When I asked my dear friend Ken Ripley to write something special to help introduce this book, this is what he "served up".

Enjoy!

致中国记者的一封信

亲爱的中国朋友们——我一般都这么看待同行记者，不管他是来自哪个国家——你们正在阅读赵克撰写的关于社区新闻的书，这让我很激动。作为他众多多年老友中的一位，也作为一名在小乡镇从事了38年周报编辑和发行的工作者，我知道你从本书阅读中获得了一种改变并充实你的记者生涯的力量。更让人激动的是，好的社区新闻有一股震撼人心的力量，它能改变并充实你所服务的对象。

新闻工作可成为谋生的好出路，我们当然希望在经济上能获得成功。但是，就我所知，世界范围内大部分记者至少因为以下两条原因从事这一行：一是对周遭人和事的极大好奇和兴趣，并为能分享他们的故事而引以为豪；二是源自我们内心不时的热情的期盼，希望自己的行动能为自己所服务的社区做出贡献。社区新闻工作同时满足这两点要求。

当然，一则好的突发新闻报道总能让人激动。每个作家看到成千上万的读者在阅读由他署名的故事作品时，都会狂喜不已。得新闻奖委实不错，但是我至今印象最深刻的是，在做完礼拜后，一位自豪的父亲羞怯地靠向我，让我在报纸上报道他儿子取得的体育成就；那位带着结婚告示和照片走进来的快乐新娘；那封写给编辑，感谢编辑帮助他的家人和一位失散多年的兄弟重新团聚的信；那众多带着一条大鱼、一个大西红柿或一头刚猎获的鹿走进办公室，让我“为了报纸”拍下他们照片的读者。我拥有一份名为《春泉希望行动报》的报纸，但实际上这份报纸的所有人是整个社区。

大都市日报和小乡镇周报本质上做的是相同的工作——报道，撰写，倡导，在其所选择的社区中扮演一个积极的角色。但是多年以来，众多大报花费如此多时间在“大局”上，以至于他们对日常生活空间的挖掘很小。然而对于读者而言，每日发生的事情常会比一些我们认为的“大新闻”更为重要。垃圾清扫日期的变化、孩子们即将迎来的新老师、为什么城镇的水质糟糕、刚颁布的关于鸡肉规范的法律条文——生活在继续，有好有坏，这些都是不论什么规模的优秀社区报都会去报道的题材。因为我们中的大部分人生活在所报道的社区中，我们同读者一起大笑或哭泣，自豪或难堪，遭遇不幸或庆贺喜事。如赵克所说，我们倡导“无以复加的本地化”。

在我的国家，一份报纸也是一个社区机构，它让人们有向心力并提供重要的领导力。通过新闻和社论，我们塑造舆论，影响行动。我的报纸已成为建设镇图书馆和公园的力量、推广政府的良好做法并揭露其不良行径的平台、学校和孩子们的坚强后盾、鼓励企业发展和产业化的推手，以及保护本地环境的中流砥柱。我相信我的报纸在春泉镇起到了积极的影响。好的社区新闻有助于促进美好社区的建设。

如你所知，近些年来众多事物在发生变化，技术在发展，商业模式在改变，互联网让更多方式的交流成为可能。甚至连我这小镇上的小报都有网络版和Facebook主页。

但是有件大事从未改变，我也希望它永不变化——不论社区规模大小，我们的使命都是帮助它正视自己的现状以及可能的未来，成为代表全体社区居民利益的一股积极力量，以及成为一个真实信息的流通渠道和开放的讨论平台。不管拥有什么样的政府，在这里，关心的人可以决定自己的事务，在社区中行使公民义务。

不论是在大都市、小城镇还是网络上，当你开始或继续从事你所选择的新闻行业，我都希望你会热爱所做的工作。如果你喜欢所服务的人，美好的事情就会在未来等着你。你可能不会挣很多钱，但你会在其他方面变得非常富有。

送上来自美国北卡罗来纳州春泉镇的最美好的祝愿！

里普利

《春泉希望行动报》编辑兼发行人

A LETTER TO THE CHINESE JOURNALIST

Dear Chinese friends — for that is how I view all fellow journalists, no matter what country — I am excited that you are reading this book by Jock Lauterer on community journalism. As one of his many friends for years, and as a weekly newspaper editor and publisher for 38 years in a small rural town, I know that what you will read in these pages has the power to transform and enrich your journalism career. Even more exciting, good community journalism has the awesome power to transform and enrich the people you serve.

Journalism can be a good way to make a living, and of course we want our businesses to be financially successful. But most journalists I have known, worldwide, have become journalists for at least two other reasons. One is a tremendous curiosity and interest in the people and events around them, and pride in sharing their stories. The second is an inner and sometimes passionate desire to make a difference in the communities we serve through what we do. Community journalism satisfies both.

A good breaking news story is always exciting, sure. Every writer is thrilled to see his or her byline on a major story that thousands of people read. Press awards are nice. But what I remember most now is the proud father who shyly approached me after church to ask that I put a report about his son's sports accomplishment in the paper. The happy bride who came in with her wedding announcements and picture. The letter to the editor that reunited a long-lost brother with his family. Many readers who came into the office with a huge fish, a giant tomato, or a freshly killed deer so I could take their pictures “for the paper”. I own the *Spring Hope Enterprise*, but my newspaper really belongs to my community.

The big city daily newspaper and the little rural weekly newspaper are essentially doing the same thing — reporting on, writing about, advocating for, taking active roles in their chosen communities. But over the years many large newspapers spent so much time looking at “the big picture” that they found little room for everyday life. And yet the everyday things that happen are often more important to readers than some stories we consider big news. A change in days their garbage is collected; the new teacher their child is going to have; why their town water tastes bad; a new town law regulating chickens — life happens, good times and bad, and this is what good community newspapers of all sizes try to cover. And because most of us live within the communities we cover, we laugh or cry, feel pride or embarrassment, suffer or celebrate along with our readers. We are, as Jock says, relentlessly local.

In my country, a newspaper is also a community institution that helps bring people together as well as offering important leadership. Through news and editorials, we shape opinions and influence actions. My newspaper has been a vital force behind building our town library and park, promoting good government practices and exposing bad ones, supporting the schools and the children, encouraging business growth and industry, and protecting the local environment. My community newspaper, I believe, has made a positive difference in Spring Hope. Good community journalism helps foster good communities.

As you know, so much has changed in recent years. The technology. The business model. The expanded means of communication made possible through the Internet. Even my small newspaper in a small town has a website and Facebook page.

But one big thing has not changed and I hope never changes — our mission is to help our community, whatever size it may be, to see itself as it is and as it can be; to be a positive force for good on behalf of all its people; and to be a channel of honest information and open discussion through which caring people can determine their own affairs and the civic life of their community no matter what kind of government they have.

As you begin, or continue, to practice your chosen journalism profession — big city, little town, Internet blog — I hope you will love what you're doing, and, if you love the people you serve, great things will be ahead in your future. You may or may not make much money, but you will be rich in all the ways that count.

Best wishes from Spring Hope, North Carolina, U.S.A.

Ken Ripley
Editor-Publisher
Spring Hope Enterprise

导读

敬爱的中国读者：

在你一头扎进这本书之前，先让这初章带你“一睹为快”，窥视接下来的章节将会是什么内容。

“一图顶万言。”

所以，我以一张照片开始，这是我家乡——美国东海岸的北卡罗来纳州——的一张地图。

这份州地图上的每一个大头钉代表一个我曾去做过社区新闻培训的拥有社区报纸的城镇。我所在的州至少有190份社区报，这个数字是全美50个州的平均数。正如你在照片里看到的那样，那些“小报”随处可见！

在美国，“小报”指发行量不超过5万份的报纸,大约有7202份。令人惊讶的事实是，在美国仅有165份主流大城市日报。

相对于165份大报，小报数量高达7202份。

还有几个更惊人的统计数据：在美国7367份报纸中，“小报”占了7202份……包括88%的日报（读者达到1620万），加上5970份周刊（读者高达4420万），还有962份其他类报纸（读者数量达到3580万）。

结果是社区报拥有9620万读者，发行量是165份大报的三倍有余。

我曾给陈凯教授于2012年出版的《走进美国社区报》一书写了篇序言，请允许我摘录其中一段：

> 当我告诉学生们，美国97%的报纸都是小型报纸时，他们无一例外地大吃一惊，有些人则坦率地质疑这个说法。和多数美国人一样，他们倾向于认为那些都市摩天大楼顶层的宽敞办公室里生产出来的“大城市新闻日报”把持着美国的报业主流。
>
> 或许中国的读者也持有这种过分简化的概念，但你将会读到，在美国，没有什么事实比这个离真相更远。

我们的开始：乡村周刊

无疑，你知道，美国是一个非常年轻的国家。比起拥有5000年历史文化的中国，我们这个只有200多年历史的国家的确就像个婴儿！但是，也正由于“新”才衍生出新的媒体形式。请记住，在17世纪，欧洲殖民者发现这片土地时，这里还是一个广袤的原野。随着从沿海到内陆的一步步探索和开拓，小型农场和集镇陆续涌现。这些“新兴地带”像新业务：需要领头羊。社区领导者通常认为，一份当地的社区报是不可或缺的重要机构或设施。

怀俄明州的科迪镇是一个完美的典范！传说中的牛仔“水牛比尔”科迪在19世纪创建这个城镇时宣称：他的新镇上第一批建成的场所会是一所学校、一座旅馆、一间酒吧和一家报纸！直到今天，“水牛比尔”的报纸《科迪进取报》仍兴旺发展。

不少这些所谓的“乡村周刊”创办于19世纪，再发展、成长、买卖、合并、悄然演化，没有进入大城市媒体和主流新闻学者的视野，直到20世纪50年代后期，一本有着巨大影响的书籍的出现才改变了这一局面。前乡村周刊编辑兼出版人出身的大学教授肯•拜尔利20世纪60年代著成《社区新闻》一书，改变了我们对于所谓的“乡村周刊”的思考方式。拜尔利是第一个将“乡村”一词删除并以“社区”取而代之的作家和学者。他以此区分和归纳了新闻的风格，将“社区新闻”和“大城市新闻”从理念、风格和做法上完全区分开来。拜尔利也率先看到并提出，将“社区意识”作为报纸存在的理由——这对报纸的核心使命而言至关重要。从20世纪60年代到90年代再到2001年，美国社区报一直在不断增加、成长、繁荣和兴盛。“9·11”事件以及随后的经济衰退使得这一发展趋势有所减缓。但是，即使处于经济低迷时期，社区报的表现也远远好过大城市媒体兄弟们。

现在看来，新世纪来临后，社区新闻再次焕发生机。具有讽刺意味的是，主要城市日报的缓慢消亡换来了人们重新对本地事物的尊重及渴望。因此，我们有这么一种说法：“老即是新。”在美国媒体行业和学术界，社区新闻现在已经受到了广泛的认同和尊重。

沃伦•巴菲特之所知

近几个月来，美国最富有的、最受人尊敬的、具有前瞻性思维的商人之一——沃伦•巴菲特收购了数十家小地方报纸。他和他的伯克希尔•哈撒韦公司正在改变美国媒体版图，让那些早早宣称美国报纸将要入古、只留下辉煌过后遗迹的愤世嫉俗的媒体评论员们目瞪口呆。

引述沃伦•巴菲特的原话：“在社区意识强烈的城镇地区，没有比当地报纸更为重要的机构。”

沃伦•巴菲特知道哪些媒体评论员所不知道的东西？美国每一位成功的社区报人都深知哪些事儿？这些，都是这本书所要讲述的。

先明确定义

首先，让我们就一些美国语境下的定义达成共识。这样的话，作为中国读者的你就可以理解美国的大背景，以便更好地构建一个有中国特色的办报模式。

新闻平衡，用来描述本地和非本地报道比例的一个术语。《纽约时报》的内容偏重于州、国内和国际新闻，而大城市之外的一份小周报很有可能大部分是本地新闻。

本地优先，指报纸的领导们都有一个明确的政策，即在报道中，报纸覆盖区域内的事情比其他区域的事情更为重要。“新闻平衡”这一术语用来描述本地和非本地新闻两者之间的议程设置。“本地优先”则意味着本地故事在社区报中总能获得最佳版面和重视。例如，只有当总统参访你的城镇时，你的社区报才会报道他或她。不然，你的报纸便属于冒险和那些规模更大、新闻发布速度更快的媒体进行竞争。

社区报，一份有着明确“本地优先”新闻指导原则的报纸，发行量不超过5万份，包括周刊和小型日报。

周报，每周发行一期的报纸。在美国，周报通常在星期三发行，一直这么做的原因是配合杂货店（或超市）对其周末特价促销的宣传。注意：在美国，每周发行两三期的报纸也被称为“周报”。一周发行两期的周刊，也被称为“半周刊（semi-weeklies）”，通常在星期二和星期四发行。一周发行三期的报纸，称为“三周刊（tri-weekly）”，可能在星期二、星期四和星期日发行。

社区日报，是一份发行量低于5万份，每周至少有5天进行“本地新闻”优先报道的报纸。许多社区日报星期二至星期日发行，这并不稀奇。星期一停刊是因为这天本地广告最不给力。

注意：在美国，按照传统，阅读量最大以及广告量最多的日子是星期日。人们认为这一天读者会花更多时间来看报纸。此外，美国的日报通常只在人们更想看新闻的早晨发行。

新媒体。当使用“新媒体”这一称谓时，我们指大致从20世纪90年代中期开始，与数字革命以及互联网的引进同时发展的所有的技术形式。

付费/免费，传统上，在美国，任何时期的报纸都是“付费”的。也就是说，读者掏钱订阅报纸（这里的费用可能包括也可能不包括该报纸网页的全部浏览权限）。读者可以选择送报上门，也可以在镇上的报箱或超市报“架”投币购买。然而，这些单独的“销售架”不向消费者提供访问网页的权限，所以还是鼓励读者提前订阅。

但是，近些年出现的报纸，特别是近20年内推出的周刊，是一种典型的“免费”报纸。也就是说，他们大量赠送（不论是通过“报纸架”还是送报上门的方式），旨在让当地广告商相信报纸在当地家庭中的高覆盖率。这种发行方式用一个术语来形容，即“全市场覆盖”。它的成本非常高昂，因此有风险。然而，为了在一个已成熟的媒体市场占得一席之地，它可能是唯一可行的商业计划。

“是否要读者支付报纸网络版阅读费”是目前美国出版商的一大挑战。由于网络上的信息历来是免费的，美国读者还不习惯付费浏览新闻内容。然而，大出版商和小出版商都正在意识到新闻内容的生产成本很高。为了支付这些成本，许多出版商正设立“付费墙”——一种网络订阅业务模式。截至此书出版之日，这一计划能否在美国推行还不明朗，因为众多用户和读者对为曾经免费的东西付钱感到反感。

鲜明的界限

社区周报和社区日报的重要差异在于：周报每一页都可以用来报道由员工或社区读者提供的本地内容，但日报则不可以。

因为日报有着巨大的待填充的版面，所以想在整份日报上只报道本地新闻几乎是不可能的。

因此，社区日报有部分版面需要依靠非本地新闻来填充——通常来自通讯社，如美联社、路透社等。

于是问题就产生了：这些新闻源通过广播和网络以在线形式发布州、国内和国际新闻，其发布速度是任何一家印刷报纸所不能企及的。报道非本地新闻无疑是将报纸直接置于和这些新闻源的面对面竞争中，而且，使社区报显得重要和独特的“本地优先”新闻也被这些非本地化报道稀释了。

结论：在未来，周刊会凭借其高度地方化报道的定位获得成功，然而准备成为真正社区报的日报必须格外努力，要在本地记者身上加大投入，从而实现本地新闻优先报道原则。可以理解的是，许多小型日报的出版人，尤其是那些以利润为第一追求的媒体公司，将面临不少的挑战。

社区报为什么会成功?

正如你在接下来的章节里会欣赏到的那样，在美国2008年经济大萧条时期，和大城市媒体相比，社区报更顺利地度过了这一危机。为什么会这样？答案涉及到我们对社区报作为一种传统、专业和独立新闻训练的核心理解。接下来先快速理解这些概念：

接近性和便利性

社区报的记者凭借接近性能和读者更好地打交道。你在社区报工作的话，你会住在那个社区，每个人都认识你。编辑部的大门是敞开着的，读者可以畅通无阻地走进来与记者、编辑甚至所有人直接交谈，尤其是一些特别小型的社区报根本没有安保系统，只需开门即可入内。这些开放的举措有利于在公众心中培养出社区信任感。对于报纸本身，也有利于其养成可靠负责的态度。

这些积极的态度合成的结果可用一句话来说明：我们永远不会错的答案是对读者说“是的，可以”。

本地新闻优先报道

当本地报纸将本地新闻置于首位时，它在向社区释放一个信息：你是重要的！对小地方来说，这种肯定与他们收到的大城市媒体的信息完全不同，因为大城市媒体常向小地方的民众传递“你是边缘化的！”这样让人反感的信息。因此，小报通过加强对本地新闻的报道获得茁壮成长也不足为奇。有一份成功的社区报将这种积极的态度总结成一句座右铭：“本地新闻是我们的发展之道。”

社交媒体

尽管社区报规模较小，财政资源较少，但是也有专门的社交媒体网页和新闻编辑部，也有善于使用类似Twitter、Facebook、YouTube等工具以及最新数字技术的工作人员。

服务至关重要

一份报纸必须赢利才能生存。如果报纸所有者的唯一目的是赚钱，报纸就很有可能失败。如果问美国模式要告诉我们什么，那就是，社区报只有将“服务社区”设为主要愿景，它才能茁壮发展。如果报纸能成功地为社区提供服务，那么商业上的成功便会不期而至。

内容独特/小众出版物

除了传统的社区周刊和社区日报，在美国也存在许多种类的社区报，包括面向非洲裔、拉美人、亚洲人以及许多其他族群的报纸，针对同性恋、军事、大学、宗教教育、老人群体、特殊兴趣等类别的小众报纸，服务于高尔夫手、钓鱼爱好者、飞行员、摄影师以及环保爱好者等不同群体的社区报，以及大城市中那些主题为时尚、音乐、艺术和美食文化的小众周刊。

报道覆盖范围

这个术语指统计学上的地理区域，在这个区域范围之内，报纸全面报道本地新闻并刊发启发性的、有趣的特写。在美国语境中，报道范围常和报纸广告人员服务地区相一致。很显然，报道范围的大小与新闻和广告所涉及的地域的大小有直接联系。因此，如果和一份覆盖五个行政区七所学校的地区性报纸相比，报道范围较小（发行量较低）的周报对所在区域的报道显然可以更透彻，更深入。

所有权

在美国历史上，报纸几乎完全由个人或家族掌控。今天，美国社区报所有者的来源各异，有个人、家族、私人公司、小团体以及媒体集团（通常称为“连锁公司”），比如由资深出版人比尔•霍纳三世管理、拥有北卡州《桑福德先驱报》的帕克斯顿传媒集团。虽然许多周刊仍为私人所有，但公司还是掌控着极大比例的社区日报，这一比例还在不断增长。这点很重要，因为许多媒体评论员和学者相信，非本地拥有的报纸会产生“利益至上”的追求，这对报纸整体质量和本地报道都是种危害。不过，过去20年间，我曾前往美国许多州的社区报机构授课。我发现，在富有公民责任感的编辑和出版人的领导下，仍有许多独立经营的优秀周报在赚钱。

社区建设

社区报是美国的心跳。它们几乎存在于每一个村庄、小镇，在许多情况下也存在于城市街区。不论它是缅因州的周刊，还是北卡罗来纳州的半周刊，抑或是加利福尼亚州的小型日报，它们普遍都拥有一个共同的、不言而喻的、超越单纯利益层面的目标：报道地方新闻，服务社区，以树立、培植、增强和鼓励“归属感”等一系列手段建设社区。我们称之为“社区建设”，本地媒体则是这辆“火车”前行的主要动力。

社区报的特点

简而言之，比起主要的都市日报，一份典型的美国社区报由小团体而不是大城市日报创办，发行量不大（不超过5万份），维持本地新闻优先报道的新闻平衡。就周刊而言，不管是印刷版还是网络版，内容都倾向于原创，员工的工作范畴也远非“记者”一职所能概括。

有更多空间要填充的社区日报同样尽可能贯彻“本地优先”原则，尽量使用本报记者报道的本地内容，包括常规的“本地头版”（头版全是本地内容）。尽管比起较大的城市报纸，社区报财政来源偏少，但是不论是社区周刊还是社区日报，都致力于通过“社区建设”来服务社区。至于编辑部的开放程度，周报的大门向公众敞开，日报在这方面可能稍弱一些。

成功的社区报记者的特点

每当我思考“如何成为一名优秀的社区报记者”时，我的脑海里就会出现那些我了解的、与我共事多年的出色的记者的脸庞。如果我能提炼出他们成功的配方，那应该包括如下成分：在社区生活，特别注意多结交他人，在社区报工作之余积极参与社区公共事务，学习并跟上时代和历史潮流——大白话说，就是爱你的社区，并希望它能不断变得更好。（如果你不爱你的城镇或城市，你应该迁往别处！）

社区新闻及其未来

可以很有把握地说，全球新闻行业的未来发展将会进一步集中于本地报道。但它的存在形式——是印刷、网络，还是移动媒体，抑或是三者融合？这点还有待观察。然而，有个不争的事实：目前，通过广告赚取的每1美元中，75%来自印刷媒体，只有25%来自在线网络广告。因此，即使所有的未来学家和学者都在讨论报纸即将消逝，网络必将掌控未来，印刷报纸仍然是赢利的主体部分。可能未来只剩下网络信息，但现在还不现实！所以，美国大小型报纸出版人目前都面临着一个挑战：他们必须为所有人提供所有平台的信息，包括印刷的、网络的和移动媒体的。而这成本很高！

关于“技术”，我们在书中会有更详细的介绍，现在先快速概览：我已观察到几家社区报成功地将新媒体整合到他们的运作中去。北卡州南港镇的《州港领航员》是一份由个人独立拥有的付费周刊，只要读者每年订阅纸质版，他们就免费提供给读者所有网上内容。他们一直按照这一方式去实践，这是他们成功的秘诀。另一个榜样则是北卡州谢尔比的《谢尔比星报》。《谢尔比星报》先在网上发布“原生态”本地新闻内容——这些内容没有经过修订和编辑。这一行为“翻转”了网络内容生产范例。快速发布突发新闻是头等大事，然后再回去编辑完善。显然，这很冒险，多少有些革命性质，也容易引起争议。但是，读者喜欢！另外，《谢尔比星报》也通过Facebook、Twitter和YouTube等社交平台吸引读者，鼓励他们给报社投稿。当然这些投稿不用付稿费。

为什么这些问题很重要

“社区报最重要的工作是向人们说明，让他们知道他们的生活很重要……我们所做的一切对于真正民主的维护至关重要。”

——伯尼•斯坦，一位来自纽约的周报编辑

作者附言及致谢

你现在拿着的这本书虽展现的是美国的心跳，核心却是中国。

翻译的原稿主要基于我编写的教材的第三版。这本书翻译成中文后，已然成为一个完全独立和独特的存在，专为中国读者而创，文本经过全新修订，章节也重新编排，以便你能更好地理解美国社区报的实践经验。

《美国社区报实操指南：无以复加的当地化》一书是一个长达五年的国际合作的成果。笔者感谢所有参与的同事和同学们。亲爱的朋友们，做得不错！希望中国社区新闻能如美国那般发展、繁荣。

特此感谢里普利增色的文章，同时还要感谢美国《桑福德先驱报》出版人比尔三世专为本书写作“社交媒体和《桑福德先驱报》”一章。

——向前看，向上看！

赵克

北卡罗来纳大学教堂山分校新闻与大众传播学院

高级讲师及社区媒体中心主任

INTRODUCTION

Dear Esteemed Chinese Reader,

Before you dive into this book, let this preliminary chapter give you a "sneak peek" into what will follow in subsequent chapters.

"A picture is worth a thousand words."

So let me begin with a picture. It is a photograph of my home state, North Carolina, on the east coast of the United States.

Every pin on the state map represents a town with a newspaper where I have visited to lead workshops on community journalism.

Our state has at least 190 community newspapers, roughly the average number of community newspapers for each of our 50 states. As you can see from this photograph, these so-called "small" newspapers seem to be everywhere!

In the U.S., a "small newspaper", is defined as a paper with a circulation of no more than 50,000. There are approximately 7,202 of these newspapers. But the surprising fact is that the U.S. has only a mere 165 major metropolitan daily newspapers.

That's 7,202 small newspapers, compared to 165 big newspapers.

Here are several more stunning statistics: of the 7,367 total newspapers in the U.S., 7,202 are "small"...including 88 percent of the dailies (which reach 16.2 million readers) plus 5,970 weeklies (which reach 44.2 million readers) plus 962 alternative papers (which reach 35.8 million readers).

Bottom line: community newspapers reach 96.2 million readers, which is three times more circulation than the 165 big papers.

Permit me to excerpt the following passage from my Foreword to Professor Chen Kai's 2012 book, *An Introduction to Community Newspapers in the U.S.*.

When I inform my students that 97 percent of all U.S. newspapers are small newspapers, they are invariably surprised. Like most Americans, they subscribe to the stereotype that the American newspaper landscape is dominated by only the big-city daily newspapers with spacious offices on the top floor of some urban skyscrapers.

And perhaps the Chinese reader will also hold to this simplistic notion. But as you will read, in the United States, nothing could be further from the truth.

OUR BEGINNINGS: COUNTRY WEEKLIES

As you doubtless realize, the U.S. is a very young nation. Certainly compared to a Chinese culture that stretches back 5,000 years. A mere 200-plus years old, our country is a baby! But out of that "newness" grew a new form of media. Remember that the European settlers of the 1600s found this land to be a vast wilderness. And as exploration and development moved from the coasts into the interior, small farming and market towns sprang up. These "start-ups" were not unlike new businesses: someone had to be the leader, or leaders. And very often among the vital institutions and facilities that town leaders deemed absolutely necessary would be a hometown local newspaper!

Cody, Wyoming, is the perfect model. When legendary cowboy "Buffalo Bill" Cody built the town in the 1800s, he proclaimed that the first establishments built in his new town would be a school, a hotel, a bar and a newspaper! To this day, Buffalo Bill's newspaper, the *Cody Enterprise*, thrives.

These so-called "country weeklies", many of which were started in the 1800s, developed, grew, were bought and sold, merged and evolved quietly, out of view of the big city major metro press and mainstream journalism academics — until the late 1950s when a seminal book was written that changed the landscape. "Community Journalism," written in 1960 by Ken Byerly, a former country weekly editor/publisher turned university professor, changed the way we thought about so-called "country newspapers". Byerly was the first author/scholar to delete "country" and substitute the word "community" to brand and to differentiate the style of journalism — distancing community journalism as a concept, style and practice that was wholly separate and apart from "big-city journalism". Byerly was also among the first to grasp and articulate the "sense of community" as being vital to the newspaper's raison d'etre — vital to its core mission. From the '60s through the '90s and until 2001, American community newspapers multiplied, grew, thrived and flourished. Only the events of 2001 and the subsequent recession have slowed that growth. But even in the economic downturn, community papers weathered the economic storm far better than their big-city media cousins.

So now, as a new age dawns, community journalism is once again resurgent. Ironically, the slow demise of the major metro daily has led to a new respect and desire for all things local. So we have this expression: "What is old, is new again." And community journalism in the U.S. is now widely accepted and respected, both in media and academic circles alike.

WHAT WARREN BUFFETT KNOWS

In the recent months, Warren Buffett, one of the wealthiest, most respected and forward-thinking American businessmen, has purchased dozens of American newspapers — all in smaller places. His success with his company, Berkshire Hathaway, is transforming the American media landscape and stunned cynical media critics who had long ago pronounced the American newspaper to be a dinosaur and a relic of the quaint past.

Warren Buffett has been quoted as saying, "In towns and cities where there is a strong sense of community, there is no more important institution than the local paper."

What does Warren Buffett know that the media critics don't know? What every successful community journalist in America already knows deep in his or her bones? That's what this book is about.

DEFINITIONS FIRST

But first, let's agree on some U.S. definitions, so you, the Chinese reader, can understand the American context in order to better construct a distinctly Chinese model of your own.

News Balance, a term that refers to the mix of local vs. non-local content. Thus, the *New York Times'* content is heavily weighted toward state, national and international news, while a small weekly outside the city is likely to contain mostly local news.

Local-first, a term that means the newspaper's leaders have an articulated policy dictating that events in their coverage area are automatically more important than events outside their coverage area. The term "news balance" refers to this agenda setting as the relationship between local and non-local content. A "local-first" news balance implies that local stories always get top priority in placement and emphasis in the community newspaper. For example, your community newspaper will only cover the President when he/she comes to visit your town. To do otherwise is to place your paper in perilous competition with the larger, faster media.

Community newspaper, a newspaper with a clear "local-first" news balance and a circulation of no more than 50,000. This includes weeklies and small dailies.

Weekly newspaper, a newspaper that is published once a week. In the U.S., the typical publication day of a weekly is Wednesday, traditionally in coordination with grocery stores (supermarkets) that wish to advertise their weekend special sales. Note: Newspapers that are published twice or three times a week, are ALSO referred to in the U.S. as "weeklies". Twice weeklies, also called "semi-weeklies", typically are published on Tuesday and Thursday. A three-time-a-week newspaper, called a "tri-weekly", might be published on Tuesday, Thursday and Sunday.

Community Daily, a newspaper with a circulation of less than 50,000 and with the local-first news balance that publishes at least five days a week. It is not unusual for many community dailies to publish Tues-Sun, taking a break on Mondays, typically the weakest day for local advertising.

Note: in the U.S., historically the largest reading day and the largest advertising day is Sunday, when readers have more time, it is believed, to spend time looking at the newspaper. Also, American dailies typically publish only morning editions, when more people want their news.

New Media, when we use the term "new media", we are referring to all forms of technology developed in conjunction with the digital revolution and introduction of the

Internet, speaking roughly from the mid '90s on.

Paid/Free, traditionally in the U.S., newspapers of any age are "paid." That is to say, the reader pays for a subscription for the print product (That price may or may not include full access to the newspaper's website.), and it is either home delivered, or the reader puts money in a newspaper box or "rack" found about town. However, these individual "rack sales" do not entitle the buyer to web access, thus encouraging readers to subscribe in advance.

But newer newspapers, especially weeklies introduced in the last 20 years, are typically "free". That means, they give away many free copies (either through newspaper racks or by home delivery) in vast numbers in hopes of convincing local advertisers of their reach and penetration into local households. The term for this type of distribution is "total market coverage", and it is very costly and therefore risky. However, to break into an established media market, it might be the only workable business plan.

Whether to require readers to pay for web versions of the newspaper is currently a major challenge for American publishers. Since content on the web has traditionally been free, U.S. readers are not used to having to pay money for news content. However, publishers, both large and small, are realizing that the production of news content is expensive. And to pay for that, many publishers are now instituting a "pay wall", a term that defines an online subscription business model. As of this writing, it is unclear if such a plan will work in the U.S. since many users/readers are resistant to having to pay for something that was once free.

THE BRIGHT LINE

The critical difference between the community weekly and the community daily is this: The weekly can fill up its pages with all-local content, generated by its staff or contributed from readers in the community. This is not true for dailies.

Because of the sheer volume of space that must be filled, it is almost impossible to fill up a daily newspaper with all-local content.

Thus the community daily must rely in part on outside content to fill those pages-usually meaning wire service, such as the Associated Press, Reuters News Service, etc.

Here's the problem: Such non-local content places the newspaper in dangerous and direct competition with broadcast and online news sources which deliver such state, national and international news much faster than any printed newspaper can ever do. And, such non-local content dilutes, or "waters down" the local-first message that makes the community newspaper so vital and unique.

Conclusion: Weeklies, with their all-local content, are better positioned to succeed in the future, while dallies that aspire to be authentic community newspapers must work extra hard and spend money on local reporters to make local-first content a priority. Understandably, many publishers at small dailies, particularly those owned by profit-first oriented media companies, struggle with this challenge.

WHY COMMUNITY NEWSPAPERS ARE SUCCEEDING

As you will grow to appreciate in the following chapters, community newspapers survived the Great Recession of 2008 in the U.S. in a far better position than their big-city media cousins. Why is this? The answers are central to our understanding of community journalism as a practice, profession and separate journalistic discipline. Here is our quick take on this:

PROXIMITY AND ACCESS

Journalists who work at community newspapers have greater contact with the reading public because of proximity. If you work at a community newspaper, you live in that community, and everybody knows you. The doors of the newspaper office are open. Readers can walk in, unimpeded, to speak with a reporter—the editor—or even the owner! Especially at most smaller community newspapers, there is no security system, just open doors. Such open access inspires a sense of community trust among the pubic, and at the newspaper itself, it encourages an attitude of accountability and responsibility.

The saying that sums up this positive attitude is, "Our default answer is YES."

LOCAL NEWS FIRST

When the local newspaper puts local news first, it sends a message to that community: YOU ARE IMPORTANT. This affirmation is quite the opposite message that many smaller places receive from the major metro daily media, which often sends the off-putting message to smaller places: YOU ARE MARGINAL. No wonder that small newspapers can thrive as businesses by promoting local news. The motto of one successful community newspaper sums up this positive attitude by saying, "Local News is our Business."

SOCIAL MEDIA

In spite of their smaller size and less financial resources, many community newspapers have very engaged social media web sites and newsroom personnel who are expert in using such tools as Twitter, Facebook, YouTube and the latest digital technology.

THE SERVICE IMPERATIVE

A newspaper must make money to survive. But a newspaper is likely to fail if its owners' sole motivation is making money. If the U.S. model tells us anything, it is that community newspapers thrive when their primary vision statement is to SERVE the community. If follows that when the newspaper successfully serves its community, that business success will naturally follow.

UNIQUE CONTENT/NICHE PUBLICATIONS

In addition to the traditional weekly and daily community papers, there are many different kinds of community newspapers in the U.S., including black, Latino and Asian newspapers (as well as many other ethnic newspapers), gay and lesbian newspapers, military, college, religious, parenting, seniors, special interest and niche papers serving communities of golfers, anglers, fliers, photographers, environmentalists, etc., as well as "urban alternative weeklies", in larger cities with a vibrant hipster, music, arts and culinary culture.

COVERAGE AREA

This term refers to the statistical geographic area, which the newspaper feels like it can provide thorough local coverage of local news events as well as enlightening and entertaining features. In the U.S. context, the coverage area often coincides with the area serviced by the paper's advertising staff. Obviously, there is a direct correlation between the size of your coverage area and the size of the news and advertising staff required to "cover" that area. Hence, weekly newspapers, with typically smaller coverage areas, (and a smaller circulation) can and usually are more thorough in their coverage, than a regional daily with say, five municipalities and seven schools in its coverage area.

OWNERSHIP

Historically, American newspapers were owned almost exclusively by individuals and/or families. Today, American community newspapers are owned by a variety of sources, including individuals, families, private companies, small groups, and media corporations (often called "chains"), like The Paxton Media Group, which owns *The Sanford Herald*, managed by veteran publisher Bill Horner III. While many weeklies are still in private hands, the great percentage of community dailies are owned by corporations, and that trend is increasing. This is important because many media critics and scholars believe that out-of-town ownership contributes to a profit-first business motivation, much to the detriment of local coverage and the newspaper's overall quality. Still, over the last 20 years, in every U.S. state in which I have visited and lectured, I have found that there are still many many independently owned excellent weekly newspapers, led by courageous civic-minded editors and publishers, as we say — and making money.

COMMUNITY-BUILDING

Community newspapers are the heartbeat of the country. They are located in practically every village, hamlet, small town — and in many cases — urban neighborhoods. Whether they are weeklies in the state of Maine, twice-weeklies in North Carolina, or even small dailies in California, they all share a common, often unspoken purpose — beyond being merely profitable: to TELL the LOCAL news, to SERVE the community and to help BUILD that community by instilling, nurturing, reinforcing and encouraging a "sense of place". We call this "community-building", and the local media is the primary engine driving that train.

CHARACTERISTIC OF THE COMMUNITY NEWSPAPER

In brief, a typical American community newspaper has a smaller circulation (sub 50k) with a dedicated local-first news balance, created by a smaller staff than at a major metro daily newspaper. However, in the case of the weeklies, ALL the content, both print and online, is likely to be original, created or gathered by the staff, whose job descriptions will extend far beyond just "reporter".

The community daily, with more space to fill each day, will still attempt to project a "local-first" news emphasis by having as much local content as their staff can generate, including a regular "all-local front" (the front page containing nothing but local content). In spite of fewer financial resources available at larger metro newspapers, the community paper, whether weekly or daily, will be dedicated to serving the community through "community building". As to newsroom access, the weekly newspaper will very likely be "wide open" to the public, while the community daily will be less so.

CHARACTERISTICS OF SUCCESSFUL COMMUNITY JOURNALISTS

As I think about what it takes to be a successful community journalist, I am seeing faces of the amazing people I've known and worked with over the years. If I could distill their formula for success, the ingredients would include: living in the community, making a point of knowing many people, being engaged in the community beyond your work at the newspaper, studying and keeping current on both history and trends for the future —and frankly, loving your community and wanting to see it be a better place. (If you don't like your town or city, you should move elsewhere!)

COMMUNITY JOURNALISM AND THE FUTURE

It's a safe bet that the future of journalism worldwide will be even more locally focused. But whether it will be in print, online or mobile-or a combination of all three... remains to be seen. However, in the U.S., this is the irrefutable fact of life: Currently, of every $1 earned through advertising, 75 percent comes from print, and only 25 percent comes from online advertising. Thus, print is still the dominant moneymaker, while all the futurists and pundits talk about newspapers being dead and that online is the future. Perhaps web-only content may be the future, but it's not practical now! So that's the challenge facing American newspaper publishers, both large and small: they must be all things to all people: print, online and mobile. And this is expensive!

We'll go into this in more detail in the book, But a quick overview: I've seen several successful community newspaper operations that integrate new media well into their operation. *The State Port Pilot* of Southport, N.C., a paid-circulation independent weekly, gives all its online content to readers for free — so long as they subscribe annually to the print edition. And they've always done it that way, which is the secret to their success. Another example is *The Shelby Star* of Shelby, N.C., which "flips" the online content production paradigm by posting local news content "raw" first-meaning BEFORE it's been reviewed and edited by copy editors. The priority is to get the breaking news content out there fast, and then go back and refine it. Obviously, this is risky, somewhat revolutionary, and obviously controversial. But the readers like it! In addition, the *Star* engages their readers with social media platforms such as Facebook, Twitter and YouTube, encouraging them to send in their own content, which of course, is free.

WHY ALL THIS MATTERS

"The most important job of community newspapers is to persuade people that their lives are important···what we do is crucial to the maintenance of a real democracy."

— Bernie Stein

Weekly Newspaper Editor, New York

AUTHOR'S NOTE, CREDITS AND ACKNOWLEDGMENTS...

While the heart of the book you hold is American, its soul is Chinese.

Based primarily on the third edition of my text. This translation into Mandarin is a completely separate and distinct entity, created expressly for the Chinese reader, with a wholly revised text and entirely new sections all designed to facilitate your understanding of the American community newspaper experience.

Community Journalism: Relentlessly Local is the result of a five-year-long international collaboration. The author thanks all colleagues and students for their devotion to the task. Well done, dear friends. May community journalism grow and flourish in China as it has in the United States.

Special thanks go to Editor—Publisher Ken Ripley of Spring Hope,N.C., Enterprise,whose essay brightens and enlivens this text. And thanks also to American community newspaper publisher and dear friend Bill Horner III, of *The Sanford (N.C.) Herald*, whose essay on social media anchors the chapter, "Technology and Community Newspapers."

— Onward and Upward

Jock Lauterer

Senior Lecturer and Director
The Carolina Community Media Project
School of Journalism and Mass Communication
University of North Carolina at Chapel Hill
Chapel Hill, N.C., U.S. 27599-3365

第1章

社区报的论述

敬爱的中国读者：

当我们提及“小的是美好的”的时候，作为中国读者的你要理解这一表达的精髓可能会有点困难。所以，这一章节将通过一个具体的定义和关于报纸规模大小的解释来阐释“什么是社区新闻”。另外，我也会在此分享关于美国社区报业的未来趋势、成长历程以及一些数据统计。

——作者

什么是社区报?

通常当人们问“什么是社区报”时，我总觉得自己可以很快地用“社区报就是这个或者那个”来回答，但我做不到。

而下面这个故事会告诉我们社区新闻是什么东西。

迈克•伊斯利（Mike Easley）在2001年一月接任北卡罗来纳州新闻协会[①] 会长，当选不久，他需要一段休整期，以便尽快从这场成功的竞选中恢复平静。

他从自己居住的不伦瑞克郡（Brunswick）的绍斯波特港口（Southport）乘坐渡轮前往度假地点——秃头岛（Bald Head Island）。在渡轮上，伊斯利不经意间看见船长坐在一份当地屡屡获奖的社区周报——《州港领航员报》（*The State Port Pilot*）上，那是一份三天前的报纸。不过对于伊斯利来说，这份周报上的信息还是新的，所以他问船长是不是可以把这份报纸借给他在渡轮上看，船长同意了。

伊斯利在报纸上看见那些熟悉的名字和面庞时很是振奋，所以，当渡轮到达码头，他还没有读完这份报纸。伊斯利问船长：“我能不能把这份报纸拿走？”很明显是希望这位经验丰富的老水手可以给他一个人情……

但是这次他得到的回答是船长毫不留情的拒绝：“不行，我也还没读完它呢。”

“小的是美好的”的定义

社区报是指日发行量在5万份以下，以服务居住在同一个地理空间中的人们为宗旨的报纸，它在新闻、专栏、体育以及广告上，都带有明显的本地色彩。

一种更加宽泛的社区报定义应该不仅指服务于某一地理概念的社区的报纸，而且还可以指服务于以种族、宗教、理念、兴趣为纽带的社区的报纸。

社区报是美国新闻业的心跳，是一种原生态新闻，你会在看见真正的社区报时明白这些说法。

一位学生上完社区新闻课程后这样写道：“如果说人是这个星球上最重

①北卡罗来纳州新闻协会：North Carolina Press Association

要的东西，那么交流就是生命的全部意义。如果顺着这样的逻辑，社区报就是这个星球上最重要的东西之一。”

人脸和人名；人名和人脸

1998年的普利策新闻奖获得者，同时也是纽约市里弗代尔出版社（Riverdale Press）合作出版人的伯纳德•L.斯坦因（Bernard L. Stein）曾说过：“我们的工作就是报道普通人的日常生活。”

随便选两张我以前出版的报纸《本周谈》（*This Week*），现在是北卡罗来纳州西部一份发行量在1万份左右的社区日报，就能发现一系列可以阐释“社区报是什么”的新闻报道。

在报纸头版上有三所当地高中的报道，第一个新闻报道讲述的是在一所高中举办的年度春季学术颁奖宴会。记者在写完校长贺词演讲的纲要后，还把参加宴会的80名学生以及他们父母的名字都列在了报道里！这篇篇幅83厘米的报道中还插入了一张很大的集体照，这张足有4个专栏那么宽的照片让你能够清楚地分辨出每个孩子的面孔。

另外一版上，有一篇由当地艺术协会发布的约76厘米的报道，是关于话剧《爱丽丝镜中奇遇记》开幕式的，这场话剧的演员是80个当地孩子。同样，这篇报道把每个参演角色的孩子的名字都一一罗列，而且也配上了一张占4个专栏宽的照片。

无以复加的当地化

在大城市日报之外，还存在着另一种小型报纸。

这是一种读者可以直接走进编辑部告诉编辑他们的想法的报纸，是一种报道小镇会议、刊登学校午餐菜单、让高中足球比赛覆盖运动版面，并且告诉你上星期谁去探望苏西姑妈以及刊登举着奇形怪状的蔬菜种植大户照片的报纸。

报纸上刊载的几乎都是婚礼信息、周年纪念日祝福、债务申明、警局记录报告、体育比赛数据、诞子喜讯和逝者讣告这些寻常琐碎的小事，但所有的这些事情都带有同样的特点，那就是非此地莫属，或者像已故哥伦比亚广播公司传奇人物查尔斯•柯瑞尔特（Charles Kuralt）所说的：“无以复加的当地化。”我们称这样的报纸为：社区报。

也许读者对于社区报的名称还很陌生，但是它已经在美国存在了400年。

请看《（宾夕法尼亚州）夸克敦自由报》[*Free Press, Quakertown (P.A.)*]的宣言——“从1881年创刊以来100%当地化的报纸”。这句话改编自《（宾夕法尼亚州）布鲁斯伯格进取报》[*Press-Enterprise, Bloomsburg (P.A.)*]的编辑吉姆•萨切特所说的：“地方化，那是只有小镇才能玩的游戏。”

尽管这种报纸很小，但它的影响力很大。

与小镇同在的社区报

1997年4月，一场巨大的洪水毁坏了北达科他州大福克斯（Grand Forks, N.D.）小镇，现由麦克拉奇拥有发行量达到35000份的社区日报《大福克斯先驱报》（*Grand Forks Herald*）。其在面对整座小镇（包括报社小楼）都被水淹没的状况下仍坚持发行。出版人迈克•梅登伯格（Mike Maidenburg）回忆当时他们做出的决定：不管多么简单粗糙，我们都要出版一些东西。

为了不间断出版报纸，“在长达两个月的时间里，我们整个团队就在一所地势较高的中学提供的一个电脑实验室中工作，里面仅有一些旧电脑和几张用来承受我们几个中年大叔肥臀的小椅子”。报社很多记者和一些读者一样，家被淹，只能住在租来的房车里。每天，这份报纸都会通过邮件发送到邻近同一报团拥有的《圣保罗先驱报》（*St. Paul Pioneer-Press*）那里印刷出版，然后这份报纸会在11时准时被运回小镇。梅登伯格说：“人们不敢相信，这个城市已经被毁了，小镇也被淹没了，报社小楼不复存在，但是报纸却还在这里发行着！”从那以后，这份报纸就以一种神奇的方式成为社区象征，证明着永不言弃的小镇精神。

《大福克斯先驱报》的团队因为他们对社区的贡献而获得了1998年的普利策公共服务奖。在小镇从灾难中恢复过来以后，一位向来对报纸颇有怨言的读者说：“虽然有时我对这份报纸很气愤，但是我不会忘记你们在这场洪水中为社区所做的一切。”在梅登伯格退休之后，市长宣布将2003年12月13日命名为“迈克•梅登伯格日”。

你在这里

当你第一次进入任何一个购物中心时，一定会在入口处看见一张地图或者一个有图解的建筑模型来告诉你各种商店和美食广场的位置。然后你要找到“你在这里”的红点。

如果社区报可以在美国新闻业这片无边的风景中精确地找到自己的位置，拥有显著的价值，我会感到十分惊喜的。

15年来，我培养了北卡罗来纳州无数社区报编辑和出版人。如今是一名新闻学老师，我是作为一个利益相关者，而不是一个冷眼旁观的学者来问这个问题：“社区报的现状怎么样？”

我们先看概况，然后聚焦于各种数据。不要紧张，算法很简单。

全国性的现象：日报趋于困境，周报力量增强

这是最美好的时代，这是最恶劣的时代。

狄更斯这句话可能是在写美国报业在后“9·11”时代的现状：大型日报读者不断下滑，小型日报奋力找寻自己的定位，周报悄悄地发展。

周报长期以来被认为是报业中的边缘产品，现在却在大报陷于困境的情况下日益变得抢眼。从20世纪90年代中期开始，直到现在，周报的种类越来越多，覆盖的人群越来越广，发行量也达到了更高水平。

用数据说话

社区报纸（被界定为周报和小型日报）是美国报业的主要部分。根据2010年《编辑和出版人》（*Editor & Publisher*）杂志年报的数据：美国总共有7367份报纸，发行量在5万份以上的报纸数量为165份，占2%左右；7202份被美国报纸编辑协会界定为小型报纸（即发行量小于5万份），占97%以上。他们的最显著特点是高度地方化新闻，所以我称之为社区报纸。

把发行量在5万份以下的小日报和周报算在一起，总发行量达到6040万份，还有一部分是针对特定人群的专项出版物，总发行量为3580万份，两部分相加总数为9620万份。

大报总发行量为2940万份。

现在可以得出结论：发行量在5万份以下的小报总发行量为大报的3倍多。

这些足以让你从不同角度思考“小型”这个词的含义。

我所居住的北卡罗来纳州的社区报数据大致可以反映出全国的情况：基于我的定义来看，在189份报纸中，有182份都是社区报。分类如下：

141份一周一报，一周双刊或三刊。

48份日报包括：3份大型都市报，每份拥有10万份或更多的发行量；5份大型地区报，每份拥有50000到99999份的发行量，当地新闻是报道重点，当然这里所

谓的当地指的是这些报纸所覆盖的周边10到30个郡的范围；40份社区小日报，每份拥有5万份以下的发行量（在本州内发行的报纸85%都是“小型的”）。

网络

在全州179份报纸中，175份拥有自己的网络版，而他们之中，又有171份（也就是98%的份额）都属于小型报纸。

所有权

日报中，88%为报团拥有。

但是在141份周报中，73份（也就是52%的份额）仍然掌握在家族或个人手中，这是十分显著的事实：大部分周报仍然是当地所有。

趋向本地化

根据百通联合（Belden Associates）为北卡罗来纳州新闻协会做的一份读者调查显示，被调查者中有81%的人表示他们在过去一周中阅读过报纸。

2000年，北卡州全国读者调查（N.C. Statewide Readership Study）机构还强调了其他类似的调查结果：

人们希望阅读当地新闻。61%的受访者将社区新闻列为整张报纸中最重要的内容。

当地新闻是报纸中被阅读最多的板块，62%的人说他们看社区新闻板块的次数比看任何板块的次数都多。

相较于其他媒介，读者们更信任自己的社区报纸。75%的人觉得，和电视、广播还有网络相比，社区报上关于社区的信息是最精确的。

发展和为人重视

“在美国报业中，没有什么比每天都要和采访对象见面的编辑更重要了。”这句充满智慧的话是马里兰大学帕克分校[1]菲利普美林新闻学院的教授吉恩•罗伯茨（Gene Roberts）说的，他提出了一个问题：“美国报业的下一步应该走向哪里？”

北卡罗来纳州东部韦恩郡一份叫《戈尔德伯勒百眼巨人新闻》（*Goldsboro News-Argus*）的报纸是他新闻生涯的起点。在那里他负责一个很畅销的专

①马里兰大学帕克分校：University of Maryland at College Park

栏——《漫话韦恩郡》（*Rambling in Rural Wayne*）。罗伯茨回忆，这个专栏包含很多内容，“家庭聚会、制作香肠的秘方、看起来长得像戴高乐将军的地瓜……”因此，社区里流传这样一句话，“世界可以灭亡，但《漫话韦恩郡》不能不出版”。

在罗伯茨开始教学生涯之前，他曾担任了18年《费城问询报》（*Philadelphia Inquirer*）的执行主编。在他的领导下，报纸赢得了17个普利策奖。之后，他又担任过《纽约时报》的执行编辑。大报给他带来名望，但罗伯茨并没有忘记自己的起点，也没有忘记社区报是多么重要。

菲尔•梅耶（Phil Meyer）教授所著《消失的报纸》（*The Vanishing Newspaper*）十分抓人眼球。在2004年的新闻研讨会上，梅耶对社区报持乐观态度，他说：“针对不同读者选用不同媒介形式，这样的发展方式正做得越来越好，这对于小报来说是好消息，但对于大报而言则不那么乐观。”

梅耶预计，如果大报不调整经营方向，2043年的4月将是最后一份报纸淡出视野的时间，这个结果可能会提早或延迟一两个月。

梅耶所说的“不同媒介形式”将是一个巨大的增长领域。正如人们所说：“我们不再询问，这个事件有新闻价值吗。”相反，我们会问：“它对谁具有新闻价值？”

分众新闻和相关市场营销开始出现了。在2004年的全美新闻学教育会上，国际报业营销协会的报告说：“一个深刻的转变正在消费者和广告市场上发生，从大众化到小众，再到一对一的模式，这意味着，媒介形式也应该针对不同受众而转变。”

可以说，社区报纸在正确的时间、正确的地点，做了正确的事情。

社区报纸，尤其是周报正在以一种从来没有过的方式获得主流地位。如今《编辑与出版家》杂志已经开始出版专门关于周报的年鉴，它对于周报前所未有的认可表明社区报在全国范围的强势发展受到越来越多的关注，人们开始获得这样一个信息：社区新闻现在很火。

然而，你仍然可以从许多东西上看出大报受到的偏爱程度有多高，在《编辑与出版家》杂志的大报年鉴中，很多州的地图上标注的小白色三角显示的是“没有报纸的地方”，其实他们指的是“只有周报的地方”。周报只是一个隐形的存在，“越大越好”的偏见仍然根深蒂固。许多州新闻协会还是以“非日报”来代表周报，要想知道这想法有多么愚蠢和具有侮辱性，只要想象一下将《纽约时报》和《今日美国》叫作“非周报”，如何？

“我们之中太多人承受着一种复杂的自卑感。”《斯旺斯伯勒潮浸区新闻周报》[*Swansboro (N.C) Weekly Tideland News*]主编吉米•威廉姆斯（Jimmy Williams）说，“这让我们不能做出更好的报纸，也无法享受花在工作上的时间。”

但是，千万不要以为威廉姆斯是觉得自己在为一份二流报纸工作而痛苦。在2002年全国报业协会举办的最佳报纸大赛中，他的报纸被评为“全国最佳小型社区报”。

改变的人口结构

当政治家谈到“两种形态的美国”的时候，他们可能是在谈论新人口结构问题：一些偏远的小镇默默地存在着，沿着城市环线公路外围扩展出去的城郊社区变成通勤者聚居地。尽管服务于“两种形态的美国”的周报数量在近30年里有所减少，但最近10年却有反弹迹象，读者总量和周报平均发行量在稳步回升，因此周报现在更加强大，更为灵活，并且更受读者青睐。

健康发展的社区推动了社区报发行量的增长。《时代周刊》一篇名为《为什么越来越多的美国人迁向小城镇》（*Why More Americans Are Fleeing to Small Towns*）的数据是：“在20世纪90年代，200多万美国人从中心城区搬到郊区，而不是反向。”

大卫•布鲁克斯（David Brooks）在他的书《通往乐园的路上：我们现在的和未来的生活方式》（*On Paradise Drive: How We Live Now (and Always Have) in the Future Tense*）中写道，“真正意义上的历史性迁移是从近郊迁到远郊，再到远郊的远郊。”例如，20世纪90年代，亚特兰大城区人口增长了22000，郊区人口爆发式增长了21万，这样的情形同时在全国各地发生。所以他得出结论：美国人居住得越来越分散。

举另外一个例子，在阿巴拉契亚山脉南部，离我度假小屋不远的地方，有一个规模将近2000个家庭的新高尔夫社区正在形成。谁将会住在这里呢？当然不是当地人，比较典型的是来自外地的婴儿潮一代，他们提前退休，通过卖掉原先的房子小赚一笔，用这笔钱在北卡州的小镇可以买到大一倍的房子。这种潜在的新读者，相较于坐在轮椅里老态龙钟的人们，可以算“年轻人”，他们仍然十分健康并且期待生命中最好的时光：有钱，有闲。对我的朋友杰夫•伯德（Jeff Byrd）而言——他是附近《泰伦每日公告》（*Tryon Daily Bulletin*）的出版人，这些潜在的新居民读者非常重要，伯德面临的挑战是，如何让这些新成员感到和社区紧密相连，只有有了归属感，他们才会阅读《泰伦每日公告》。

在中西部的很多地区，农业小城镇正在逐渐消亡，出版人面临的挑战与伯德的有所不同。在堪萨斯州拥有三份周报的出版人比尔•梅耶（Bill Meyer）说：“小城镇已经失去了他们作为零售商业中心的地位，投放广告的当地商店越来越少。针对这样的情况我们该怎么办？为了生存，必须转换方式，做不同的事情。不根据时代而做出调整的报纸是不会长久存在的。答案不在于e-mail或互联网，社区报还得依靠那些讲述当地事和当地人的有趣报道。”

消失的独立声音

在未来几年里，我们所面临的挑战是从新闻业务中拯救新闻业务。——记者皮特•苏斯曼（Peter Sussman），来自《自由论坛日程报》（Freedom Forum Calendar）。

在20世纪50年代还未曾听说过的连锁报团如今正在改变美国报业的面貌。根据吉恩•罗伯茨的统计，在全国日报中，80%由报团拥有。他承认，20世纪80年代兼并初期，一些由连锁报团拥有的报纸质量的确有了提高。但是，他也感叹道，“另一些报团报纸却开始追求更大的商业利益”。

罗伯茨认为，美国新闻业的企业化意味着新闻逐步被商业考量主宰，利润压力迫使高层无暇考虑手下每份报纸的长远利益，而社区报纸的本地编辑和出版人也被迫无奈地跟从，只看利润不顾新闻品质。

“为了保持高得不正常的利润，报纸正在毁灭自己”。他发现，缺钱已成为时下常见的编辑室现象。最近几年中，他声称“为了达到资本市场的期望，越来越多的报纸犯下类似的错误：缩减工作人员以及新闻版面”。

这种现象在其他方面也有所表现，比如减少对于政府要闻和国际新闻的报道篇幅，这样做，是否考虑到如果投票人对国际新闻一无所知的话，让他们投出政治选票将会变得危险？又或者报纸拥有人武断地认为政府新闻很无聊，不值得做，这样的认知对民主社会危害无穷。

为了扭转现在的趋势，报纸必须坚守自己的看门狗角色，报纸尽责了，就可起到防患于未然的效果。

《消失的报纸》的作者菲尔•梅耶说，大型日报正陷入困局，因为对许多上市报团而言，底线远比质量重要，季度收益也比新闻内容意义重大，报团管理者对生产更便宜的报纸驾轻就熟。最为糟糕的是，这些报纸的拥有者提高报纸的价格，降低报纸的质量，然后把钱抽走，在合适的时机再把报纸卖掉走人，这正是梅耶所说的“杀鸡取卵”的做法。

在梅耶的想象中，最差的报纸是这样的：缩减版面，这样可以减少印刷费用和新闻内容。对以赢利为首要目标的企业，新闻品质是无关紧要的，他们雇用便宜的记者，工资更低，培训更谈不上，这样一来员工流动率大大增加。对远在报团总部的老板而言，只要利润高其他都可以舍弃，但这样的烂摊子却需要当地社区报负责人用有限的资源去收拾，真是巧妇难为无米之炊啊。

梅耶说，他希望通过寻找另一种赢利方式把现状扭转过来，这种新的赢利模式可以让投资者们愿意用长远的眼光来看待报纸的发展，而不是在季度财报压力下榨干报纸油水。“报业公司有足够的资源来扭转这一趋势”，但问题是，“他们是否愿意去扭转？这是关键”。

媒体评论家和《纽约客》杂志的作者肯•奥莱塔（Ken Auletta）说，随着越来越多的报纸被报团购买，他们今后的发展趋势会给社区报带来“深远影响”，“当你从飞行在30000英尺高空的喷气式飞机窗口往下看时，地面上的人就像蚂蚁一样”。这就是从企业角度而言的“蚂蚁人群”理论，这种理论也困扰着我和奥莱塔。从30000英尺的高空（或是从北部、东部、南部或西部的1000千米之外看），整个社区以及生活在这个社区中的每个人，都只是一些不带有情感的客观存在体，他们的梦想与问题，他们的身份地位，都被距离还有强大的底线压力所模糊。

大报团逐渐看清社区报的潜力，所以迫不及待地想吞食成功的社区报，如今那些报团拥有的社区报面临的巨大挑战是，随着越来越多的报纸被报业巨头远距离控制着，有追求的社区报如何在促进社区利益的同时，也让它的拥有者得到他们所满意的持续的高利润。

在北卡仍有33%的独立出版人，他们在观望。《南松镇领航员报》（*Pilot of Southern Pines, N.C.*）的出版人大卫•沃伦诺夫（David Woronoff）说：“目前这种变态的企业化现象在某种程度上反证了我们坚持独立运作的正确性。”

技术革命

20世纪90年代被称为“新兴科技”和“新媒体”的技术现在已成为我们日常讲故事的工具。这是一个造词跟不上变化的时代。

今天即使在最小型的周报上都能看到科技创造的奇迹，电子邮件、手机、笔记本电脑、数码相机、通过谷歌下载的照片资源和在线网站都是我们常用的方法。数字革命的第一波浪潮已经退去，但我们仍然在从事讲故事的职业，以不变应万变。

数字报纸

美国报业协会（*Newspaper Association of America*）的报告指出，近1500家北美日报拥有数字报纸，这个数据显示了数字报纸吸引年轻读者的巨大潜力。2004年加州大学洛杉矶分校（UCLA）的新媒体报告显示，在18岁到34岁的网民中，有55%的读者每周在网上浏览新闻。更重要的是，83%的网民表示这些在线资源是他们了解当地新闻事件的最主要工具。毫不令人惊讶的是，美国报业协会早在1999年的一份报告中就指出，这些数字报纸中有75%是由当地“小报”经营的。

我在对北卡州的报纸进行深入研究的过程中发现，在北卡州的189家报纸中，有135家拥有网站，而其中94%，即127家网站属于小型报纸，包括许多周报。不过尽管许多网站开始有收入，但是距离网站成为可以支撑内容出版的主流经济引擎还有很长的路要走。

数字报纸现在更像是作为一种附属品而存在，一种可以与如今主流的印刷报纸互补的不错的东西，仅仅考虑年轻人喜欢网络这一个因素——他们不喜欢传统的纸质报纸，而是专注于网络读物——互联网的未来几乎就是可期待的。

社区新闻与高等教育

曾经一位知识渊博的科学工作者问我的研究领域是什么，我回答说："社区报业，正如你所认知的小报。"

这个研究者对我的回答表示出一种真正的惊讶。"哦！还有这样的报纸吗？""有一些。"我心里窃笑。

这件轶事反映出如今人们对于美国新闻业的一些粗浅的认识，尤其在20世纪80年代，许多学院和大学的新闻课程为了提升地位，增强吸引力，纷纷以达到将自己的毕业生置于那些所谓的有声望的主流媒体市场为目标，许多新闻院校几乎忽略了社区新闻课程。这样的做法无异于把洗澡水和婴儿一起倒掉。

在一个97%的报纸都被界定为"小报"的国家，大多数的高等院校都不把开设社区新闻作为专业设计的重要部分，这难道不是一个令人惊奇的悖论吗？

幸运的是，过去10年高等教育中社区新闻课程的复兴正在全美各地悄悄展开，新的课程、新的班级、新的讲座、新的出版物、新的举措以及由一些志同道合的研究社区新闻的教授所组成的国际一流的协会正逐步成形，大家的努力使得社区新闻的重要性日益被认识。

2004年8月，在加拿大多伦多，25个新闻教育工作者组成了全美大众传播教育协会史上第一个社区新闻兴趣小组（*Community Journalism Interest Group*），它致力于通过成立一个由志同道合的学者组成的队伍，让他们每年定期交流自己的想法、科研成果和教学心得，以此来激励和振兴社区新闻领域的教育工作者；通过学术竞争，展示最好的研究论文以及最具有创造力的教学理念，以此达到培养、鼓励和奖励在社区新闻领域内取得卓越的学术成果的目标；通过支持和肯定该领域内优秀的教学方法、出版物和研究，来推动该领域的发展；通过培养和指导领域内的年轻学者来鼓励更多新研究成果和出版物的产生；通过打造新型合作关系，搭建学术和行业之间的桥梁，鼓励对专业直接有效的实用型研究成果，从而推动社区新闻行业的积极变化。

公民或公共新闻

尽管有的人不愿承认，大型报纸已经意识到，他们还有很多东西要向成功的社区报学习。

20世纪90年代中期，当意识到当地新闻的重要性时，大报便用自己发明的新词冠之以“公民新闻”或“公共新闻”的概念，但事实上在大报编辑室，很多记者对此概念颇为怀疑，不愿改变以往的做法。现在已很难找到仍在做公共新闻的大报。

其实，所谓的“公民新闻”或“公共新闻”的操作手法对社区报而言并不是什么新奇的玩意，它就存在于社区报的基因中。

纽约大学公民新闻专家杰伊•罗森（Jay Rosen）曾在我任教过的宾夕法尼亚州立大学做过一场题为“我不知道什么是公民新闻，你们也不知道”的演讲。在问答环节中，社区新闻这个主题出现了。这位纽约大学的副教授向观众发出了一个挑战：“什么是社区新闻？”

麦克•达菲（Mike Duffy）是校园报网络版副主编之一，他接下了战书。我紧张地屏住呼吸，但其实我并不需要担心。

“社区新闻，”麦克轻松回应，“它使社区和报纸彼此更为真实。”

“彼此更为真实。”罗森重复，若有所思地点点头，他对此留下了深刻的印象，而我也是。

发生在身边的转变

2001年1月，我成为北卡罗来纳大学教堂山分校新闻与大众传播学院卡罗来纳社区媒介项目（*Carolina Community Media Project*）的创始主任，该项目的启动资金由卡罗来纳公共服务中心（*Caroina Center for Public Sercive*）提供，通过教学、研究并走出象牙塔，与业界保持沟通，帮助、支持本州189份社区报以及他们在线网站的出版。这个项目致力于实践如下理念：强大的社区媒体有助于建设公民生活丰富并且有归属感的社区——无论是农村还是郊区——对维持一个有活力的民主社会是至关重要的。

以家乡为傲

开学第一天的课堂上，老师往往会问学生来自哪里，很多人都会说谎。用“说谎”有点言过其实，但确实很多学生的回答会避轻就重——如果认为自己来自一个小城镇，他们就不会说出它的名字，而是默认用最近的大城市来代替自己的家乡。

古语有云：“可怜的青蛙不会赞美自己的池塘。”为什么会这样？比较一下虽然来自小地方但能骄傲地说出家乡名字的学生的特点是：他们具有强烈的公民荣誉感。这个观念或许已经有些落伍，但依旧是当今社会的一种无价之宝。为家乡感到骄傲就是要成为它的利益相关者，一荣俱荣，一损俱损，一名愿意为家乡出力的公仆，一个值得被家乡人托付重任的人，等等。

公民没有自豪感就不会有正面的认同感，无数的因素导致每个地方都有“当地感”，这也就是为什么生活在俄勒冈州波特兰市会与在缅因州波特兰市有如此的不同。同时，也引出了另一个道理：公民缺少自尊心和认同感，集体性的公民生活就会处于危险之中。美国是个参与式社会，它能运行有赖于认同自己是利益攸关者的普通人对公民意识的保持。乔治•伯纳德•肖（George Bernard Shaw）提出公民参与势在必行时说：“我认为我的生活属于社区，只要我还活着，我很荣幸为它做任何我可以做的事。”

社区报在其中扮演了一个重要角色。《纽约周报》的合作出版商伯纳德•斯坦因说：“社区报最重要的工作是说服人们他们的存在是无价的。”他声称，只有赋予人们权利才能让公民参与到公共生活中来。“我坚信我们所做的事对维护真正的民主社会至关重要。”

我们让民主真正实现的方法是通过高透明度的政治和相互制衡的组织架构，以及沟通，沟通，再沟通。媒体伦理学家、哥伦比亚大学协和神学院已退休的荣誉教授唐纳德•施莱佛（Donald Shriver）认为，社区报的职责就是“建立一种对话式的公民文化”。

没有公民生活，冷漠和疏远将使民主社会难以为继。

查尔斯•柯瑞尔特深谙公民生活的重要性。这个哥伦比亚广播公司的传奇新闻记者，在1985年北卡罗来纳大学教堂山分校的毕业典礼上发表演讲：“许多年以前，就在这个大学，我第一次模糊地意识到在这个州、这个国家甚至这个世界上有一群相互关联的人们，尽管他们也许并不认识对方，却是一群愿意为促进公共利益而奉献的好公民。”

我觉得事实上也有一群类似的“好社区报”，他们把焦点对准各自的社区，形成一个同心轴，其产生促进公民社会发展的积极效应可以像涟漪一样放大到地区、州乃至全国。这才是社区报的重要性所在——报道当地政府、社区学校、董事会会议、俱乐部活动、当地公共事物辩论、高中体育比赛、当地人的生死婚嫁等等。

社区报可以成为沃尔特•李普曼（Walter Lippmann）“新闻出版自由不是特权，而是一个伟大社会有机组成部分”说法的最好注解。

“好社区报”都是当地的，无以复加的当地化。

第2章

到底是谁的报纸？

敬爱的中国读者：

报纸是谁的？乍一看是个小儿科的问题。但若从更深层次上考虑，则意义深远。即使某个美国大型媒体集团在法律上和名义上拥有某份报纸的资产，但如果城镇居民认为该报不属于他们，那么这份报纸也无法顺利创办下去。所以，社区报记者应明白他们是在为谁工作——社区居民！为表示对报纸真正所有者的敬重，社区报办公室的大门需一直敞开，并允许公众自由出入。报纸越小，就越容易接近。

——作者

拥有一份报纸就像拥有一头奶牛

一位来报社续订报纸的老农注意到身边年轻的编辑似乎总是一刻不停地在忙乎。“小伙子，”他颇有哲理地说，“拥有一份报纸就像拥有一头奶牛。”看着编辑一脸疑惑的表情，他解释道：“你一天只挤两次奶，但是一步也不能离开。”

社区报与大型日报最明显的区别就在于所有权的差异。在这里我不是指那种商业性质的所有权，而是报纸对社区在情感和理念上的拥有感。

我们一直在讨论你和你的报纸怎样看待自己所处的社区，现在可以拿镜子照照自己，想一想，社区是怎样看待我们的，读者如何看待这份报纸。

第一点，也是最重要的一点，不要说什么“这份报纸”，这里只有“他们的报纸”。对于社区报的一切看法都是基于个人体验，即使是“读者把他们的报纸当作什么”这种根本性的问题也是如此。

再强调一遍，这是“他们的报纸”，或者更常见的说法，读者称为“我的报纸”。即使你拥有这份报纸，社区读者才是它的主人。无视这一点的社区报必败无疑，而认识并且利用这种认识将会使你获得巨大的成功。

所有权是制胜的关键

你的读者们对很多事物都有一种排他式的热爱，这是小城居民的天性。他们对本地高中的足球队、校园军乐队、教堂都有一种非我莫属的拥有感。郡公所、市议会、规划署、市政厅在他们眼里自然更是只属于本地人。这儿是他们的社区，社区里的报纸，自然也是他们的报纸。

如果他们有一期报纸没有收到，或是报纸中写了什么让他们反感的东西，抑或是改变了一些他们早已习惯的内容，你就会听到读者们源源不断的抱怨：

“怎么把我的报纸弄丢啦？”

“你怎么把我的报纸搞成这个样子？！”

“如果你不相信社区报在人们生活中扮演着至关重要的角色，”宾州韦恩斯伯勒格林郡[Waynesboro (P.A.) Green County]《信使报》（*Messenger*）产品经理丹尼尔•V.莫里斯（Daniel V. Morris）说，“问问前面桌上办公的那位秘书，如果送报人没有准时把报纸送到她手里，后果会有多么严重！”

大城市日报和电视台雇用广告代理商和公关公司，拼命地想怎样才能使读者或观众保持忠诚、投入。但是这对社区报来说完全不算什么难事。很多时候，读者们表现得就像自己才是报纸的主人一样。

能用建设性眼光对待读者的出版人更像一个公仆而非只图挣钱的商人。挣钱并没有错，那是天经地义的。事实是，你越认识到报纸与社区之间这种独一无二的关系，越是认同它、相信它，你就越有可能从中赚到更多的钱。

其他的社区报工作者们——编辑、记者、摄影师、广告人——请听好，无论你的最高准则是追求新闻事业的价值还是仅仅为了糊口，毫无疑问也是为读者工作。

一份报纸最宝贵的资源

一份社区报最宝贵的资源不是先进的印刷技术和设备，也不是拥有者的雄厚财力。一份报纸最宝贵的资源是它的读者。

胡佛•亚当斯（Hoover Adams）是一个成功的报人。他知晓读者们真正需要什么，并且一直满足他们的需求。本地优先的报道策略最终成就了邓恩郡（Dunn）这份成功的一周五刊的日报《每日记录》[*Dunn (N.C.) Daily Record*]。

对于一份社区报来说，像《华尔街日报》那样被全国所熟知确实不大可能。但是2001年8月，这种事情真的发生在《每日记录》的头上。《华尔街日报》报道了这份由家族拥有、发行量达9832份的日报，原因在于它的社区家庭渗透率达到112%，在美国发行稽查局统计的所有日报中，这是最高的数字。

《华尔街日报》的大标题感叹道："北卡州邓恩郡几乎人手一份《每日记录》。在这个电子时代，它赢在了全方位的本地报道上。"

《每日记录》的创始人——81岁的胡佛•亚当斯发现了社区报的成功秘诀，那就是你的发行量取决于你提到了多少本地居民的名字，展示了多少他们的照片，即我们最为看重的人名和人脸。

在随后的一周中，兼任《每日记录》编辑和出版人的巴特•亚当斯（Bart Adams）在专栏中对报道做了回应："《华尔街日报》的文章会让我们头脑发昏吗？有的读者会担心，本报被外界过多关注会使我们变得骄傲自大。但是对这份社区报来说，我们员工数量很有限，我们也没有时间去那样做。我们经常会出现排版错误或者措辞不当的句子，这促使我们放慢脚步，反躬自省。另外，本报受到的关注不但不会诱使我们躺在功劳簿上睡大觉，反而会让我们更加坚定地去报道本地新闻。请相信我们会穷尽所有可能，把报道做得全面、准确。"

亚当斯写道，他希望员工能够把自己当成一个公民记者，真正关心社区的福祉："因为这份报纸的所有主人都在这个社区里生活和工作，这一直是我们所坚持的理念。当然，我们的入户率能够如此之高，更深层次的原因在于这里的确是一个伟大的社区。这句话听起来很像是奉承，但是并没有夸大其词。遗憾的是，如今无数的小城镇已经变成了中心大城市周边的‘卧室社区’，一旦如此，人们就不会那么关注本地建设和其他事务了。

“虽然这里的通勤人口相较以往有所增多，但是我们仍然还保留着强大的社区认同感。而且我们都愿意付出努力来维护这种认同感，一起参加烤肉聚餐或为提供洗车服务的邻家小孩支付酬劳。我们长住此地，看到年轻人为了一份体面的工作而离开每每让我们感觉不舍。简单地说，我们热爱此地。铭记这一点正是《每日记录》的职责所在。

“我父亲的策略是尽可能多地提到人们的名字。1980年前后，他在新闻编辑室的一本备忘录中写道：‘如果我听说今天早上卡特总统将要来到社区，我想知道的第一件事就是，参与接待的人都有谁，是谁组织的活动，哪些人参加了活动。当然，我也会关注一下总统的演讲——仅仅着眼于他的来访能给社区带来什么影响。’

“他的观点，毫无疑问是正确的。居民们才是我们关注的焦点。我们在发行上的巨大成功，以及随之而来的全国范围的关注，是很多人通力协作的功劳：我的父亲，他仍然是报纸的灵魂人物；我们报社的工作人员，顶着截稿时间的压力每天辛苦赶稿；是投递员们的奔波让我们的成品能够准时到达读者手中；那些选择在我们报纸上刊登广告以期达到最佳传播效果的商家和个人……他们都值得我们感恩。

“然而，最值得感谢的还是我们的读者。你们让一切成为可能。任何时候，只要你觉得我们变得傲慢自大了，尽管打电话来纠正我们！”

报纸的个性

报纸也是有生命的，当然更有独特个性。你为一份报纸工作的时间越长，就越能感受到它的真正天性。社区报的品格常常由两个因素决定：谁拥有它和它所报道的社区本身。

就像人们有着千差万别的个性，不同的城镇同样拥有大相径庭的性格。它可能有见识、有教养、思想开放而且有远见，也有可能闭塞、故步自封、对新事物和外人满腹狐疑。经济层面，有濒临破产的，有自给自足的，也有走向衰落的。性情上，有友好乐观的，也有暴躁冷酷的。有的社区欢迎新来者并慷慨给予友谊，有的则傲慢地漠视他们。有的社区对待你像亲人一样，让你认识到自我价值，有的则无论你在那儿生活了多久，他们都不会接受你。

一个社区是怎样养成这种集体品格的呢？研究一下这个地区的道德、文化、宗教、商业和历史背景，答案自然会浮出水面。

一个渐趋衰落、由中东欧文化主导的宾州产煤小城与一个欣欣向荣、主要是苏格兰和爱尔兰人居住的北卡州旅游城镇，必定在性格上有着天壤之别。

社区报和社区：阴阳两面

有些现象有力地证明了社区报能够很好地反映出一个社区的个性：一个环境恶劣的社区往往有一份脾气暴躁的报纸；反之，一个蒸蒸日上的宜居城镇中，很可能有一份性格开明的高质量报纸。

不同身份的读者要考虑的事务是完全不一样的。你是一个即将毕业、准备在社区报开始新闻职业生涯的大学生，还是一个正在考虑改行的社区新闻从业者，抑或是一个想要拥有一份自己的社区报的社区新闻老手？

牢记下面这些话吧！这将会使你节省大量时间和金钱，避免自己陷入麻烦之中：在你正式进军一个社区之前，务必要对这个社区进行全面的调查。即使你不提前找出这个社区的性格之源，早晚你也会发现它们——而那时往往已经太晚，错误的决定早已付诸实施了。

这儿的人口是从哪里迁移来的？人们对于新人、新事物是持欢迎还是躲避态度？居民们怎样看待他们自己？他们是热爱自己的社区，还是自惭形秽？再也没有比一个充满抱怨和嫌恶的社区更糟糕的地方了。他们是否开车到48千米以外的大城市消费？如果这样的话，你的报纸很可能会缺乏稳定的广告客户。

社区居民们对他们的政府、学校、医院和其他社会服务设施看法如何？当地的政治图景如何？有哪些头面人物？是否有一个政治组织在维持社区的正常运转？如果有的话，你最好对此有所了解。

社区里面或者附近有没有大学？居民们的艺术修养如何？社区里有什么社会活动？这里的主流价值观是什么？占主导地位的宗教信仰是什么？对于当地人的行为和价值观有何影响？居民们都在哪儿工作？社区人口是在增长还是在萎缩？这都是我们要提前了解的信息。

报纸的所有权

社区报的个性不仅是所在社区个性的一种反映，同时也是这份报纸持有者身份和态度的一面镜子。正如传媒学者吉恩•罗伯茨和菲尔•梅耶所说，在美国，有一些富有远见的报社在努力地为社区服务，与此同时也有很多报团只图从社区获利，而不愿意回馈社区，根本不被自己所报道的社区待见，读者们经常会公开地向他们表达自己的厌恶情绪。这是社区新闻中最糟糕的情形，在那种报社工作的人总是能让你想起“屹耳”——动画片《小熊维尼》中那头整日无精打采、顾影自怜的驴子。我曾经听说过这样一个报社，它的员工们被称作“58只屹耳”，想想那会是一份什么样的报纸。

在你选择去一个报社工作之前，了解一下这份报纸的所有者。如果这是一份家族报纸，那么这个家族怎么样？社区居民对这份报纸和报纸的所有者有何看法？记者们喜欢在这家报社工作吗？报社的人员流动情况如何？新闻编辑室的氛围怎样？工作环境是否令人愉悦？如果这是一个报团所属的报社，你同样需要考虑这个报团的名声和发展方向。与其他报业集团的管理层相比，他们对员工是否足够大度和友善？

你很难把自己的个性强加于一个社区或者一份已经存在的报纸。更理智的途径是找到一个与你性格相符的社区和报纸。这样的话，你会过得很快乐，而你所服务的那些人也会由衷地感谢你。

社区报的个性与年龄

就像人一样，报纸也有自己的生命跨度，他们会逐渐成熟、变老。一群傲慢自大的家伙运营一份新生的周报时会气势汹汹地快速扩大规模，然后每周出版两期、三期甚至扩大到日报。

报纸为什么会发生这样的变化？

原因可能是内在的，也可能是外在的。

有时候报纸的持有者、出版人和编辑会发现通过改变报纸的版式和出版周期可以提高发行量。更常见的情形是，随着所在社区的经济发展，报纸要适时而变，否则有可能被淘汰。一份无法赶上社区发展步伐的社区报是不会获得任何成长的。一旦无法发展壮大，它就会陷入衰退，甚至可能逐渐消亡。

一份报纸的消亡往往是因为社区本身商业的衰落，广告基础已经无法支撑起原有的媒体规模，尤其当市场竞争很激烈的时候。但是很多时候内部管理的失败也难辞其咎。如果一个报团选择关闭一家社区报，可能出于多种原因，但最根本的往往是报纸每况愈下的营收状况和黯淡无望的未来。

作为一名社区报从业者，你一定要准确判断你的报纸所处的阶段。它是一个垂垂老矣的白发老人，还是一个天不怕地不怕的年轻人？它是一个安分保守的生意人，还是一个敢于冒险的探路者？你必须了解。

当报纸转手

就像离婚撕裂一个家庭一样，一份报纸可能面临的重大创伤是报纸所有者的易手，其糟糕的程度仅次于关张。尤其是当一份家族报纸被转让给一个报团的时候，这种创伤更加痛苦。报社里的每一个人都在考虑自己的饭碗，而非报纸质量，这被发展心理学家称作“发展抑制”。直到报纸的新主人展示出诚恳的态度并且把事务都安排妥当，报纸才可能恢复元气——而这一过程可能会花去数年时间。

所以你要搞清楚，你中意的那份报纸是否正处在身份认同危机的边缘，它是不是正要改变出版周期或者转手他人。了解这些关键信息将会使你避免失败的悲剧，并且能够提升你的工作表现，让你收获更和谐的人际关系。

另一些声音，另一些编辑室

伊利诺伊州迪克森的《迪克森电讯报》（*Dixon Telegraph*，以下简称《电讯报》）的第五代出版人威廉•E. 肖（William E. Shaw）说，他花了很多年才弄明白到底谁才是这份报纸的真正主人。下面这些内容节选自他在1994年佛罗里达州奥兰多举行的主题为“社区报与社区发展”座谈会上的发言。

“我们的《共和党人》完了！”

每天早上我都提醒自己是《电讯报》出版人的身份。这个工作和头衔很多年以来都是我们家族成员的专属。我的父亲，在他之前是我的祖父，整整一生都是报纸出版人。这可以一直追溯到143年以前，那一年我的曾曾祖父创办了这份报纸。

整个小镇的人都对我们肖氏家族了如指掌。我们的姓氏与这份报纸几乎可以画上等号。报纸的创始人，我的那位曾曾祖父，曾经拜谒过亚伯拉罕•林肯，当时他要去与另一位总统候选人道格拉斯进行辩论，正好途经这里。曾曾祖父不仅拜会了他，还帮助他制定了辩论策略。我的祖父给了罗纳德•里根人生中第一份工作——我家这份报纸的投递员。

这么多年以来我们不间断地出版《电讯报》，一期都没有停过。这个社区发生的一系列事件都被完整无误地记录下来，这是家族整整五代人的经营成果。这份报纸承载了迪克森过往的历史，也包含着一种能量，引领着迪克森走向未来。

每一天的生活都为《电讯报》带来新鲜的故事。每天早上开始工作时，我们丝毫不知道什么新闻会占据报纸的头版头条。然而，当一天结束的时候，那些突发事件都会被报纸永远地记录下来。

在这个报纸纷纷被报团收购并上市的时代，绝大多数报纸的所有者与他们服务的人群之间相隔太远，大多数人甚至不知道自己所在社区报的出版人是谁。有的报纸所有者对所报道的社区一无所知。

即使像我们家族经营报纸这么多年，我也不敢说自己真的了解所有权到底意味着什么。但是7年前发生的一件事情，改变了我把报纸的投资人当成报纸主人的观念。

为了扩大家族的产业规模，适应家族本身扩张的速度，我们在伊利诺伊州、爱荷华州和威斯康星州并购了一些社区报。其中一份叫作《比罗郡共和党人》（*Bureau County Republican*，以下简称《共和党人》），在伊利诺伊州的普林斯顿镇，一个位于迪克森以南不到48千米的地方。在我1986年回到迪克森之前，我在那个报社做了5年的出版人。

在我离开普林斯顿镇几个月之后，一场火灾突袭了报社所在的街区。瓦斯爆炸造成的大火迅速吞没了报社旁边的那栋大楼，火苗窜到了我们的屋顶。

后来，报社的新任出版人、我的继任者鲍勃•索伦森（Bob Sorensen）报道了这场灾难，这场灾难让报纸从报道者变成了被报道者。

当时天色将暗，鲍勃冲到火灾现场后，立即开始从大楼中搬出电脑和其他一些贵重物品。当大火逼近办公区域时，他不得不停下来，由消防员来与大火英勇搏斗。当鲍勃惊恐地望着眼前的一切时，他听到一位女士大声尖叫：

"我们的《共和党人》完了！"

这在当时恐慌的情境下，实在是一个有趣的想法。当鲍勃把这句话说给我听的时候，我们都意识到，那位女士似乎是目睹自己的报社毁于大火。事实上，整个社区的居民恐怕都是这么想的。《共和党人》属于社区所有居民，我们只是管理和出版着这份报纸而已。

整整4年，那句话一直萦绕着我。即使是在迪克森，这份报纸服务此地近一个半世纪，我们实际上真的拥有它的所有权吗？答案当然是肯定的。我们是伊利诺伊州家族持有报纸最长时间纪录的保持者。在此期间，我们辛劳、奉献，付出热血、汗水和眼泪，一刻都没有停止过。

但是从更高层面上来说，这份报纸永远都属于迪克森这个伟大社区里的所有人。如果想让这份报纸保持健康和活力，最高境界就是本地居民把它当成自己的报纸。这就是他们的报纸。

幸运的是，消防员们扑灭了屋顶上的大火，《共和党人》得救了。但是那位惊慌的女士的叫喊——“我们的《共和党人》完了！”却像火一样在肖的脑海中燃烧起来，生生不息。1993年，受那场大火启发，出版人肖编列了一本《〈电讯报〉所有者手册》，分发给报纸的所有新老订户和广告商。在序言里，肖的开场白是：“广义上说，你们这些读者才是这份报纸的主人。通过订阅《电讯报》，你们雇用了我们来出版一份能够满足自己需求的报纸。我们准备了这本手册以便你们能更好地利用自己的报纸。我们同时也很渴望聆听你们的意见，以便提升你们的这份《电讯报》。尽管写信或者打电话来分享你们的想法吧！”

有关大火的另一堂课

在一个平常的周五早上，宾夕法尼亚州格林郡韦恩斯堡市（Waynesburg）发行量达到6000份的周报《信使报》报社里，生产经理丹尼尔•V.莫里斯正在为下周一要出版的家族报纸忙碌着，突然警报大响，报警器中传来急促的声音：“第61消防连队向您的位置报告，布莱尔酒店发生火灾！”

莫里斯回忆：“我和秘书都愣了一下，突然明白大火就发生在我们这栋楼里。跑出去，看到从上方的三楼窗户中冒出滚滚浓烟。店主说可能是油脂失火造成的火灾。当火焰窜出窗户的时候，我们意识到：要赶紧转移！”

他们拔掉了所有机器、电话和电脑的插头。“我就像疯子一样，把所有的线从每一个插头上拽下来，把硬盘摞在扫描仪上，还有一盒又一盒的光盘。”莫里斯说道。

然后一件神奇的事情发生了：

> 当我抱着一大堆器材向门口走去时，我很惊讶地看到一大群人正排着长队把办公室里的物品搬到外面去。
>
> 一个年轻人过来说：“我们来把报社的东西搬到街对面的韦恩斯堡街区，鲁斯蒂•瑞奇（Rusty Rice）已经准备好房间来存放这些设备了。”
>
> 他接过我手里的器材，像其他人一样开始搬运起来。他们甚至不知道自己怀中抱着的是价值数千美元的精密设备。银行家、律师、店主、孩子们和来自我们对手报纸的职员们都来帮忙。把视线拉回办公室，一大群社区“蚂蚁”在我和秘书的身后集结，等着我们递给他们那些散乱的物品。人们把巨大的文件柜和其他一些家具装箱运出来。当最后一件必需品搬出来的时候，浓烟已经开始涌进办公室……
>
> 匹兹堡电视台拍摄了现场画面并采访了员工，报道了我们的幸运大撤

退，作为外来者，他们并不能如我们那样深切地感受到这种社区认同感。社区里的人们刚刚拯救了“他们的”报纸，这是我们都心照不宣的。

本地商人夏尔•海德里（Shirl Headlee）前来安慰我那做编辑的父亲。夏尔追忆了三年前他的建材生意毁于一旦时我们的报纸给他的帮助，并给了我们一把钥匙，那是他的家族拥有的在中央商场的一所空房子的钥匙。他告诉我们：“随便用，不必拘谨。”

有些皮卡车主目睹了刚刚发生的一切，他们把我们的设备装上自己的卡车，浩浩荡荡地开往中央商场。搬运这些设备花了好几个小时，之后我们都觉得疲惫极了。就在那时，夏尔先生走了进来，为每个人带来了芝士汉堡和炸薯条。他告诉父亲，不必担心房租的问题，他会想办法解决。“此时此刻，”夏尔先生说，“你们还有更重要的事情要做。”

夜幕降临之前，我们又重新变成了一个运行无碍的报社。赶在周一截稿期限前顺利完成了任务。

这次火灾事故占据了报纸头版，其后一整版的告示告知居民他们的报纸现在搬到了哪里。社论版上刊载的是一份致谢声明，感谢那些在危难中向我们施以援手的人们。这次经历使我们更加看清楚一份社区报对于它所在的社区有着怎样不同寻常的意义。当大火突发时，朴实低调的邻居们站出来给了我们无私的帮助，大家一同见证“社区”这个词语的伟大内涵。

大火已经过去十年了，格林郡《信使报》依旧发展得欣欣向荣。它有了一个新的落脚之所——夏尔•海德里先生捐出来的一栋房子。丹尼尔•莫里斯的父亲后来将报纸卖给了科尔金传媒集团（Calkins Media），但是莫里斯本人仍然担任报社的总经理，为报纸掌舵。

开放的新闻编辑室

很难找到将读者拒之门外的周报、一周双刊或是三刊的新闻编辑室，其中绝大多数，确切地说，其实是完全开放的。

为什么会有一些日报在达到一定发行量之后就要借着“安全”“防盗”这样的理由把自己的新闻编辑室与大众隔离开呢？难道那些小一点的报纸不面临同样的问题吗？为什么它们就能敞开大门呢？

撤掉隔离的屏障吧！出版人伯纳德•斯坦因呼吁道：“要敞开大门，同时也要让人们知道，你的大门是敞开的。”

正如社区新闻学学生克里斯蒂娜•利克斯路德（Christina Rexrode）所说，北卡州《阿什伯勒信使论坛报》[*Asheboro (N.C.) Courier-Tribune*]确立“开门办报”的宗旨是一个非常明智的决定。该报专栏作家、前任主编鲍勃•威廉姆斯（Bob Williams）说:“你不可能坐在象牙塔里，然后宣称自己写的就是公众们的真实想法。如果你不与他们交流，你如何得知他们的所思所想呢？”

威廉姆斯，一个打小就住在本地的居民，自从1969年起就开始为这份报纸工作。他所写的那些如实反映生活实景的专栏文章，每周在报纸的头版刊登四次。他那些源源不断的想法到底从何而来呢？答案是，从这份发行量为16300份的日报的大门口涌进来。

显然，我们可以看出，新闻编辑室的开放度与其承担的对社区的责任之间有着极为重要的相关性。当有人要求我定义“社区报”这个词语的时候，我建议提取一个关键因素——新闻编辑室的开放度。

也就是说，读者们能不能直接走进来与编辑、记者、摄影师进行面对面交流？是不是需要经过一道道安检程序、需要专门的许可？通往编辑室的途径会不会是彻底关闭的？

为什么要强调这一点呢？因为有些大报往往虚张声势，为了阻止自己发行量的日益流失，给自己披上“正宗社区报”的外衣。但这蒙不了人。

就如前面已经说过的，真正的社区报是指紧密地报道本地事务、发行量不超过5万份的地区性报纸。发行量只是一个表层的指标，社区报的社区融合度必定还有其他可以度量的因素。那个因素就是“开放度”，这是最关键的指标。

也就是说，报纸编辑室多大程度上是对读者们开放的呢？是不是有一套安全系统把读者们挡在大门之外呢？记者和其他报社职员是不是与公众们分隔开来没有接触呢？读者们通过电话与编辑、记者、摄影师取得联系方便吗？打进来的电话会不会被送进“来电地狱”——那种电脑控制的非人工服务系统？编辑室是不是像在象牙塔里一样脱离社区？

周报的自我陈述

现在让我们聆听一下宾夕法尼亚州的报纸从业者们对于报纸开放度的看法。首先是来自周报的同仁们:

- “我们必须开放，因为我们是社区报。”
- “我们与读者之间不能横亘任何阻碍。”
- “我们的办公室是没有门的，这就是我们的开放程度。”
- “开放度是我们报纸存在意义的关键。这给我们一种近在眼前的紧迫性。而那些大报，显然太把自己当回事儿了，他们把自己的作品看得比读者更重要。尽管我们也对自己的作品感到骄傲，但我们从来没有忽视什么才是真正重要的：读者永远第一位。”

- 读者径直走进办公室对报纸内容说三道四并不总是令人愉悦。“话虽然难听，却是苦口良药，使你保持清醒。除此之外你还有什么好办法与社区保持信息交流和情感联系呢？”
- “走进我们的办公室，你就会看到这儿只有三个房间，而且都小得可怜，我们无处可遁！”
- “我们的办公室在主街旁的一栋两层小楼里，与其说它是个办公室，不如说它更像个家。这让来访者和报社的三个员工都觉得很舒服。”
- “我们的办公室是开放的，即使是松鼠也能进来，更不要说人了。”
- 伊丽莎白城（Elizabeth town）《编年史》（*Chronicle*）的出版人万达•里德（Wanda Reid）说雇用当地记者很重要，这会使他们与读者随时可以接触，报纸服务于公共需求。
- “我们的办公室是非常开放的，连风都可以随时吹开前门进来。”

日报的自我陈述

“很多日报有身份认同危机。”一位要求不披露名字的宾州的日报记者说，“中型日报想变成大都市日报，有的大都市日报却想做社区报。”

但是很多小型日报或者社区日报也像周报一样向读者敞开大门。《时代》（*Era*）是一份发行量达到12800份的报纸，主编马蒂•怀尔德（Marty Wilder）说：“我们很清楚开放的意义，我们做的就是社区新闻。报纸把自己和读者隔离开的话会产生一种疏离感，这可能会影响报纸在社区的被接受度。”

埃德•克里斯汀（Ed Christine）和他人合伙拥有发行量达3900份的报纸《丹维尔新闻》（*Danville News*），“我们完全开放并以此为傲”。

发行量达1万份的《亨廷顿每日报》（*Huntingdon Daily News*）的记者说读者可以直接从后门走进报社，畅通无阻。

建筑结构也能影响开放度，以发行达28200份的《森伯里日报》（*Sunbury Daily Item*）为例，编辑室位于二层，所以上楼之前总得接受前台接待员的一番盘问。

还有一种情形是报社的选址，南希•马驰（Nancy March）是发行量达到3万份的报纸《水星》（*Mercury*）的主编：“如果报纸远离小镇主街，读者必须开车、停车才能到达，即使编辑室完全开放，其程度也要大打折扣。”

《论坛民主党》（*Tribune-Democrat*）发行量达到50400份，主编大卫•勒旺（David Levine）说：“开放是我们的责任、使命，没有开放，让社区报介入社区事务就是空谈。”

大卫•特洛伊西（David Troisi）是威廉斯波特（Williamsport）发行量达到35900份的报纸《太阳公报》（*Sun-Gazette*）的主编，他办公桌上的电话是直拨外线，也就是说社区里的任何人都能直接找到他，他承认："有时候这也很痛苦，但这意味着我们是公众的一部分，即使有时你和读者意见相左，你也能从他们身上学到东西，这时刻提醒我们要对报道负责，对社区负责。"

我的北卡同仁比尔•霍纳（Bill Horner）是《桑福德先驱报》的发行人，他处理读者来访的事比较巧妙："我从不拒绝，但如果碰巧很忙，我会从办公室里走出来，和读者在走廊交谈听取他们的意见，一般人都能明白我这么做暗含的意思，抓紧说完就告别，这样就不会耽搁我很长时间。"

丹尼尔•黑泽尔（Dennis Hetzel）是发行量达到50400份的约克镇社区报《约克每日纪事报》（*York Daily Record*）的发行人兼编辑，当报社搬进新楼时，本来他可以选位于三层视野相对较好的办公室，但那样的话，读者想见他还要坐电梯，实在不利于开放，现在他的办公室位于一层临街的位置，"完全开放"。

在很多主流大报中，可以明显地察觉到一种"我们与他们"之间的对立态度，这其中当然也包含了一些偏执的情绪。一位大报编辑解释道："完全开放是很好的想法，但我们做的很多都是揭发性的报道，只要有一个人前来报复滋事，后果就会很严重。"

结论

报纸从业者可以走进读者的家里去采访，但是有些人却不愿意让读者走进我们的新闻编辑室。如果你不让他们走进你的世界，你又怎么能期待自己可以真正走进他们的生活呢？想一想，为什么那些大报会渐渐失去与社区的联系？高度的开放性是社区报的重要组成部分。我们可以得出下面一组等式：

主流大报：开放度受限=与社区疏远/失去联系
社区报：开放度通畅=融入社区/紧密联系
开放度是报纸"社区融合度"的重要指标。

真正意义上的社区报，既指外在形式，又意味着独特的新闻编辑室，两者缺一不可。

小型报纸工作者必知的15件事

- 不管你是否知道，也不管你是否喜欢，总之，你在做的是社区新闻。
- 社区报绝非城市大报的微缩版。
- 虚假报道在社区报根本没有藏身之处。
- 牢记“本地化，本地化，本地化”，紧接着的是：“所有故事必须是关于本地的。”
- 报纸目标就是服务所在社区——它既简单，又纯粹。
- 无论是谁拥有报纸，这份报纸真正的主人都是它所报道的社区。
- 在社区报，没有严格的分工，你什么都得做：记者、摄影、设计甚至发行。
- 你不必等到在《华盛顿邮报》《体育画报》或者《国家地理》工作的时候再全力以赴，你现在就应该付出全部的才能和热情。
- 小的是美好的。你要相信它并且把它铭记于心。
- 你可能不会变得很富有，但是你得到的精神回报将是巨大的。
- 每个人都是有故事的人。
- 一个一无是处的地方对另一个人可能意味着天堂，要学会换位思考。
- 当记者说“这儿什么也没有发生”的时候，他实际上是在说自己的脑子。
- 每一个故事都会导向另一个故事，所有的事物都是有联系的，你要相信这一点，并且多加注意。
- 新闻编辑室大门，应该像你所报道的那些人的心门一样，向别人敞开。

第3章

小而美的社区报

敬爱的中国读者：

你现在可能会好奇：美国社区报扮演着什么角色？它与主流都市日报有何不同？它是否有不同分类？这一章节将试着回答这些问题，甚至也会阐述这一职业的负面信息。

——作者

说说职业认同危机

当鲍勃（Bob）出现在主街[1]上的艺术中心时，他已经焦躁不安。他还有其他事要做，而这一个看上去不是那么重要的颁奖典礼——四个中学生因为他们的创意写作而获得了奖项，令人感觉实在是浪费时间。

尽管鲍勃觉得这件事无聊透顶，可编辑还是想要一篇报道和一张照片。

他带着厌烦的情绪抵达艺术中心，没有和任何人搭话，只是看着父母们、老师们和校长们一簇簇地聚在艺术中心大厅里聊天。

一群屌丝。鲍勃偷偷地嘲笑这一场景。他有更重要的事情要做。难道这些小人物们意识不到他的重要性吗?

郡督学谈到了优秀作品的意义。

艺术委员会主任谈到了有效沟通的重要性。

各位校长——四位校长无一例外，都一一列举了各自学校在提升书面写作方面所做的努力。

鲍勃变得越来越焦躁。

然后每个获奖的学生都走上台去，谦逊地接过支票，并被要求“简单地说几句”。

这仪式一拖再拖，鲍勃的坐立不安开始变得引人注目了。他把重心转移到身体的另一侧，发出一声清晰可闻的叹息，转了转眼珠，盯着手表看……

最后，当他再也无法忍受的时候，鲍勃听到了自己的一声惊呼，声音大到坐在他身边的人都能听见——“我正在这里做什么？！”

此时此地

事实上，这是一个非常棒的问题。

鲍勃去艺术中心的颁奖典礼做什么——为一家地方小报写稿吗?

答案应该是这样的：他在为他的家乡服务；无论在何种情况下，都要尽他所能。

如果毕业后能立即靠你的裙带关系、良好的长相和魅力去《纽约时报》、

---

①主街：Main Street，位于城镇中心地带的街道，往往是小镇的起源，代表着社区中的主流意识形态和价值观。

ESPN频道、《国家地理杂志》、《体育画报》（*Sports Illustrated*）或CBS《60分钟》栏目工作，那么恭喜你。绝大部分人可没有这样的运气，草根媒体可能是更现实的第一份工作选择。

我是做什么的？

喜剧演员豪伊•曼德尔（Howie Mandel）喜欢以询问观众的职业作为例行的开场白。

“你是做什么的？”他简洁地问。

系统分析师、中层经理等诸类人就要费尽心思解释一番。

“哦，这么说来你是分析系统的。”豪伊的回应带着一种嘲讽的魔力。

“呃，也不全是。”随之而来的是尴尬回应。

“好吧，那么，又是什么呢？”豪伊带着孩童般的无邪追问，他的意图很显然是让对方用寥寥数语概括自己一天八小时的工作，可这却让人相当抓狂，因为他们从未思考过，根本做不到。

我们是做什么的？

如果我们这些做社区新闻的人都不能立马说清楚我们是做什么的，那就只能承认我们缺乏身份认同，没有目标且很难长久地把这份工作干下去。所以马上，在我们谈论社区报写作、编辑和制作等具体细节之前，先明确一下我们是做什么的。如果豪伊•曼德尔今天站在这里，用手指着我们问：“社区报的编辑、出版人、记者、摄影师、广告销售人员……你们是做什么的？”

我们应该异口同声地回答：我们的工作核心是本地，本地，再本地。

街头狗咬狗

肯•拜尔利（Ken Byerly），这位已故作家、教授和出版人，曾经引用过一句话，精确地抓住了社区新闻“本土第一”的本质：“一场发生在主街的狗咬狗事件，比保加利亚的一场革命更为重要。”

“如果我们找不到一个本地视角，我们将无法报道新闻——无论新闻有多大。”埃德•哈珀（Ed Harper）是绍斯波特一份家族所有、发行量达9000份的周刊《港口引航员报》的编辑，他的经验是：“报道‘9·11’事件时，关注的是本地那些与死亡或幸存的人有联系的人的故事。对于伊拉克报道，则关注那些有本地根基的军人。”

社区日报面临着特殊挑战。许多日报编辑都说，他们希望报纸有全本土化的内容，但是每天出版的报纸对新闻的需求实在是太大了，这使他们不得不用通讯社通稿来填补缺口。也有另外一些社区日报的编辑反驳，读者也会期望社区报刊载一些非本土的内容，某些情况下，社区报可能是读者当天唯一的印刷媒体新闻源。因此，社区日报刊载国内外新闻大事也是一种义务。

然而，社区报的本土使命永远不应该被忘记。《金士顿自由报》[*Kinston (N.C.)Free Press*]——自由报团一家发行量达13000份的日报——的总编李•雷诺（Lee Raynor）这样对社区新闻系学生卡伦•斯塔夫（Cullen Stafford）说："每个人都想知道在阿富汗或是伊拉克发生了什么，但他们真正关心的是他们的垃圾是否能准时被清理。"

1999年，小约翰•肯尼迪在大西洋飞机失事的那一周，发行量达5050份的《每日公告报》（*Daily Bulletin*）当期的头条新闻却关注一名于交通事故中丧生的杰出本地学生。导语这样写道："一名杰出的波尔克（Polk）年轻人，于周二凌晨在斯帕坦堡（Spartanburg）丧生。本周我们的社区失去了梅雷迪思•麦卡利斯特（Meredith McCallister），就如同本周我们的国家失去了小约翰•肯尼迪一样，未来丧失了许多的可能性，留给我们无尽的悲伤。我们的心情与大家一样沉重，让大家一起向麦卡利斯特的家庭致以哀悼……"

北卡州的布里瓦德（Brevard）通过了一项饮酒法令，邻近的城市大报《阿什维尔公民报》（*Asheville Citizen*）对此事的小篇幅报道被排在第24版，与其他17篇关于其他社区的报道编排在一起，但是对于布里瓦德的一周双刊社区报《特兰西瓦尼亚时报》（*Transylvania Times*）来说，这可是当之无愧的头条，详尽的、长达76.2厘米的报道满足了本地读者的需求。简而言之，布里瓦德的居民通过口口相传，或者通过收音机、电视，也许还通过周边城市报纸得知法令是否通过的结果，但若想读到完整详尽的报道，则不得不捱到不求时效但求深入本地的社区报的出版。

社区报的角色

《共和党先驱报》（*Republican*）对波茨维尔市（Pottsville, P.A.）的报道可谓登峰造极；《迪克森电讯报》对迪克森市的报道也是天下无敌；《每日快报》（*Daily Courier*）熟知拉瑟福德郡（Rutherford Country）的程度，无人能出其右；论及对麦库克市（McCook, Neb）少棒联盟季后赛的报道，则无人能做得比《每日公报》（*Daily Gazette*）更好。

和城市大报相比，社区报在满足人的基本需求方面表现得更卓越，比如对社区的认同和归属感，零距离所带来的积极而真切的互动效应，人际间关联的强化，等等。这就是斯坦福大学（Stanford University）纳丁•克鲁兹[①]（Nadinne Cruz）所谓的“大我”[②]意识。

尤其在当下，社区报在人文主义新闻中所扮演的角色变得比人们想象的更加微妙、重要和影响深远。社区报是本地事务的大集合：市议会、规划委员会、童子军运动会、教堂聚餐，甚至莫德（Maude）姨妈的100岁生日，这些都需要社区报进行报道以扩散传播效应，报纸通过图文反复表达的愿景是人们对自己社区身份的认同——人的重要性再怎么强调都不过分。

社区报的编辑、出版人、广告销售、记者、摄影师……还有社区新闻的学生们，请把下面这一点钉在你的墙上：人是最重要的因素。如果你还未曾那么做过，请将这句标语带入你的生活和工作之中——然后就会看到你的报纸得以起飞，你的员工士气得以飙升，你的社区关系得以改善。

大小可不是小事

“小的是美好的”，不仅仅是堆在笑脸上的陈词滥调。有研究证实了这一点。

心理学家们已经发现，在任何特定的环境下，当许多人被置于同一个地理单元中，却没有足够的职位时，一部分人就会觉得自己在这个环境中毫无价值，无足轻重，往坏处说就是被孤立。

反之，在一个没有足够的人口来担当必要性职位的环境中，许多人——如果不是大多数的话——不仅感到自己实现了价值，而且还会觉得自己得到了重视。

个体在群体生活中能把潜力发挥到何种程度与他是否处于人尽其用、规模适度的环境紧密相关。对报纸而言，这意味着报道覆盖范围应该适度。举个关于学校规模的例子吧。

心理学家已知，那些来自学生数在1000人以下的高中的孩子，有着更良好的自我价值感与幸福感。因为他们做了更多的事情。

在1999年的哥伦拜恩校园事件[③]之后，来自波特兰市西北地区教育实验室的凯思琳•柯顿（Kathleen Cotton）接受《时代》杂志采访时提醒：“也许小的会更美好些？”

堪萨斯大学行为心理学家罗杰•巴克（Roger Barker）与赫伯特•赖特（Herbert

---

①纳丁•克鲁兹：美国基于社区学习的倡导者。

②原文为“the Big WE”。

③美国历史上最血腥的校园枪击事件之一。1999年4月20日，美国科罗拉多州杰佛逊郡哥伦拜恩高中的两名青少年学生配备枪械和爆炸物进入校园，枪杀了12名学生和1名教师，另有24人受伤。

Wright），在他们于20世纪四五十年代进行的里程碑式的研究中发现：出身于小规模的学校，或来自小城镇的孩子比来自大城市与大学校的孩子更有可能取得较高成就。巴克和赖特称此为“人员短缺行为环境”，在这样的环境中，学校的年鉴编辑也可能同时兼任拉拉队队长；如果是在小城镇中，学校看门人可能同时担任镇长一职。

与之相反的环境中，最有天赋的人才能成为运动员，最聪明的学者才被获准加入私人俱乐部，最优秀的演员方可成为毕业大戏中的明星，然后赢家通吃。许多人没有机会充分发挥能力的地方被称为“人员过载行为环境”。身处这种环境中的人没有在任何领域被委以重任，他们会觉得自己没有目标，无法表达诉求，也没有事物能将自己与别人区别开来。

不难理解，那些大型高中里的普通学生，大型城市里的普通人会被置于何种状态中：被无视，被社会巨大裂谷所吞没。直至意识到这个社会并不关心他们，他们在挫败中做出激烈的反抗，形成可见的悲剧。

你可以看到这将如何适用于我们这一行业。想象一下，你是一名新手，身处于一个有着400位记者的新闻编辑室中——这在城市大报中并不罕见。你能够认识每一个人吗？你不能。

你也许仍旧会是一个“陌生土地上的陌生人”。在同一栋大楼里已经共事多年，经常合作报道的资深记者与摄影师可能从未谋面。如果想在这样的环境中工作，你需要对此有所准备。

从另一方面来说，如果你想了解所有与你一同工作的人，那么社区新闻就是你的选择。如果你希望了解社区，同时还能在社区内为人所知，那么社区新闻就是你的选择。如果你期待人尽其才，刚一毕业就在报社举足轻重，那么社区新闻也将是你的选择。

新闻中的社区

“社区”之所以成为一个热门话题，是因为美国文化具有重视个体的趋向。美国人要求所消费的产品能让他们感觉被承认，被肯定，体现自我价值而且有一种亲密的关联，比如：人性化设计的个人电脑，不给人以压迫感、尺度合适的建筑，人际关联紧密的社区等等。

有理论认为，这类“社群主义”精神的增长在某种程度上是“以自我为中心的80后”带来的效应。对美国人来说，家乡不仅仅意味着高速公路的一处出口，还包含更多精神层面的追求。弗罗斯特市（Forest City, N.C.）的城市规划师丹妮尔•威思罗（Danielle Withrow）认为，人们渴望被接纳和包容，渴望成为一个实体社区的一部分，成为社区中有责任感的公民。

作为个人，我们渴望和需要首先在自己的家乡得到认可、被重视和倾听。然而，一个城市很难成为一个社区。与一个小地区相比，城市虽然有能力提供许多产品与便利设施，但很难让它的居民感受到被接纳、滋养和珍视。因此，在任何大都市中，分散的各类小型“社区”，从少数族裔聚居区到不同性取向群体，每个团体都渴望构建自己的身份，都会出版为各自不同利益代言的“社区”报，在主流媒体触角无法深入的地盘，社区报用一种亲密包容的方式来阐明和加强各自社区的核心价值观。

社区新闻视角

尽管在读者定位、报道主题或发行量等方面有所不同，但所有社区出版物都有一个共同点，他们的视角、关注点和新闻价值判断都以本土利益为驱动。据宾州州立大学（Pennsylvania State University）副教授安东尼•奥罗伦尼索拉（Anthony Olorunnisola）说，尼日利亚人甚至总结出了这种观点，将“T'iwanit'iwa; t'eminit'emi（我们的是我们的，但我的是我的）”这句约鲁巴[①]谚语应用到社区新闻时，可以这么说：“全国性新闻挺不错，可这报道内容和我有什么关系？”美国人对此也有相似的表述，已故的马萨诸塞州议员狄普•奥尼尔（Tip O’Neill）曾说：“一切政治都是地方的。”

如果真的有一种普适性的社区新闻模式的话，那就是它了。无论读者是在尼日利亚的拉各斯，还是在马萨诸塞州的波士顿，他需要知道的是，国内外新闻事件将如何对他的生活产生直接影响。事实上，我们可以从每一个大新闻中找到本土化视角。

社区报是什么

你无疑已经很熟悉“杯子一半是空的”和相对应的“杯子一半是满的”这两种说法。一个人的观点和态度决定生活中的行为。一切都取决于你看待事物的方式。无论是写一篇与之相关的论文，还是在学习社区报，请遵循以下思路。首先，列出一张“社区报是什么”的清单。

举例来说，我们假设有那么一份社区周报——为了好玩，我们就称其为《号

①尼日利亚的一个民族。

角报》（*The Bugle*）吧——这份刊物的特点如下：

1. 无以复加的本土化。对《号角报》读者来说，这张报纸是获得本地深度报道的第一手来源。他们能从中获取一切信息，从社区体育比赛到校车路线，从市议会到女童子军烘焙冠军介绍，仅有这份报纸能做到这一点。

2. 小发行量。它使社区报便于管理，更加人性化和令人愉悦。记者可以驱车在一天之内轻松地跑遍本地采写新闻。报纸的发行规模也不至于庞大到影响投递线路的程度。

3. 家庭的第二份报纸。当读者想要了解国内外大事时，《号角报》不是首选，他们可以订阅《纽约时报》或其他地区性日报。《号角报》只关注本地新闻，这方面的报道没有任何一份报纸能做得更好。

4. 大门敞开的编辑室。大多数社区报没有戒备森严的警卫，任何读者或广告商都可以自由出入。这种开放更好地体现了社区报的人文关怀，对个体的尊重，同时鼓励记者养成对读者更负责任的工作态度。

5. 做社区的引领者。无论编辑或出版人是否意识到或者承认，一个社区报都应该积极地参与社区活动，反映社区生活并引领社区发展。一份报纸能办成什么样子往往取决于它的编辑/出版人和这个社区的愿景。这很像为人父母。一旦你有了一个孩子，你得选择如何做父母，它将会使孩子和你自己的人生与众不同。正如一个伟大的母亲或父亲那样，具有启迪性的社区报发挥着独特作用，它是社区向着健康和适当方向成长的必要条件之一。

6. 周刊。周刊的定义是每周出版频率在1到3次的报纸。多数情况下，周报记者比日报记者有更充裕的时间完成采访、写作、编辑任务。报纸的出版频率越小，新闻保质期越长。周刊很容易被放在咖啡桌上一整周，但日报就得承受一日鲜的命运了。

7. 网络版。你的报纸不是日报，但这并不等同于它没有一个优秀的网站。许多周报都有卓越的网络版。请点击stateportpilot.com。

社区报不是什么

第一阅读选择。社区报不提供国内外爆炸性新闻，它也不应该提供！这不是很好吗？《号角报》可以节省派驻国外记者的大笔费用。但是如果有本地的孩子在曼谷做交换生，那又是另外一回事了。

大型。社区报的规模越大，它在运营、印刷、投递方面的开支也就越大。我们不是大城市日报，不必装成大日报的样子。你曾经看到过费尽心思把自己打扮成年轻女孩的老女人吗？漂染的头发、松弛的皮肤、紧身的裤子、浓妆艳抹的妆容。路人皆知她在竭力保持着她所没有的东西。她没能展示出自己年龄段独有的那种高雅而富于尊严的美，多么令人感到悲哀。

其他媒体。我们不是电视和网络，社区报拥有其他媒体没有也不可能有的东西：真实的个人化社区体验。这里是你的地盘。请把这种优势放大到极致。

社区报应该是什么样子

前社区新闻编辑比尔•福勒（Bill Flower）现在是塔拉哈西市（Tallahassee）一家报纸的顾问，他总喜欢说社区报对他们的社区和广告客户都至关重要，但报社从未放弃追求更高标准。我们应该利用社区报在图文深度报道方面先天具有的传统优势，在你所擅长的方面——全方位地进行本地报道——尽你所能。最后，我们应紧随科技的进步保持着学习的状态，以此应对未来。

社区新闻的不利之处

正如城市大报有着明显的缺点，我们也有不利之处，比如势单力薄，无须否认我们的资源更少——记者更少、计算机更少、摄影师更少、高端的相机更少——与之相伴的是更少的经费，无论在报纸的制作方面，还是在员工的薪水方面。在他们升任至编辑、广告和出版的管理岗位之前，社区报的新手记者、摄影师和广告销售人员的收入相对于城市大报中的同行来说更少。这对于心怀梦想的新手来说是令人沮丧的。

除此之外，还有一些城镇小报记者没有职业荣誉感，如果把新闻只是当作可以糊口的工作，报纸的质量就可想而知：懒散的管理、糟糕的文章和平庸的摄影。

报团带来的消极后果

报团拥有报纸，如果管理得当，也许能成为一件好事。但坏事也数不胜数。

为了节省开支，最常见的恶劣行为，是在有新闻编辑室员工离职的情况下不雇用新的人员，而是继续阴险地榨干余下的员工，让他们超负荷工作，同时虚假地承诺在合适的时机会雇用人手，而实际上这些空缺席位永远不会得到填补。可以预见的是，这样过度用人的新闻编辑室士气低下，人员流动频繁。

对于那些尚处于训练阶段的年轻记者，这样的工作氛围使他们难以了解社区新闻的重要性。他们从未产生介入社区生活的欲望，而是以一种自以为是、居高临下的态度轻慢地对待社区和读者。只要逮着合适的机会，就会抬腿走人，在社区报的工作经历只是未来职业进阶的一个垫脚石。

这样的体制会培养草率的、懒惰的编辑。如果相信自己所出版的只是“区区一张小报”，那么日常工作中，什么事都少做一点并不算得过且过，可长此以往，报纸的品质、精确度、专业性都会受影响。

要求体面的收入：你的付出终有回报

出版人怎么能够指望，刚从大学毕业的学生们（还背负着购车和助学贷款）能够来到社区报，为每小时8.5美元而工作，并且逐渐成长为骨干角色？算算这笔账，这样的收入在贫困线之下。难怪有些胸怀大志的年轻人踏入社区新闻这个行业，却在艰苦地撑过几年后热情殆尽，这样的情况并不鲜见。一名曾经隶属于一份拥有35000份发行量为报团所有的小型日报的记者，现在则在本地餐馆当侍者，他对笔者直言：“比起在报社一周工作65个小时，我在这里当服务员可以挣得更多。”当出版人抱怨新闻编辑室中频繁的员工流动时，他们应该好好考虑这一点。

对有职业追求的年轻记者来说，为一家平凡的社区报工作也许会很艰难。你在一个懒散的编辑室里无法得到有创意的培训，也无法得到来自前辈建设性的意见或者专业性的鼓励。但请谨记这一点：你的付出终有回报，你的经验将会在未来令你受益匪浅。当你选择动身离去，无论你去往何方，你所经历的一切都会对你有益。许多城市大报的总编辑会告诉你，社区报是起步的最佳选择。

第 4 章

社区报的读者们

敬爱的中国读者：

请允许我先做些解释：迪比克（*Dubuque*）是一个位于美国中西部中心的小城市，与纽约这种熙熙攘攘的世界级大都会相比，显得微不足道，住在这里的读者个体更是无足轻重。20世纪90年代，不少美国大都市日报都有这种优越感，现在他们麻烦多多。最好、最成功的美国社区报却把先天优势发挥到极致，从而在互联网时代也能站稳脚跟。

——作者

我们不是《纽约客》

1925年，当苗条而又优雅的《纽约客》杂志创刊的时候，编辑哈罗德•罗斯（Harold Ross）在卷首语中堂皇地写道：“《纽约客》不是写给来自迪比克的老妇人看的。”

好吧，朋友，我们的工作却正是以爱荷华州（Iowa）迪比克（或者说伊利诺伊州的迪克森，还有北卡罗来纳州的邓恩）的老妇人能理解的语言报道他们的身边人和身边事，时尚精巧的工作得有人做，但是，请不要忘记那个老妇人，她也是你的读者。

1041航班上的真实故事

在东海岸上空，华盛顿飞往迈阿密的1041航班正在11千米的高度上平稳飞行。乘客们有的喝着饮料，有的看着窗外风景，还有的打瞌睡或者读报纸，就连空中小姐们也难得清闲下来。

“抱歉打扰，先生。”年轻的空姐对一位商人说道。那位先生身旁放着一份东北地区的大城市日报，而他自己则凝视着窗外。“这是你的报纸吗？”空姐礼貌地问道。

“是的。”他回答。

“能借我读读吗？”她问。

“行啊，但是记得还回来。”

“当然，”她开心地答道，“我看看漫画和头版就够了。”

她说的的确是这个顺序，简单地说，就是娱乐第一，其次是一点新闻。

这位年轻的空姐看报的效率堪比她做事的敏捷，还没到5分钟她就把全部内容浏览了一遍，并把报纸还了回来。要知道，这份沉甸甸的宽幅报纸一共有68版，外加68版的周末软文杂志！

有时候你的读者可能不仅仅是那个来自迪比克的老妇人，她也可能是一个年轻的空姐。

矿井中的金丝雀

就在那份日报中，有一封读者来信。信中写道，30年前18到29岁的年轻人里有60%的人每天读报；而现在只剩下不到30%，而且这个数字还在不断下降。那封信的作者列举了一些原因，解释为什么很多读者渐渐放弃了读报。

变了的不是读者，而是报纸本身。25年前，你可以在大多数报纸中读到如何烘烤蛋糕、如何修车，同时也可以了解到自己社区发生的事情。年轻人也会热切地翻阅报纸寻找自己的名字和照片。

而今天，所有的报纸几乎都在责怪电视抢走了读者。有的报纸赞助了"报纸参与教育"之类的项目来争取年轻读者。炫目的图片、价格不菲的配色被用来提高读者的阅读兴趣。然而当普通读者寄来发自肺腑但文字略显生涩的信件时，编辑们却不屑一顾。当学校老师询问是否可以报道一下学生表演活动的时候，总是得到否定的回答。要想发表新闻公告，需要提前三到四周预约，而且必须亲自去报社预约，打电话是行不通的。到最后能不能发表，也没有一个确切的保证。

如今的记者和编辑们比以前受过更好的教育，也更精于世故。他们很少是在自己所报道的那个社区长大的，他们与自己的读者群体并不拥有一致的价值观或者生活方式，也没有同样的生活经历。而且他们总是收拾好了行囊，随时准备从一家报纸跳槽到另一家，期待着尽快开始在大报的职业生涯。

如果报纸真心实意地想赢回读者，必须重新认识他们。尽管电视、快节奏的生活方式等因素会削弱报纸的影响力，但是报纸自恃精英的傲慢才是真正让读者感到厌烦的原因。

关于今日报纸的问题，那些最简洁有力的批评不是来自某个媒体专家或者某位大众传播学教授，而是那个来自迪比克的老妇人！

一边读，一边哭

曾几何时，当医生们开始为"新闻斋戒"（长达两周的时间里不看电视，不读报纸，不浏览网络新闻，不看杂志，不听广播）开出处方的时候，那些关心严肃新闻的人士就意识到了这是一个警钟。

社区报也是"媒体"总称的一个组成部分。人们其实搞不清楚各种媒体的区别，当读者谴责"媒体"时，作为社区报人，我们感到委屈吗？我们必须搞懂的是，读者在想些什么、说些什么。下面这些就是他们最常抱怨的话：

- 媒体根本没有深入社区。记者总是端着一副高人一等的架子，身在曹营心在汉，寻找着走进大报的机会，随时准备离开。他们是无根之木，与社区没有情感联系，他们更不会为读者着想。他们做的，就是俗称的“降落伞新闻”（意指居高临下，与读者缺少情感关联的新闻及报道方式）。

● 总体而言，媒体对小的、少数族裔或者边缘社区总是一副居高临下的态度。他们总是拿“昏昏欲睡”或者“死气沉沉”这样老套的词汇来形容小城镇。大城市日报只有在小城镇发生灾难或是负面新闻时才会做一些报道。

● 主流媒体总是在煽情。尤其是电视新闻，就像歌手兼作曲家比尔•拜尔斯（Bill Byers）说的那样“一边吓唬，一边诱惑”。一句老谚语依然适用：“流血的新闻就是好新闻。”举个例子，晚上8时的新闻预告说：“男孩在田径场上被标枪刺中，详细信息请留意晚上11时的新闻。”我们居然要等到晚上11时才能知道男孩还活着吗！他是谁？不得不问的是，这种新闻对公众利益有无好处？报道这个是否必要？不，这简直是“性、腥、星”式的低级娱乐节目，这不是新闻！《华盛顿每周评论》（*Washington Week in Review Host*）前任节目主持人保罗•杜克（Paul Duke）表示对现在的媒体生态感到十分悲哀，认为这种泛娱乐化趋势，给了谣言乱象以可乘之机，招致了社会对媒体的普遍怀疑态度。

● 媒体傲慢自大，自以为是，只要有一点点机会，就会用观点来掩盖事实。保罗•杜克引用了一份投票结果，有70%的受访者表示新闻机构“妨碍了问题的解决”。

● 媒体有时候会摆出一副关心大众、心系社区的姿态，但他们并没有真的那样做。“邻里”版面只是主流大报争取中心城市之外周边市场的一种虚情假意的尝试，一种卖广告、扩大发行量、迂回进入社区领地的小算盘，抑或是排挤其他竞争者的一种手段。出版“邻里”版面的真正目的是利润，至于说社区新闻价值则无人关心。

● 媒体没有人情味，不亲民，没有责任心，也没有爱心。日报越来越不受读者信任，这大概没什么好意外的。根据皮尤调查中心“大众与新闻”项目的研究结果，相信报纸内容的人数比例已经从1985年的80%下降到了2003年的59%。

媒体对他们所报道的人有多尊重呢？据《今日美国》的一份调查显示，早在1985年，35%的受访者表示媒体的确是关怀被报道者的，而到了1999年，这个数字降低到了21%。在1999年，67%的受访者认为媒体不关心被报道者，相比于1985年的48%，上升了19个百分点。

关于怎么做邻居

傲慢自大和精英主义甚至影响到了社区新闻。有这样一个故事：一位曾在东北部都市大报工作过的资深报人跑到南部海岸买下了一份小型社区报。在社区工作不到6个月的时间，他就疏远了自己报纸的绝大多数读者和所有广告商。他总是唐突而无礼，一心向钱看，傲慢自大，目中无人，面对当地人时总有种高高在上的优越感。他可能有着出类拔萃的学历、光鲜亮丽的履历，但是他没有学会一种大学和大公司不会教给他的能力——与人为邻。每一个有经验的社区新闻工作者都知道，在小地方，闲言碎语传得很快，一旦遭到集体排斥，你就很难开展工作。新来的报纸出版人如果自我膨胀得厉害，看不起当地人、难以接地气的话，纵使编辑能力再超群也于事无补。如果这个出版人对每个人都充分尊重，无论他是一个银行家还是一个低收入者，无论他是一个厨师还是郡长，结果应该会很不一样吧！要记住，在社区报工作，无论身边人是什么身份，都是你现有的或潜在的广告商和读者——换句话说，是你的客户。

关于单词“CARE”

对于一份稳定运行的社区报来说，它与社区之间一定存在一种积极互惠的关系。也就是双方互相信任，互相帮助，互相支持。

如果可以通过打电话、发邮件或者登门拜访与报社进行沟通，社区的居民们一定不会觉得自己受到了忽视排斥或者被当成麻烦。相反，他们会觉得自己受到了欢迎，自身的价值得到了认可。

报纸和读者双方同时也应该形成一种诚挚的利益攸关的关系，共同促进社区的良性发展。报纸的员工们必须全心全意地为他们所服务的社区着想。这要求我们放下身段，以平等的视角与社区对话。

在宾州小镇，卡尔•斯托尔茨福斯（Carl Stoltzfus）经营的管道公司门口挂着这句格言：“我们心系本地，我们关怀邻里。（We’re local and we care.）”靠着这种人性化的态度和过硬的产品质量，卡尔奇迹般地抓住了所有能抓住的生意。

卡尔的信条一针见血地指出了社区报与其他大型报纸的核心区别。我们不妨把“CARE”这个单词分解一下。

要理解社区和社区报之间的契约关系，以C、A、R、E开头的单词可以提供一种简单又直观的解读方式。

C代表community，也就是“社区第一”。

A代表accessibility和accountability，指的是“开放度”和“责任感”，强调为社区服务。

R代表responsibility，强调为报道负责。

E代表even-handedness，equanimity，egalitarianism和elitist-not，核心意思都是去精英化。

首先说“社区”，对社区新闻工作者来说，社区是立足点。具体一些，报道内容应该紧扣所在社区，对身边事怀有高度好奇心，在新闻事件中挖掘本地化视角，比如它对社区有何重要性、对建设一个更加和谐美好的社区有何帮助，等等。

其次是“开放度”和“责任感”。社区新闻工作者应该向读者敞开交流的大门。阻碍报纸与公众交流的壁垒，无论是客观的还是主观的，都应该尽可能地消除。我们要这样想：每一个陌生人都是你尚未谋面的读者。更进一步，我们要向读者保证，将会对他们负责任，对社区负责任，对报道负责任。

继续说责任。我们需要尽自己所能为居民提供完整、准确、公正的报道。不要鲁莽地进行采访，不能偷偷摸摸或者像狗仔队那样采访，我们也不会快来快闪，不应该再次伤害受害者。我们会采访社区中最普通的民众，把他们当作自己的邻居对待，他们是活生生的人，而不是新闻产业的消耗品。

最后摒弃媒体精英主义。我们要带着谦卑的态度做每一件事情。当报道出发点落在“我们都是社区一分子”而不是“我们与他们”的对立视角上时，日积月累，报纸内容就能反映社区日渐发展的轨迹。

读者想要什么

在一场名为“读者想要什么”的新闻研讨会上，田纳西州诺克斯维尔大学传播学院（University of Tennessee-Knoxville College of Communications）名誉院长凯利•雷特（Kelly Leiter）直奔主题，用机关枪般的速度做了下面这篇演讲：

> “读者想要什么？他们想要的是本地化的新闻！他们想知道自己周围有哪些人结婚了，哪些孩子出生了；他们想知道，是谁买下了4号公路上雷特家的房产，买主是不是准备在那儿建一座汽车旅馆，规划委员会有没有批准那个修建化工厂的计划。他们想知道，通过新增的消费税为学校筹集的资金被用在了哪儿，谁将会在本周高中橄榄球比赛中打四分卫，为什么那个傻瓜教练把那个家伙放在这么重要的位置，下周哪些街道会被拆掉。他们想看到健康资讯，但必须是他们自己用得着的才行——比如说如何好好休息，如何选择适合退休后居住的房子等。他们想要的是本地化的新闻，尽可能多的本地新闻！”

雷特用一种夸张的幽默结束了他的演讲：“如果可以的话，我想告诉每一位报纸主编，让他们在每天晚上召集所有编辑记者一起诵念咒语：‘本地化，本地化，本地化……’”

雷特还讲述了他采访一位75岁老妇人的见闻："当我问她报纸中你最喜欢的版面是哪一版时，她的回答颇为意外：'体育版。我有两个孙子，他们都在校足球队踢球，我想在报纸中看到他们的名字！'"

读者研究

当被问及最想看到什么内容的时候，可以预料的是读者们大概会简单地说："更多的本地新闻。"但是真正的结果要复杂得多。

2001年，西北大学读者研究所（Readership Institute at Northwestern University）的研究者们对37000位读者进行"你想从报纸中得到什么"的调查，之后，报告列出了一些报纸吸引并留住读者的重要方法。

研究所主任约翰•拉维尼在2004年出版的小册子《让研究落地：小型报纸在干什么？》（*Implementing the Impact Study: What Small Newspapers Are Doing*）中写道："内容为王，服务出色，品牌信誉，都是培养读者忠诚度的法宝。它们对吸引读者有着巨大的潜力。"

读者研究所同时也调查了100份规模大小不一的日报，研究这些报纸在面对发行量下降和读者疏远的问题时做得怎么样。（注：读者研究所的影响研究计划没有包含全美周报，可能是因为本来他们在读者工作方面就做得很出色吧！）

研究所最终给出的"行动指南"完全基于读者对优秀的评判，为提高报纸质量提供了一份实用的路线图，帮助从业者选择如何做出改变。

内容：极致本地化

- 报纸对内容的选择应该遵循这样一个规律，那就是：尽可能本地化，不管是关于政府和政治的新闻，还是关于生活方式、教育和宗教等方面的新闻。
- 想一想如何通过导读栏或者头版来展示报纸内容的丰富性。
- 报纸最重要的版面要用来刊登本地化报道。

报纸中的内容推广

- 指引读者去读报纸内页内容。
- 引导读者去关注即将发生的事情。
- 重点推广的内容应该吸引眼球且能真正有助于提高报纸销售。

写作手法的多样化

● 除了倒金字塔结构，报纸应该尝试用各种不同格式来报道新闻，传达信息。比如说，有特色的文体、问答、图片报道、表格，等等。

● 简单明了。

● 每个故事都有一个要点，抓住要点并做出一份清晰的报道。

实用信息

● 去哪儿、怎么去、打电话给谁、方向、定位地图、到哪儿取得更多的信息，这些琐碎的事情都要替读者考虑。

● 表格、图表等都可以运用起来，从而给读者的生活带来方便。这是对读者兴趣的一种回应，也可以帮助他们更好地利用信息。

寻找读者的兴趣所在

● 报道影响广泛的事件时，应该从本地居民的视角切入。

● 少报道镇议会的决议，多多解释政府决议如何影响人们生活、对居民有何意义等与日常生活相关的内容。

● 最基础的工作是，引导读者去做些对社区有益的事情。

● 更高级的工作是，要扮演好社区“看门狗”角色。

寻找公共话题

● 你的内容应该是读者们乐于与他的邻居朋友们分享的东西，也就是那种“嗨，你看！”式的故事，那些会被当地电台的谈话节目拿出来说的事情，那些热门的话题。

和我一样的人

● 报纸为本地普通居民服务，他们是我们报道的主要对象。

● 写普通人的故事。

● 照片和文字报道应该是当地社区日常生活的写照。

让年轻读者感兴趣的内容

● 报道可以吸引他们的事情。

● 报道与他们息息相关的事情。

● 报道公共利益的议题时要呈现年轻人的观点。

报纸的个性

● 反映社区的主流观点。
● 激发人们讨论。
● 不仅是新闻和信息的载体，还要表达对社区和读者的关怀（这方面的做法有很多，比如编辑在专栏中讨论读者关切的话题，为了社区的良性发展而做的报道，刊登读者来信等都可以体现出这种关怀）。
● 标题应有力、新鲜且吸引人。
● 报纸用自己的热情和创造力把日复一日的生活有滋有味地呈现给读者。

抓住难以捉摸的年轻人

要满足他们的需要就得报道他们的生活，报道他们感兴趣的内容。

北卡州一份非常成功、广受欢迎的一周双刊《富兰克林周刊》[*Franklin (N.C.) Press*]，大胆引入年轻的学生进入报社做记者，写他们自己的故事。每周让各个高中的学生记者轮流写专栏，报道校园里发生的故事，或者反映高中生活的一个侧面。这个专栏由高中教新闻写作的老师们协助学生完成，这是课程中的重要组成部分。它不会给报社带来任何负担，只要给学校写一份委托书就够了。报社编辑芭芭拉•麦克雷（Barbara McRae）和富兰克林高中新闻写作老师李•伯格（Lee Berger）说，这对所有人来说都是一个共赢的局面。

镜中窥报，令人不安

特德•瓦登（Ted Vaden）是发行量达22000份的双周刊《教堂山新闻》（*Chapel Hill News*）的编辑兼出版人。位于教堂山大学城的这份社区报，现由麦克拉齐报业集团所有。在一场关于新闻公正性问题的引人深思的研讨会之后，特德在《每周评论》中写下了这些话：

> 你可能没有注意到，上周我们镇来了很多新闻工作者。确切地说，一共有600多人参加了这次每年一度的北卡罗来纳州新闻协会冬季大会。周三晚上，你在主街上可以听到此起彼伏的“嘶嘶”声，那是人们开啤酒的声音。在年度颁奖典礼上，人们向那些获得了新闻奖项的编辑和记

者们表达了诚挚的祝贺。本地经济——至少是酒吧和餐馆的生意——因为大批“无冕之王”的涌入而变好了许多。

记者们是出了名的宴会达人，但是聚会毕竟不是主要的事情。在周五的会议中，我们进行了很多的议程。事实上，会议中听到的话都是很令我们警醒的事。有感于《纽约时报》记者杰森•布莱尔涉嫌虚假报道被曝光这件丑闻，记者们都很担心现在媒体的信誉问题。我们这个行业并非有着多么严格的防范机制，很难确保记者的行为都符合规范。

前《圣皮特斯堡报》（*St. Petersburg Times*）执行总编鲍勃•海曼（Bob Haiman）为我们详细陈述了这个问题。他曾经在自由基金会（一个报业智囊机构）主持了一项关于新闻公正性的研究。从来自全国各地不同阶层的读者那里，海曼了解到了人们对媒体公正性诟病最多的一些方面：

● 事实错误和事实不清。“人们都说，报纸每天都会出现很多错误。”他说道，“如果你想让别人认为你是公正的，首先要做的就是避免报道中的事实错误。”

● 不愿意承认和改正错误。人们的抱怨往往无济于事，我们总是羞于承认自己的错误。“如果你犯了错误，你不仅仅应该改过来，你更应该向读者道歉。”海曼说。

● 记者的无知。在一个科技迅速进步的时代，有些记者不具备相应的专业知识，他们知道的实在不够多。

● 文化上的偏见和迟钝。记者的构成没能反映出社区居民成分的多样性，这一点不仅仅体现在种族和价值观念上，更体现在政治、意识形态甚至宗教信仰上。“记者中有很多人都以自由主义者或中间立场者自居，相比之下支持共和党立场的保守派就少很多。”海曼说，“新闻工作者中很多都不是虔诚的新教徒，至于天主教徒和犹太教徒，那就更少了！”

● 没有把充分的时间和空间用来刊发正面新闻。“我们想知道什么事情现在出了问题，但是同时我们也想知道什么事情正在顺利进行。”海曼解释道，“如果你不把两方面的信息都告诉我们，你只是把这个社区里发生的一半事情传达给我们，这显然是不恰当的。”

● 伤害弱者和无防备的人。比如强迫车祸受害者接受采访这样的事情。

● 报道采纳未经确认的消息源。“他们不愿意看到某个声明或者某次袭击没有一个确定的来源。”海曼说，“信息源的胡乱引用是杰森•布莱尔事件中的核心问题。”

对于上面大多数控诉，《教堂山新闻》表示，我们非常愧疚，很多事情确实在这里发生。我们让很多错误溜进了报纸，而自己对错误又有着太高的容忍度，我们的记者们博而不专，无法搞清楚一些比较艰深的问题，团队组成也没有反映出社区逐步增加的多样性。相对于保守主义，我们更倾向于自由主义。（当然，教堂山—卡布罗地区本身就是一个较为自由的地方。）

我们要不停努力，努力使自己变成一个专家，清除掉报纸中的错误，摒弃偏见，对稿件进行二次审核和确认——这对于小型报纸来说是很奢侈的行为。我们尽力招募最优秀的人才并且给予他们充分的锻炼。我们还通过定期举办交流会的方式与您——我们的读者们进行商榷。我们将来还要加大这种交流会举行的频率。

第 5 章

新闻中的社区

敬爱的中国读者：

要说明中美之间的语言歧义，对“社区”的深层次理解便是一个绝佳的例子。其实，即使是美国人也在纠结着这个词的定义。所以，我们需用一整章来讲解“社区”的内涵。在美国人看来，“社区”不仅仅是一个明确的统计区，更代表着一个包容的、开放的、受人欢迎的场合。在这里，人们可以一起分享快乐、悲伤、负担以及彼此的共同信仰。人们共聚在一起，生活因此变得更美好。初次接触者能理解到这程度也算不错了。但“社区”的内涵远不止于此，你将会得到更多的解读。

——作者

当寻求“我是谁”的答案时，最好从地方认同开始。

——*伊丽莎白•舍维尔*（Elizabeth Sewell）

报纸并不存在于真空，而是立足于某一地。不同的地方像人一样也千姿百态。学新闻的学生对自己未来的工作地要好好研究一下，“地方认同”是一个非常重要的概念。

“所有的社区，就像人一样，都有自己的……态度！你在1千米之外就能识别这个社区的特质！”北卡森林小镇的规划者和社区媒体项目顾问丹尼尔•韦斯洛（Danielle Withrow）如是说。当人们提起自己所居住的地方，不管是勤劳的蓝领社区、文化气息浓厚的社区，还是富裕的小镇，心里都对它有一个明晰的定位。

定义“地方”

如何定义一座城市、一个小镇、一条村庄、一处社区？我们明白这些词的确切定义吗？有趣的是，在大多数情况下，我们对它们的定义模糊而主观。根据苏珊•梅休（Susan Mayhew）在地理字典中的定义，城市是一个“能够提供专业的产品和服务的大型中心都市功能区”。在人口规模和城市面积方面，全球对城市的定义并没有统一标准。对乡镇的定义也是如此，梅休将其描述为“相对小型的都市地带，没有人数或面积的限制”。

给社区下定义无疑就更具有挑战性了。有人曾开玩笑说：“社区的定义可以有99种，而且每一种解释都是正确的。”多年和这个定义打交道，我得出的结论是：“社区”是一个有争议的概念，其表达有的很强烈，有的很浅层次。

然而，多亏了乡镇规划者丹尼尔•维斯洛，我们得以将社区划分为三种类型：

地理上的社区；

观念上的社区；

种族上的社区。

地理上的社区

我们都生活在地理意义上相互绑定的社区之中。关于领地的传统定义适用于对社区的解释。梅耶和布赖特比尔（Brightbill）在《社区休闲》（*Community*

Recreation）一书中写道："……一群人生活在相同的地方，统一受当地政府和法律的管束……通过地理上的，还有经济、社会和文化上的纽带，被一个共同的环境结合在一起。由于大家共同的利益、需求和关注，他们创造了为己所用的政府、教育、经济、娱乐和宗教等性质的机构。"

禅学陶艺师肯尼斯•贝提尔（Kenneth Beittel）曾写过，社区可以被定义为一个通常较小且相互联系的人口中心，在这里，每个个体都能感觉到自我被重视，他们共享核心价值观和社会习俗，有着高度界定的地区感和强烈的城镇认同感。

社会心理学家阿米塔伊•埃兹欧尼（Amitai Etzioni）写道，社区的本质是"建立在共享价值观之上的社会关系网"。

马丁•路德•金的解释是："我们不可避免地陷入了相互缠绕的关系网，被共同命运所束缚。"

引用喀麦隆的古老谚语："雨水不是落在一个屋顶上的。"

根据《国家地理杂志》的世界地图集，仅某一非洲国家就有200个不同宗族，大家操着80种不同的语言，这使得对社区概念进行定义难上加难。

观念和种族上的社区

"社区"这个词几乎可以被随时随地使用：无论是在知识分子聚居的社区，还是在大学社区，抑或是农业社区。虽然他们跨越空间界限，但这些团体由于共同价值观而关系密切地连接在一起。该术语通常被用来指称具有正面意义的群体。因此，很少有人听说过"监狱社区""毒品滥用社区"或者"色情社区"。

虽然不同民族的社区可能在地理位置上是分散的，但他们被共同的血缘和历史连接，聚合在一起。我们听说过苗族社区、拉丁裔社区或者希腊社区等。

但同时，也合理地存在着一些人造社区：近年来，"社区"这个词已经被滥用了，比如网络上的"虚拟社区"，被门禁隔离出来的"社区"，甚至大城市都被称为"社区"。

社区的地理范围很小，也只有小才能使这一撮人聚集形成一种特别的人文关怀，每个个体都能够感到被重视并意识到自身价值。研究表明，小规模易亲近，大规模易疏远。

这种"人性尺度"在城镇中得以自然保存，但笔者认为，这种城镇是有限度的，当人口超过5万时，小城镇以及地区感和公民身份感会逐步消失，各方面会更接近大城市的感觉。而城市是一种完全不同的存在。

通常你听到"社区"这个词都是一种幸福的表达，并且通常带有吸引力。当某地可能没有社区认同时，也需要倡导某种想象的共同体把大家维系在一起——人口约四五百万的底特律市长深谙此道，他在媒体中号召整个"底特律社区"团结起来，阻止其走向“恶魔之城”的命运。

底特律是一个社区吗？不是，它是一个城市。“城市”并不具有“社区”的包容性和强烈的吸引力。从属于一个社区等于从属于一个团体，即“大我”。在城市中这种“大我”的情感体验只在多元化和个性化的街区生活中才能找到。这又被称为“社区中的社区”。

以互联网为例，所谓的“社区”成员能够假造身份，随意泄愤，对他人造成伤害，然后不承担后果就消失无踪，这样的社区与社区的最基本含义——成员承担相应责任相去甚远。

此外，以封闭式社区为例，如果一个社区只对特定人群表现出善意，它不能被称为一个真正的社区。传统社区往往是环绕着铁路、河流或者交通十字路口自然地慢慢成长，开放、包容而且友好，不可否认的是，封闭式社区确实能给传统社区带来某些新气象，但它们作为简单纯粹的建筑物，以提供便利的生活条件来吸引买家，只是市场化的工具，喂肥了开发商而已。

地区如何成长

值得庆幸的是，“地区”被定义得更加具体，它被梅林描述为一个“可识别的位置……位于地球的表面……能够赋予人类意义”。

美国的大多数地区（指城镇和城市）的形成都始于非常微小的东西的集聚。宾夕法尼亚州立大学的地理名誉教授佩尔斯•刘易斯（Peirce Lewis）说，最常见的就是简单的道路，无论是通航的河流还是美国原住民通商的交叉道口，定居者把这些通商道路转变成驿道。当城镇兴旺变成城市时，无轨电车和铁路线向外延伸，使乡亲们能够住在城市核心区域之外。

乔治•华盛顿大学（George Washington University）地理系教授约瑟夫•伍德（Joseph Wood）认为，交通工具的发达催化了20世纪50年代居住郊区化的“第一次浪潮”，小型载客汽车的发明正是适应了那样的生活方式。

百货公司或多或少仍为住在城里的人服务，但随着住房模式和交通方式变化而来的零售业务也跟着进化，50年代购物广场（现代购物广场的前身）依一条街排开，每个商店都有自己独立的入口，门外就是停车场，购物的便利使得顾客逐步远离了老式的市中心百货店，并最终导致其退出市场。

美国第一条环路也是这一时期建立的，意在减少交通问题，远离拥挤的城市中心。但是路易斯认为这些环路产生了没有预料到的结果，修建环线的目的在于维护和提升老城区的吸引力，没想到“第二次浪潮”却把城市中心的居民以及紧随其后的零售业从中心吸引到城郊，由此一来，彻底改变和削减了美国传统城市中心的吸引力和影响力。

伍德所说的“第三次浪潮”表现为办公中心的迁移。换言之，办公园区沿着环路发展，公司把分部安排在靠近新郊区而不是市中心的地方，随后沿线大量商场拔地而起。伍德指出，随着越来越多的女性加入劳动大军，离家近的工作更吸引她们，因为它缩短了上下班以及接送孩子的时间。如果你住在郊区，在附近的办公园区工作，也能刚好在旁边的商场购物，还有必要自找麻烦穿越堵塞的交通到市中心去吗？逐渐地，郊区或者远郊富人住宅区成为同质化的、没有多少地区从属感和社区感的“睡城”。

此外，当新型购物中心拔地而起，用人造景观煞费苦心再造出来的小型城镇表明美国人的集体意识正在异化。

新都市主义

如果有“第四次浪潮”的话，就是伍德所谓的“新都市主义”，他定义其为精心规划的新传统社区，这些社区被开发商设计为“结构紧凑、适宜步行、综合用途的城市和城镇”，每个人都能够在那里很好地生活、购物、工作，但情感上没有人真正属于所居住的地方。

情理之中，新都市主义也受到了批评。然而，倡议者如蒂莫西•S.美斯克（Timothy S. Mescon）在2002年8月出版的飞机杂志《抵达》（*Arrivals*）上写道：“新都市主义支持开放空间、适当架构的区域规划，支持工作和住房均衡发展。他们相信，这些策略将减少人们耗在交通上的时间，增加保障性住房供给和抑制城市蔓延。”

如果作者能够大胆地提出“第五次新浪潮”，那一定是“城市远郊住宅区”，居住在“封闭式社区”中、成长于汽车文化的一代只想在离家一小时车程之内的地方工作。我把这些人称作“远郊游牧民族”，汽车文化的基因是疏离感，这些每天奔驰在公路上的“战士”会对自己居住的“社区”有多少归属感呢？事实证明，几乎没有。

社区报适合什么样的地方

宾夕法尼亚州立大学地理学名誉教授皮尔斯•刘易斯说，所有地方、所有社区都面临“变化的挑战”，这通常意味着“经济增长的挑战”。这正是社区报可以一展身手的时机。刘易斯认为，社区报的介入可以让社区在考虑经济增长和发展前景问题时更全面，更充分。

刘易斯担心，如果没有积极的区域规划，按照自然发展则会变成无拘无束的城市扩张，住房、交通等问题都会出现，最后导致类似洛杉矶或华盛顿这样的摊大饼都市，只知道不断通过一圈圈的环路让城市无限扩充，居住区和商业区散乱地修得到处都是，这些都是城市规划的败笔。

社区报能够造就社区吗？

得克萨斯州奥斯汀大学（University of Texas-Austin）副教授吉恩•伯德（Gene Burd）在一次关于社区报和社区建设的研讨会上表明，媒体观察员指出郊区社区报的主要增长领域就位于大型都市报的“后花园”中。这样的报纸面临着一个难以应对的挑战，出版商不可能在地图上画一个圆，把一帮居民圈进去就声称这个地方是一个社区，当一个郊区与附近城区的‘卧室社区’高度相似时，社区报如何突出其独有的地方感？

与会的一名出版人就有这样的烦恼，他说在那里“人们买下一套房子，搬进来，开车去城里工作，他们的房子只是用来睡觉。他们一点也不关心我们的城镇”。

如果邻里之间完全没有社区意识，也就是相互隔离的话，报纸需要长期坚持不懈地报道本地事物，这既花费时间，又充满风险，还需要一定的财政保障。

但是对处于这种困境的报纸来说，只是一周又一周地发布时事新闻是远远不够的。它应该用积极主动的创新手段来销售报纸，把社区概念灌输给这个社区，并且使新住户了解这个社区的社区环境。

令社区报出版人高兴的是，居民对当地新闻信息的渴求使得赢利成为可能。大量的成功案例是存在的。当被问道：“您如何与《费城问询报》竞争？”《费城领导者》（*Philadelphia Leader*）——一份周发行量达3万份的免费报纸——的编辑马歇尔•罗斯曼（Marshall Rothman）几乎笑出声来。“《费城问询报》是什么？我们之间没有任何一点是相同的。” 这份社区报在大报“阴影”下已经蓬勃地出版了40余年。

另一些声音，另一些编辑室

当“杰夫”威廉•J.布雷迪（William J. “Jeff” Brady），阿拉斯加《史凯威新闻报》（*Skagway Alaska News*，以下简称《新闻报》）的创始编辑与出版人，于1978年毕业于北卡罗来纳大学教堂山分校之时，他年少轻狂，谈吐中处处流露出轻蔑与冒犯。用他自己的话说："我刚走出大学校门，我将会改变世界——至少得改变南阿拉斯加。"

他具有十足的冒险精神，离开他土生土长的南方，在家乡千里之外起步创业。带着母亲给予的小小一笔资金，布雷迪将自己的狗及一切财产都塞入一辆小卡车，他穿越整个国家，在西雅图买了二手的印刷排字设备，之后向着北方的史凯威进发。

在大学春假期间，布雷迪发现了史凯威——一个19世纪90年代淘金热中遗留的小镇，他决定在此创办一份报纸。

镇长听说有个刚出大学校门的愣头青准备在这里创办报纸，他劝诫布雷迪："如果你要在这儿办份报纸，可得先准备一组铜指节和一个保镖啊。"

但布雷迪安然度过了大风大浪。他的报纸不久前刚刚举行了25周年庆典。

这份报纸的出版就是一场荒野求生的冒险。这份每月双刊、发行量达800份的《新闻报》，8开16页，它的印刷地点在加拿大育空地区白马市（Whitehorse, Yukon Territory）。

布雷迪说："我想告诉大家的是，我的通勤状况世界一流。"他去印刷厂的跨国之旅需要经过30个潜在的雪崩区域，其中最高的山口海拔高达1千米。

报纸发行量会在旅游季到来之时翻一番，每年这个时候史凯威会成为全球第16大游轮港口。被设计成1898年淘金热风格的游客手册为他带来滚滚财源，据布雷迪说，这占他年收入的2/3。

他的报纸也不时出现反映他内心野性的报道。举个例子，布雷迪向采访他的人展示了《新闻报》的头版——头条报道是镇外的一座冰山突然移动，从而在当地引发了一场洪水。在解释报纸在社区中所扮演的角色时，他说："你既是社区的拉拉队队长，也是历史的记录者。"

《新闻报》是场一个人的战斗，布雷迪说："我们有三台电脑：一台给我，一台给业务部门，一台给记者——不过总共只有一台。"

布雷迪也欢迎夏天到报社实习的大学生们——如果他们不介意只能将就睡编辑室沙发的话。

第 6 章

社区报的新闻特写：留意表征

敬爱的中国读者：

尽管特写常被视作“软新闻”或“无价值的东西”，但实际上，特写撑起了社区报道的主要板块。可能是因为“硬新闻”多发生在主流都市地区，在小城镇不常发生，所以众多社区报得依赖关于当地人、事的特写来填充版面。这也为社区提供了敏锐的视角与独特的审美价值。

——作者

没有掉头走掉的年轻人

一位年轻的特写记者困惑地站在一扇敞开的大门前。他本该在这儿见到一位叫霍利•格林（Hoyle Greene）的老人家，采写一篇关于苹果酒制作的特写，但他却找不到老者的踪影。年轻人很失望，准备掉头走开。但是，等一下——邮筒上那个纸条写的是什么，看起来像一团胡话：

"围。见。房。我。在。工。→"

年轻人怔怔地盯着纸片，然后，他明白了：老爷子文化程度不高，他以为每个字的后面都要加上句号。弄懂了纸片的意思后，年轻人在附近找到了正在工作的老者。老者见到他就眉飞色舞地说：

"喜罕俺嘀迹条吧，小豁子？"

年轻的记者真心"喜罕"这张"迹条"，还专门为它照了相。紧接着，这位不怎么会写字的老爷子向年轻人展示了他的苹果世界——苹果的种类、苹果酒的分类和简易的制作方法。

接下来的好些年里，霍利•格林成了那位记者丰富的稿件来源。最终，老者的照片登上了一本展示西阿巴拉契亚地区老人和文化的图书封面。

回头想想，年轻记者如果错过了那张纸片，那么多的后续故事又怎么可能会发生呢。

社区新闻记者：有创造力的作家

在爱德华•斯特陈（Edward Steichen）的经典摄影展和《人的家庭》（*The Family of Man*）一书中，有这么一张载入史册的照片：篝火旁，一群非洲孩子聚精会神地听着村中长者讲鬼故事。长者双手高举，犹如张开的魔爪，两眼放光，牙齿外露，好似鬼怪的恶嚎。孩子们惊愕地张着大嘴，目不转睛，生怕漏掉一字一句。

这种讲故事的艺术与人类有着同样长的历史，它同时也是所有报纸的基础。本质上说，这就是我们行业存在和兴旺的理由。（仔细想来，广告实际上也是讲故事的另类方式。）现代生活中充斥着网络的喧嚣、电视的浮夸、图片化的阅读和杂志中花里胡哨的文字，还有那些仿照电视炫目效果的报纸，人们很容易忽视"讲故事"的重要性。

小尤金•L.罗伯特茨（Eugene L. Roberts Jr.）在自己的母校北卡罗来纳州大学教堂山分校设立了一个年度奖项，奖励那些能把故事讲得精彩的学生记者。从下面这段刻在奖匾上的话，你可以看到罗伯特茨的精彩阐述和对获奖者的严格要求。

> 尤金•L.罗伯特茨奖向如下人和事物表示鼓励和敬意：那些娓娓道来而不凌乱割裂的故事；那些揭露事实而不叠床架屋的故事；那些委婉而不拐弯抹角的报道者；那些寻求真理而不拘泥于事实的记者；那些高瞻远瞩而不目光短浅的记者；那些会被大街上咖啡馆中的人津津乐道的故事；那些不仅仅讲述了“时间、地点、有谁在做什么、为什么做”而且同时提出质疑的故事；那些为描绘真实生活而做出的努力；那些能够唤醒心灵并能让人们看见真相的新闻；那些逐渐消失的讲故事大师的复活。

给年轻人的建议：讲故事

为了把故事讲得生动有趣，人们会引用奇闻轶事，使用叙述性的笔法，直接引用鲜活的话语或者生动的比喻。

如果你在做一篇关于阿巴拉契亚地区贫困状况的报道，就不要简单罗列数据。那会是一个浮于表面的故事。你应该找到当地的一个穷苦人，请他讲故事。这样，把问题具体化，把数据落在个体身上。通过一个人真实的故事，你对阿巴拉契亚地区贫困状况的报道力度将超过全世界有关于此的数据表格的总和。

普利策奖获得者、记者小莱昂纳德•皮茨（Leonard Pitts Jr.）说：“通过人的视角看事件报道，才有人味儿。”如果你能谨记这点，你就能把故事讲得活灵活现，讲到读者心里去。

菲利普斯•拉塞尔（Phillips Russell）是北卡罗来纳州大学教堂山分校的荣誉教授，他曾经这么告诉上写作课的学生：“如果你想写一只熊，那就去找一只熊去！”

社区新闻和特写

社区新闻为有创造性的、引人入胜的故事提供了独一无二的平台，它是那些懂行的社区记者的福音。因为社区报与生俱来的特点，相对于大城市大报，我们有了以下某些优势。

第一，相比于大报，我们的受访者很可能已经认识或者了解我们，这种熟人关系让受访者愿意快速接受采访。因此，我们可以腾出更多时间去采访和写作。

第二，在报道方面，我们可以更加私人化。很多社区报支持特写记者写出受访者的名字，而不必去恪守“美联社风格”的“只呼其姓”的没有人情味儿的规则。

第三，记者更有可能自己拍照片、做采访，因此可以更好地从整体上把握报道的完整性。如果足够幸运，我们还可以按照自己的想法做标题和内容设计。说到版面设计，你要是进过大报的联合印刷车间，你就看吧，大报特写记者要是敢进报刊印刷间随便碰点什么，印刷间的人都会停下手中的活，齐刷刷地瞪着你，看你敢动一根指头？

大部分情况下，我们的人员会有更大的空间去经营内容，不管是照片还是报道，这点弥足珍贵。在社区报特写中发挥个人特色的空间大得多，也有机会进行实质上的创新，说到底，比大报要有意思得多。

引用伟大的体育播报员瑞德•巴伯（Red Barber）经常说的一句话作为结尾吧：“我们占尽天时地利人和！”

什么是特写？

什么是特写？是肤浅的娱乐、耸人听闻的鼓吹，还是无足轻重的补白？那些专攻硬新闻的记者和编辑往往会让你认为，特写只不过是“软新闻”和一些二流的故事。一些生意人还会公开鄙视特写，说特写不过是凑点内容给广告做个陪衬。一言以蔽之，特写就是浪费版面。

如果上述属实，《人物》杂志怎么会火得一塌糊涂？看看《滚石》（*Rolling Stone*）、《大都会》（*Cosmo*）、《时尚先生》（*Esquire*）、《纽约客》，充斥着这些成绩斐然的杂志的是什么样的作品？事实上，精明的大报和杂志正逐步意识到，在跟电视节目抢观众的战争中，加入更多特写是行之有效的策略。

我们可能永远无法用印刷的新闻把电视打到溃不成军，但我们确信，因为有特写，所以我们不会消亡。一篇精心制作的特写故事或许不会成为报纸头条，但是如果写得足够好，我敢说读特写的人比读头条的人更多，因为人们会情不自禁地被一个有人情味儿的故事吸引。

特写的形

你应该还记得特写诸多的特性：可以用各种形式的导语；作品可以用轶事的

形式和叙述的手法；文章不受时效性约束；可以警示大众也可娱乐大众；观点可以不必完全客观；报纸任何地方都可以刊登。

借用间谍小说行业里的一句话，区分特写和新闻就是它“包含的信息不是你必须了解的”。不知道住在街对面的美国第三胖的猫“肥肥”正在减肥，或许你的生活依然过得不错。可是，知道这只肥猫后，生活就多了那么点情趣和乐子，过得就更有滋味了。人们都说，最幸福的生活就是带那么点疯癫地活着。特写可以用来娱乐，可以让我们更清楚地知道“我活着”，能启发我们，加强一种归属感，还能用人文情怀感动我们。

更长的时效性是特写的另一个要素。即使不是绝大多数，大量的特写都被人称为“长青篇”。就是说，里面的主干信息不会过时，特写也就依托故事而永存。虽然特写也常常存在局限，但相比于那些时效性要求高的、稍纵即入古的新闻故事，它对时间的要求宽松得多。比如说，本章开头提到的霍利•格林的果酒制作特写就是一个很好的“长青篇”例子，它可以在整个夏末苹果丰收季刊登。

独立性和创新意识

不论是为社区报还是大报工作，因为怀有创新热情，你展现出的特写天赋，或后天所学的技能，都会对记者生涯的成功起到关键性作用。

新手记者总是期望太多，期望编辑提供所有的解答、想法、指导和大量的校对。然而，在多数社区报里，情况并不像想象的那样。由于各种各样的原因，你很可能要孤军奋战，特别是在报道点子方面。编辑会要求你去自己构思，做背景调查，然后写出特写。这就意味着，你要提前做功课，对故事追根溯源，设计并进行成功的采访，甚至自己拍摄，最终完成特写。

“但是社区里啥事儿也没发生！”年轻的记者会这样抱怨。

想象一下，一个钢琴家坐在钢琴前说：“没啥可弹的啊！弹来弹去就老是那88个琴键！”或者是一个吉他手看着吉他说：“总是这六根弦，我把我能弹过的全都弹了啊！”

明白我的意思了吗？社区就像钢琴键盘或吉他琴弦。面对那几个键、几根弦、几个音，就像面对社区中同样的人、同样的脸、同样的球赛、同样的活动，年复一年，但相同中孕育了不同，这不同来源于你不同的洞察力、角度和态度。微不足道的六根弦或者同样微不足道的88个琴键可以让你为其穷尽一生。全新的思路、复杂的指法、抑扬的音调全是由音乐家心底而出。无限的“新”其实就孕育于看起来完全相同的几个音符中。

每个人都有故事

查尔斯•柯瑞尔特从20岁就知道“每个人都有故事可讲”这条基本的新闻从业真理，那还是在19世纪50年代，那时他还是《夏洛特新闻报》（*Charlotte News*）的年轻记者。[多亏了哥伦比亚广播公司，它使得柯瑞尔特这条宝贵的真理流传到了史蒂夫•哈特曼（Steve Hartman）的系列节目《每个人都有故事》中。]作为社区报记者，你当然也可以用上这条真理。南达科他州立大学的摄影指导弗兰克•罗伯特森（Frank Robertson）说：“‘小’人物才有大故事。那些名人故事真的很无聊。你街坊邻居过的生活才叫有趣呢 。”

让我们想一想，就算一个社区有6000人口吧，里面有多少值得分享的故事？无穷无尽啊！想想吧，6000个不同的音符！

所以说，行动起来，拿出你的上进心！不要让你的编辑听到你发出“这不过是一个小镇”“我们不过只是一份周报嘛”“没啥事情发生啊”这样的抱怨。

每次听到年轻记者告诉我“没什么事情发生”的时候，我就知道，其实是他们没有用心，用脑，结果两只耳朵中间“什么都没发生”。

从宾夕法尼亚大学州立大学《中心时代日报》（*Centre Daily Times*）的资深体育编辑罗恩•布拉肯（Ron Bracken）那里，你会得到启发。他认为，尽管很多比赛的比分是4：2，但没有哪两场比赛是一样的。事实上，布拉肯也报道了成百上千场4：2比分的比赛，找出当天要报道的球赛同以往球赛的不同才是巨大考验。“有千万种比赛方式可以把比分打成4：2，但每场总会有那么点特别之处，你只需把它找出来就可以了。”

特写哪里来?

如果你够幸运，你的编辑会给你提出建议。但你别以为那就是靠山。事实上，“喂”给你的想法并没有太多营养，只会扼杀你的好奇心。作为记者，好奇心是你力量的源泉。所以你要知道去哪找特写。

一个优秀的记者能在那些看起来不像能产生新闻的地方找到点子，比如，《自由长矛之星报》（*Free Lance-Star*）——弗吉尼亚弗州雷德里克斯堡（Fredericksburg, V.A.）一份发行量为44000份的日报——的摄影师苏珊娜•凯尔（Suzanne Carr）说：“我总是能在自助洗衣店的公告板上找到故事。”在这些社区中心，来来往往的人在洗衣的同时把自己生活中的小需求贴出来，有时这种免费的广告效果不错，当然记者用心挖掘的话，能带来好故事的线索也不少。

下面是一条报纸尾页的分类广告，看看，简直是在跪求别人来做特写：

待售：原价$600从未穿过的婚纱，配珍珠，带长裙裾，现售$300；买就送“新郎新娘蛋糕小人”；另售伴娘裙，8号大，白色，配珍珠，从未穿过，原价$150，现价$75。卖家电话……

新闻事件

读一下自己和别人的报纸，找到一条新闻素材，看看发生了什么。事件对你的社区居民有什么影响？它怎么影响一个具体的个人？切记人是最重要的因素。

假设你的镇上有一个患唐氏综合征的孩子，该怎么抚养？找到一个愿意受访、被拍摄的家庭；找寻正能量，社工们对精神病患者有过什么帮助？哪些人参与了？谁为此埋单？患者家庭如何克服困难？在适当时机，特写可以并且应该给人们以鼓舞。查尔斯•柯瑞尔特曾说过，海边一石能够激起积极的、有创造力的社会变革大浪。你的特写可以成为社区里正能量的代言。别不相信！积土成山，积水成渊，难道你不想去做吗？

新闻中的人

社区重要人物是新闻和特写的最佳采访对象。只要是对有影响力的人的深度采访就会有价值。你周边有一大堆潜在的素材，怎么会有人说没有什么可写呢？

一些缺乏职业灵感的社区报编辑做出的东西总是题材趋于老旧，他们往往忽略身边发生的事情。如果你是个新记者，珍惜你初入世事的眼光。

如果要做一个人物特写，经常在报纸新闻中出现的社区领袖或者杰出市民会是比较靠谱的采访对象。经常被报道并不意味着他们就没有故事可讲了，读者会对这些知名人士私底下的生活细节更感兴趣，比如家庭生活、个人兴趣和爱好等家长里短都是引人入胜的佐料。

新闻编辑室里给出的建议

一旦你在报社有了特写能手的美誉，你会发现同事们会开始为你提供故事素材。让人感到最无上光荣的是，记者室、印刷间、发行部甚至收发室的人都会来评论你的文章并说出他们的看法。有智慧的记者知道不能嘲笑这些人的想法。他们就像隔着一层透明玻璃看你，从他们的评论中你有机会了解这个社区是怎么看待你、你的工作和这份报纸的。请倾听他们的想法并且向他们表示感谢。

读者

社区报中，一个好的特写作家会吸引到一批拥趸。可是，别骄傲自大，我说的拥趸可不是成千上万为你尖叫的粉丝，而是欣赏并期待你的作品的人。他们是你巨大的资产，特别是当他们开始为你提供故事素材的时候。他们可能写信、发电邮或打电话告诉你消息，但更经常发生的情况是，他们会在冷不丁地出现——可能在你买菜的时候或者交燃气费的时候。记住！你无时无刻不是个作者，或者更直接地说，你的笔杆子应该时刻准备“战斗”。扪心自问一下，你现在有没有准备好呢？一个写作的人应该时刻准备着。所以，要注意你的言行举止，因为一旦读者喜欢你的作品，并觉得你知书达理、平易近人、兼容并蓄，他们就很有可能为你提供故事素材。你不必采纳每条素材，但要感谢每个人的帮助，接着继续做你的事情，不过要记住：当时看起来像是个无趣的故事或许最终会展现出其有价值的一面。

你自己

最后，当然还要说回到你自己。如果你是个新手，或许你要过一段时间才能学会如何找寻特写素材，因为素材不会自己送上门来。记住，素材不一定及时、新鲜或者重要，所以它们可能不如新闻那样容易挖掘。尽管这样，干这行的老手到哪儿都能很轻易地挖出素材。到底有什么法宝呢？别担心，这是后天可以学到的技能，但你必须想学才能学到。

随身带一支笔、一个本子，睁大眼睛，按苏珊娜•凯尔说的做：仔细看社区里各种公告板，不管是在洗衣店，还是在杂货店，抑或是在教堂；在镇上留心人们的聊天，我们可以称之为“有创意的窃听”，换句话说，要眼观六路，耳听八方；做一个特写素材列表，标明可以联系的人和电话号码，并按重要性进行排序；最后记住，在一个小社区里，一个特写故事经常会像连环套一样引出另一个故事。

来自作者的建议

● 采访前，尽可能多地对受访对象进行背景调查，挖掘为什么这个人对社区那么重要。

● 弄清故事的时效性。听起来这样的说法很傻，其实不然，因为很多特写都是长青的，或许编辑正考虑下周用你的特写而不是这周。这会帮助你安排好时间。

● 为了给特写画上一个完整的句号，你要知道大概多长时间才能完成它。特写不像是倒金字塔形新闻，那些新闻可以不要结尾，硬生生地停下。特写需要有完整的结尾，这使它对作者的要求与新闻截然不同。

● 弄清特写要在哪个版面刊登。不同位置——位于头版、中间其他版面或是其他叠的首页——特写的影响力完全不同。

● 弄清特写是否会配照片，如果没有照片的话，你必须在文章中用更形象化的语言。如果有照片，谁来拍？照片。会让特写更具象，但如果没有专职摄影师的话，记者得边做笔记，边拍照片对记者而言，这可不轻松，你得有心理准备。

● 做采访时，要给自己预留较多的时间，写文章的时候也一样。

下面是一条真理：特写不像新闻，必须采用倒金字塔结构，它行文无定式，因此采访和写作都需要而且应当花费更多时间。

开写之前，问问自己这些问题：

● 谁是我的读者？体育类特写吸引的读者不同于钢琴师个人特写吸引到的读者，也不同于关于一个在森林中独居、养了两只熊的老人的故事的读者。问问自己，从更广泛的意义上说，我的读者是哪些？

● 为什么我要写这个？是因为这是分配的任务吗？如果这是写作的唯一原因，可以想象最后的文章会写成什么样子。你的动机应该是：因为我在乎社区，因为我好奇，因为这可以反映我的社区或者影响到我的社区，因为人们需要知道这个故事，因为这可以帮助他们，娱乐他们，让他们开心，让他们勇于面对。或者你可能想去写它是因为它能扩充你的素材档案或者丰富你的作品集，虽然这并不是最好的原因，但它很有可能是你真实的动机之一。

● 这篇文章的目的是什么？在写作工作告一段落后，作品本身会有它自己的生命。曾有一个社区报记者写了一对夫妇计划在家中分娩的故事，她写这个的原因有很多：她相信家中分娩是最好的选择；她知道这则故事和相片可以说是惊世骇俗，不同凡响；她意识到能找到一对愿意让自己写作和拍摄的夫妇是多么不容易，这对记者来说是个千载难逢的机遇。最后她做得很棒。孩子也安全降生，大众对此特写表示一致的肯定，这篇特写也获得了当年全美出版物竞赛的一等奖。

● 我能保证读者看得懂我的特写吗？这对社区报记者来说是很高的要求，你必须对你的读者很了解。比如在一个关于退休古典钢琴师的特写里，你可以保证读者能看懂采访中他用到的专业词语吗？或许在采访中，你最好能问一些后续的问题来给读者一些信息，像是“您怎么界定巴洛克式的音乐呢”。又比如你采访一位资深的小提琴家时，很多读者不知道老式管弦乐和蓝草音乐的区别，而这又是了解小提琴家故事的重点。在这两个例子中，你应该让受访人来做出解释，而且，请务必加上这看似又笨又业余的解释：“当我问到如何界定巴洛克式音乐时，玻兹诺维斯基（Boznowski）先生说……”你对读者了解多少在此尽显。

● 我怎么能让读者坚持读到文章最后？对于一个新手来说，的确很难让他意识到他的话并不是《圣经》，读者并非要一字一句地读到最后。别忘了，报纸上还有更有趣的漫画、填字游戏在向他们发出召唤呢。更糟糕的情况可能是，读者放下《号角报》转投电视了。你就这样失去了读者，而且他们像脱缰的野马，再也不会回来了。那么，在这一切发生之前，问问你自己该怎么做才能让读者一直读下去。你必须逐字逐句地“诱惑”你的读者，从始至终，那么文章的使命也就完成了。

● 最后一个问题：当读者读完文章后，我想让他们感受到什么？这个问题要在动手写之前就问自己。其实就是问，我的导向是什么？我是想让我的读者对一个人的境遇感到悲伤同情，还是让他读出其中的酸甜苦辣，抑或是感到义愤填膺，还是让他觉得大受启发、充满幸福？文字可以将它们一一表达，你不觉得很神奇吗？

形象化的重要性

如果你想提高写作水平，从这些“感”写起：视觉、听觉、嗅觉、味觉、触觉、直觉、常识。要“感写”，也就是形象化。当你的作品能从感官出发，你就不是在讲述，而是在展现画面。

人们会被用形象化手法写出的东西深深吸引。当他们读到你描写的南加州大金桃时，就忍不住幻想咬下的那一口，幻想因为太鲜美多汁，你不得不去厨房的水池旁吃，以免溅得满地蜜香的情景。那桃子绒毛可爱得像你童年泰迪熊的毛绒，汁水溢出流到下巴，但你不在乎。这蜜桃甜得像夏天的太阳，让你咯咯直乐……

人们吃“感写”这一套是因为人们都有“感”。

请你读到这里停下来，抬头看看。你都看到了什么？不管你是在屋里、甲板上、林中空地上、教室里，还是在峡谷里，你使劲儿看。你看到的东西给你什么样的感受，石膏板墙顺滑而平整，小木屋粗糙而质朴，无窗的办公室枯燥而压抑，林中空地自由而安宁。

再调动你的耳朵，你能听到什么？听不到的话闭上你的眼睛集中注意力听。不要理会邻屋收音机中播放的古典音乐和头顶风扇的吱吱作响，你可以听到一只鸟儿在屋外高声啼唱。

看到你旁边装咖啡的杯子了吗？来一口吧。它的口感是温滑还是甜热诱人？

你手中1988年买下的陶瓷杯子手感如何？岁月将它周身打磨光滑，多年的奔波也在它的边缘留下了凿痕，它是你用过的最好的杯子，就像为你量身定做的一样。

如果你在里屋，走到客厅来。闭上眼睛闻一闻，你昨晚炸洋葱头的味道，去年冬天壁炉里残留的灰烬的味道，还有该换的猫沙的味道。到了屋外，你能闻到一股如麝香甜美的香味吗？那是一种被人们叫作雏菊的植物。

这就是人们的五种感官。还有另外两种“感”，一种就是第六感，或者叫直觉。另一种“感”就是你的常识，干我们这行对此需要的可多了。

社区新闻的特写真正讲述的内容

一流的编辑、堪萨斯州三份周报的出版人比尔•梅耶说过：“特写的内容可比那些肤浅的娱乐新闻多多了。”梅耶曾获得过国际周报编辑协会的最高奖项，他这样解释：“小镇已经失去了零售中心的地位。小镇上的鞋店、汽车店之类的店铺来登广告的已经越来越少了，作为报纸，我们该怎么办？为了生存，我们必须‘变挡’来做出调整，不会审时度势的报纸不会存活太久。而‘变挡’并不是转投电子邮件和网络，而是转投那些关于当地事物和群众的有趣的特写。”

是否有出色的特写是区别一般社区报和杰出社区报的标准。很多人坚持认为，各家报纸中，新闻大同小异，但是特写从来不会重复。它们就像蘸酱中的蒜汁、书桌上的鲜花、床铺上干净的床单、一个出乎意料的吻、一位挚友的电话……我们没有了这些事物也能生活，但有了它们后，心灵得到了丰富，生活品质得到了提高。

特写就像社区的镜子，告诉人们“我们做得还不错”。用相似的经历鼓励人们渡过难关。如果我们的故事并不是那么耀眼、有启发性，我们还能称得上“不错”吗？为了鼓励普通居民，就要像大卫•兰姆（David Lamb）在《归属感》（*A Sense of Place*）一书中所说的，我们要不断地赞美“日常生活中的平凡英雄主义”。

特写的种类

人物专访

记住，不管你的采访对象是个时代先锋，还是叱咤风云的人物，抑或是当地艺术家，或是一个杰出的老师，又或者是一个小镇名人，你都要进入他们的内心世界。如果是一个新闻事件，就把人作为故事主体，从人的角度切入。报道可以用叙事手法写成轶闻的形式。有的报道只需要采访一个新闻来源，有的需要尽可能多的视角。不论哪种情况，都要对采访对象做研究和背景调查。新手必须记住：别把自己的那点事儿说进去，不要喧宾夺主。专访的主角不是你，而是你的对象。

案例：一位任职30年的小学校长退休了。他在小镇出名是因为只要有学生把得了“A”的成绩单给他过目，就能从他那里领走一个25美分的硬币。

新闻特写

在社区报里，新闻特写和大报中的叙事方式较为相似，不同的一点是社区报可以不那么正式，作者可以加入更多的个人感受。不像“长青篇”的特写，新闻特写一般含有时效性事件，而且有可能像写突发新闻那样必须在一定的时间内完成。同样，你可以在新闻中写具体的人。如果写一个遭龙卷风袭击的小镇，你可以讲述一个幸存家庭的经历，这样的叙事性轶闻的手法效果会很不错。个人化的新闻特写能够突出读者的共性，增进社区认同度。再举一个例子，在一座小镇上，一条修路的工程进展缓慢，于是两个编辑决定骑一辆双人自行车，去实地勘察那16千米的工程路况。这种创新的方式让他们不仅获得了关于路况的第一手资料，并且写出了几篇幽默的文章，丰富了编辑专栏。除此之外，读者也因编辑能做出这样有些滑稽的事情而十分感动。

案例：镇上的兽医市长决定不追求连任时，人们都想知道为什么。经了解发现，她和丈夫希望有更多的共处时光，任职这么多年，她丈夫活像一个“鳏夫”，但他一直没有怨言。

不拘泥于演讲稿的特写

演讲本身很乏味，很多没经验的记者容易把演讲仅仅当作新闻故事，事实上，来访的演讲者会带来很多有趣的特写素材，关键是你要从本社区的视角出发，找到他和当地“挂钩”的地方，挖掘出演讲事件背后的具有人情味的元素。当一个成名的本地作家来到镇上，跟图书馆俱乐部的人们交流，一个有进取心的记者就会去挖掘这个作家三年级时的老师是谁，并在采访时向她询问这位作家八岁的时候是什么样的。那老人或许摇着头不解地说：“这孩子哪儿学来的写作这一套？在我教他的时候，他写的那叫一个杂乱无章！”再次重申，在社区新闻中，写作的关键就是找到各社区的不同之处，并将其挖掘到极致。诚然，这会增加工作量，但如果不这样，是个人都能拿着录音机到观众席听完演讲，回到办公室敲出一篇过得去的文章。显然，能从社区中找到金点子，将一篇关于演讲的特写“点石成金”才更加有意思，并且更有意义。

比如说，前美国队女足明星米娅•哈姆（Mia Hamm）到镇上的中学做演讲。孩子们激动得手舞足蹈，夹道欢迎。当她走上台，一个女孩塞给她一个足球，米娅在上面赠言：“不停地踢下去——米娅。”看到这，你难道没有发现充满人情味儿的本地视角吗？那个崇拜米娅•哈姆的女孩是谁？她是个足球运动员吗？她看了奥运会吗？从米娅•哈姆的角度出发，她的反应是什么，她演讲完后可以截住她，问问她有没有对那个女孩有印象，问她经常有人让她签名吗。那个女孩或许可以当作导语中的人物，这样的话，她不仅给你提供一个本地视角，也成为当地新闻传播的一个媒介。请参考下面这个特写：

12岁的简•琼斯（Jane Jones）一直想见美国女足明星米娅•哈姆。这周五，她终于美梦成真。

米娅昨天在东卢瑟福高中受到热烈欢迎，并做了演讲，过程中，琼斯递给米娅一个足球，米娅快速写上赠言然后交给了她。“我的梦想成真了，”琼斯事后有些害羞，红着脸说，“我热爱足球，最崇拜米娅•哈姆。你可以说她就是我的偶像。”

米娅本次演说是全国巡回演讲中的一站，她表示，随着演讲的进行，她被人们热烈的欢迎深深感动了。“不管你信不信，这在我生命中并不常发生，”她在后台告诉记者，“我真心被触动了。”

写此类特写的秘籍：脑子里装着尽可能多的受访者的背景资料。列出一个信息清单。试着在演讲过后，看能不能从演讲人那里问出是谁邀请了他或她来做演讲，可以采访一下这个牵线人的感受。特别要注意的是，观察观众的反应。谁来听演讲了？他们觉得演讲怎么样？你要考虑去写因演讲衍生的报道。有了上面素材的基础，你可以去做一个由本地教练、足球妈妈和社会心理学家参与的特写，让他们谈谈，这位成功的女明星会对年轻女孩产生怎样的影响。

艺术特写

艺术特写可能看起来不伦不类，但在社区层面上，艺术版面的重要性丝毫不逊于体育版面！

一份有创意的社区报与本地社区艺术活动携手的话将会产生共赢的局面。戏迷、音乐爱好者、收藏家都会成为报纸的忠实读者。只要你给予他们支持，他们就会给予报纸以支持。

除此之外，如果一份社区报能给某个艺术委员会或艺术机构提供采访支持，那一定皆大欢喜。这证明了一个真理：一个宜居的小镇、一份伟大的报纸和一个艺术繁荣的社区彼此是紧密相连的。

社区里的大多数表演家和画家不是专职的。他们可能是当地小剧院、摄像社一员，也可能是社区大学合唱队或者艺术委员会的一员。他们不是为钱而艺术，而是为了自我表达和社区文化生活水平的提高。这也是为什么绝大多数社区报不会对社区艺术活动吹毛求疵，那样的评论毫无意义。最好是给予社区艺术活动积极的正面评论。

社区报应当尽力介入每次艺术活动，帮助宣传社区志愿者活动是报纸的职

责。最早的特写应该包括5“W”和1个大纲，特别是要强调都有谁参与。活动之后，最简单有效的报道就是用上现场照片、带妆彩排照片或者集体合照，感谢每一个为此奉献时间和精力的组织和个人。

报道主题可以包括对剧中主演、化妆师、舞者等的人物专访。专访通常是彩排或表演之前进行的，主旨是要给读者展示舞台背后的情况。演出前的专访可以加深观众对演出内容的了解，也给读者提供了一个是否决定要去的参考。

一篇艺术特写需要作者在演出前对演出内容和艺术家有全面的了解。读相关书籍、看艺术展览、听音乐会、听艺术家以前的带子，带着这些准备去观摩彩排，然后去做人物采访。这么做是为了表示对艺术的尊重，避免发生冷场。你要是问出“咱们准备出演哪一部剧呢？”这样的问题，你就是自掘坟墓了。“据我了解，卡巴莱特歌舞表演在二战前夕来到柏林……”这样的引子会更合适。

社区报可以做一个艺术活动日历，并且定期在报纸上公布当地艺术家和艺术团体的活动信息，将此作为社区艺术的一个平台。社区报还应鼓励当地新人艺术家，把聚光灯投给他们。同时，部分社区报为了版面美观，也会发表诗歌和短文。

本地的社区学院、私立学院或者大学或许早就开始这么做了。可以让当地学院的宣传部门在社区报资助下成立一个研究会，专门研究如何为各种艺术组织和机构做宣传和报道。这是个双赢的方案，对学院来说是不错的公关宣传，对搞艺术的群体也有帮助，而且这还能提高报道质量，为报纸赢得更好的口碑。

教育类特写

前出版人兼编辑、社区新闻学教授肯•拜尔利多年前就说过这么一句真理："没有什么比学校更能团结社区，也没有什么比学校更能割裂社区。社区如果是太阳系的话，学校就是太阳。只要学校停止运行，很多小镇就随之消失，足见学校的重要性。"

学校的放假时间、人员变动、课程变更、校车、餐厅、校规、新项目、教科书选择、经费支出等大大小小的新闻都是社区报必不可少的元素。除了常规的学校董事会采访，和教育有关的场所都会给特写提供取之不尽的素材。

教育是个大热门话题，它理应在报纸中得到更多的关注。美国的小学教育系统正在发生着巨变，社区报应冲在报道的第一线。故事灵感数不胜数：

● 到底是美国职业篮球联赛的明星对孩子们重要呢，还是他们的老师重要？答案显而易见，那我们为什么不能提高教师工资？伟大的老师教书并不是为了钱，但他们需要支持、鼓励和认可。对班主任教学理念和课堂情况的特写会极大影响老师对社区的看法。从报道每所学校"年度老师"的提名开始是个不错的选择。

● 是不是该对8月份来到本地高中的老师做个摄影特写和短篇介绍呢？读者对此极为感兴趣，毕竟老师可以改变人的命运，人们对此关注理所应当。

● 春季，你可以去给长时间任教过的优秀退休老师做特写。如果他们在某些场合受到有关部门的表彰，一定不要放过对此的报道。

● 报道教育动向。对大学生而言，在社区完成一定量的志愿服务是毕业硬件之一吗？当地的学校贯彻了吗？这种标准制定的性质是什么？学生们对此怎么看？

● 报道出色的学生。给一个最为出色的残疾学生做特写，将他的一天记录下来，看他是怎样克服重重困难的。

● 报道学校取得成效的创新项目。比如听闻当地一所大学即将为来自贫困家庭面临无法毕业窘境的高中生组织一场为期两周的活动，记者的采访提纲则需要列出这样一些问题：大胆提出这个点子的学校高层为什么这么做？活动由谁出资？亲自去活动现场拍摄，采访孩子、辅导员、教师、父母。后期采访也要跟上，本次活动多大程度上可以说是成功了？参与活动的孩子命运因此发生了怎样的改变？

● 报道国际交流生。不管是大学还是高中，有关交换生的特写效果总是不错的，因为他们的看法比较客观，能发现很多美国人熟视无睹的现象。他们最喜欢和最不喜欢的是什么？最让他们留恋的是什么？在交流期间，他们觉得最有趣的东西是什么？来到美国交流给他们带来了什么变化？他们觉得在此收获了什么？

● 报道夏天的校友聚会。跟往届学生交流，看看发生了什么变化。跟其中的精英交流，问问他们最珍贵的记忆、印象最深刻的恶作剧、最喜爱的老师、高中或大学得到的经验。最好的故事素材来源于50周年校友或同学聚会，在人们交谈的时候留心记下素材，聚会结束后拦住这些素材的主人翁，询问可否发表他的故事。

一份创新的报纸会和社区中学合作，比如给他们的新闻课程预留整个版面作为展示平台。学生记者做采访，报社摄影师就照学生编辑的要求进行拍摄。除了纸质版，报纸网站上也会加上学校主页的链接。就凭这些持续不断的坚持，报纸的教育类报道会越做越扎实，最好的奖励就是社区积极的反响，除此之外，社区报做了些其他媒体不愿意做也没法做的东西。

生活小贴士类的特写

如果说平面新闻媒体有什么趋势的话，那就是刊发“生活小贴士”这样的文章。报纸学会了杂志吸引小众市场的一套办法——给读者提供生活小贴士。最典型的是女性杂志。如果大标题足够吸引人，人们一定会去读，比如：《如何激活你的男人》《九种做爱的好姿势》《约会时，有什么是安全的？》《如何开启你的灵感密匙》《如何应对自己不喜欢的第一份工作》《白嫩皮肤如何畅玩沙滩》。

在社区层面来看，写这种作品先要选个好主题。为了体现内容的真实性，使之和本地环境相称，你要采访本地你能触及的一切与话题相关的人。要是你决定写上述畅玩沙滩的话题，就可以去找皮肤科医生或是其他医生咨询，了解一下皮肤暴晒的危害和皮肤癌的发病率；可以去问高中科学老师臭氧层空洞的问题；可以采访当地社区学院的社会学家，谈谈美国人审美标准的改变，如果“苍白肤色”的潮流再起，背后的原因是什么。

写生活小贴士时，一定要记住自己只是一个作者。让资料或者专业机构说话。没人愿意听你颐指气使；不管你怎么写，不要说教，你应该像个幕后军师，隐匿，但把控着文章的走向。

其他适合地区特色的社区报特写主题包括：环境、医疗、科学和种族。这样的小贴士特写可以为社区报“生活”板块提供大量好素材。

实战经验

你怎样让一个不愿接受采访的人开口？怎样给一个不愿照相的人照相？有时，只要你说对了话，问题就迎刃而解。对待不同的人，“对”的话也不同。

郡里的人都知道凯特•伯内特（Kate Burnett）大婶是麦奇山克里克人中一位高傲的老妇人。这位88岁高龄的老酋长以自己能靠一把结实的弓锯劈柴做饭而感到骄傲。

我必须拿下她的故事和照片。

老人没有电话，找到她的唯一方法就是开着车到她位于美其山山阴处的小屋中。我在锯木架处找到了正在工作的老人。

前院一块木板上写着："别来烦我，否则你死定了。"

我把车在路肩上停好后下车，还没等我走到院子，凯特就叫嚷起来："你这秃头的家伙，别以为我没看见你，你最好赶紧给我回车里去。"

我不是个容易退却的人，"凯特大婶，"我尽可能礼貌地喊话回去，"我是报社的，想采访一下您。"

"我有你们那些老报纸，"她嚷嚷道，紧接着她咧嘴笑了一下说，"我每天早上都用它们生火呢！你立马给我回镇上去！"

听到这儿我差点就离开了，但转念一想，情况再坏也不过这样了，我就试图迎合她的虚荣心。"凯特大婶，我正在写一本书。"我喊道，停顿了一下，好让她掂量一下我的话，"我想把您写进我的书里！"

你可以想象这样的情景：老人想了想后，几乎是害羞地喊回话来，声音也不是那么大了："嗯……你想让我坐在哪里接受采访呢？"

我说对了话，成功地进行了采访。

不要低估自己的影响力

任何一个老练的记者或摄影师都承认这么一个事实：房子着火后，除了孩子和宠物，人们抢救的第一样东西往往是影集。

电视、音响、电脑什么都顾不上了，但是，要抢救照片。

这些所谓的平凡镜头记录了日常生活中难忘的瞬间：四岁的乔恩钓到第一条大鱼，六岁的赛琳娜在她学会骑车的那天洗车，等等。这些看似琐碎的照片为个人或者家庭保存了视觉记录，是无价之宝。

作为记者，需要时时提醒自己，我们对被拍过的人的影响会有多大。

下面我要讲一个故事，关于一张摄于1982年的黑白照片，那是我去拜访北卡埃弗里郡（Avery County, N.C.）圣诞树种植户乔伊•亨森（Joe Henson）时拍下的。

当年乔伊60岁，身体壮得像头熊。照片里，他穿一件格子衫，戴一顶"狂野骑牛士"宣传帽，冲着相机举起一个天使般的娃娃。很难想象，那一双磨砺多年鹰爪一样的手，是如何温柔地举起小孙女的。

如果可以用"放光"来形容眼睛的话，乔伊•亨森的眼睛可以称得上"闪耀"了。他的眼里好像点了两盏灯，笑容堆满了英俊的脸庞。他好像变成了另一个乔伊，像是在告诉我他最开始种树时，土地荒凉到"兔子都要自带干粮才能闯

过”的情景。

当时我在克洛斯诺尔（Crossnore）写一篇关于乔伊和他的圣诞树的报道。1982年，乔伊60岁，身体还健康。我37岁，头发还没掉完。

最初，这篇报道被划为商业类，主要是谈圣诞树产业对当地经济的重要性，可最终，这篇报道成了影响我个人生活的一个篇章。

在我的职业中极少碰到像乔伊一样的人。随后，我就把他的故事和图片放入我的一本书中。

但是时间不巧，琐事缠身，再加上我的懒惰使我好久没有再见到他。直到上个假期，一场传统的平安夜圣歌演唱活动在乔伊家结束后，我们才重新见面。

75岁的乔伊正在与白血病做斗争，但他看起来依然结实，还是那副打不垮的样子。他在大门口迎接我，脸上挂着灿烂的笑容，见到我就一把抱着我，差点没把我骨头挤碎。

一进屋，在咖啡桌最显眼的地方摆着我那本书。经过多年阳光的洗礼，褐色的封面已经变淡。墙上挂着那幅乔伊和他天使般孙女的合影，我脑袋“嗡”的一声。

完全出乎意料！我竟然在这家人里占有一席之地！

白血病消耗了乔伊的身体，但从未打倒乔伊。“我命硬，死不了。”乔伊乐呵呵地说，“今年夏天你一定要再来看我。我要给你看看我种的圣诞树！！”

去年夏天没有拜访乔伊，但我从他的妻子艾米琳（Emmaline）那里得知，乔伊极为珍视我与他的一张合影和那张有他孙女莎拉的照片。

平安夜那天，我寄给乔伊和艾米琳一个装满相片的信封，让他们着实惊喜一番，我对礼物的效果感到十分满意。照片记录了他在遥远的老爷山的映衬下修剪树木，他用“鹰爪”一样的手搂着四岁的孙子杰米，杰米为了装扮超人，还披着一条浴巾当斗篷，还有他与孩子们的点点滴滴。

艾米琳告诉我，因为白血病，“乔伊今年差点就没了”。但是乔伊是个坐不住的人，他还是在圣诞树农场干活，依然帮家里砍做饭用的柴火。

5月份，乔伊的病情恶化，被火速送往阿什维尔的医院。在那里，他输了血，戴上了氧气罩。眼前的乔伊目光灼灼地回忆道：“那个时候，我感到一位天使拜访了我。我听见一个声音对我说‘你还不该走呢’，从那时起，我的身体一天比一天好。”

吃了饼干，喝了热巧克力，听着圣诞颂歌，中间穿插着拍照的咔咔声，终于到了分别的那一刻，我再次向乔伊许诺我会在夏天拜访他。

“何必呢！你个大骗子！”乔伊开玩笑说，“但你这回最好给我过来！”

这次，我必须遵守诺言。我对自己说：“珍惜眼前人。”

正如南达科塔州报纸协会（South Dakota Press Association）的苏珊•史密斯（Susan Smith）所说：“当一个成功的记者并不仅仅等同于在大报挣大钱。写出一篇社区居民喜欢读的人物报道，主人公对你充满感谢，并极为珍视报道的那种感觉，更让人精神愉悦。”

第7章

作为本地新闻的“9·11”事件

敬爱的中国读者：

既然已经读到这里，我相信你已准备好一窥社区新闻真面目——社区报中的新闻视角与主流都市日报及电视台的报道截然不同。你能猜到原因吗？

——作者

你敢说什么都没有发生？

不管在美国什么地方，只要你拿起一份社区报的“9·11”版，就很有可能在里面找到至少一篇本地视角的报道。最明显和最让人悲伤的报道，莫过于恐怖分子劫机撞上双子塔、五角大楼和宾夕法尼亚西南部的一个偏僻小村庄时，当地的某个家庭在灾难中失去了亲人。

最早感受到“9·11”冲击力的是那些所谓的普通人，他们感受的方式也不尽相同：有的家人在纽约、华盛顿或宾夕法尼亚工作，有人在那里有熟人，他们的亲朋告诉他们逃生的经历和对当天事件的反应；本地公民、教会或学校组织恰好那个时候在上述城市旅游；还有些本地人亲眼目睹、记录了悲剧的发生，并将故事和图片用电邮发给家乡的报纸。

很多读者自愿将故事和消息发给社区报，他们觉得自己有义务讲出这些故事并分享看法。正因为社区报敞开的大门、真人接听电话的声音、能够得到回复的电子邮件，想要贡献一份力量的读者愿意立刻把自己的经历告诉善于倾听的记者们。

“9·11”似乎触及了这片土地上每个社区的神经。很多远离事发地的人慢慢意识到了这一点，这么重要的事件发生在周一，对大多数截稿时间在周二的周报，时间太紧了。

玛丽•哈特•奥•布莱克伯（Mary Hart O. Blackburn）是北卡州华莱士镇《进取报》的联合出版人。“当‘9·11’刚发生时，它只是……在其他地方发生的新闻。”她右手指向遥远的北部，“但两个小时内，我们意识到，它发生在……我们的家乡。”

附近一份周报的副主编比尔•罗林斯（Bill Rollins）在旁边接茬说：“接下来发生的就是关于我们的故事，这里是我们的镇子。”

离家很近

贝德福德（Bedford）是宾夕法尼亚州西南部一座历史悠久的小镇，《贝德福德公报》（*Bedford Gazette*，以下简称《公报》）由一个小型报团拥有，是一份发行量为1万份的日报。第一次去《公报》报社的人都要找上半天，它位于充满艺术感的港湾站，就在那棵大树下的小指示牌那里，你要是从后面靠近公报社那又长又低、金属面的房子，很可能把它误认为是一个汽车维修厂。不管这里多么偏僻和简陋，被劫持的93号航班简直可以说就坠毁在它的后院里，《公报》和另外几份宾夕法尼亚的社区报都站到了“9·11”事件的暴风眼中。

93号航班在飞行26秒后坠落在贝德福德西边。

莫斯特（Maust）是一名在公报工作了31年的资深记者。事发前一天晚上，她跟平常一样工作到深夜。周二上午快10点时，她被一个朋友的电话吵醒，让她“赶紧起床打开电视”。

莫斯特被冒着滚滚浓烟的双子塔吓到了。她心里愈发感觉到：“直觉告诉我，双子塔是撑不了那么大的火的。”她摇着头，“五角大楼也遭到袭击了……当电视上说宾夕法尼亚也出事了，我的感觉就是：‘天啊！该死的电视说的是哪里？’然后电视说出事地点在尚克斯维尔（Shanksville），我就像遭到电击一样。‘什么？他说哪里？老天！’我跟每个记者的第一反应一样‘天啊，我一定要去做些什么’。”尽管坠机地点在40千米之外，职业意识告诉她：“离得太近了，你必须去。”

当地目击者都曾看到被劫持的波音757在贝德福德的低空不稳定飞行。上午10时刚过，飞机就以约每小时805千米的速度撞向了地面，坠机地点位于萨默塞特（Somerset）镇以东16千米的一片草地上，33名乘客、7名工作人员和4名劫机者全部遇难。

莫斯特和记者保罗•罗恩（Paul Rowan）向执行编辑克里斯•费尔（Chris Frear）报告后，他们就沿着穿山而过的30号公路向西行驶。“当然，我们并不知道那个鬼地方在哪儿。”她说，尽管贝德福德机场的人说那个地方不会太远，因为他们听到了爆炸响声。

罗恩和莫斯特决定分头行动，用莫斯特的话说是“在乡下东一榔头西一棒槌地逛”，直到他们接近了93号航班的坠机地点。可是，现场已经被封锁了。

“越来越多的记者出现在事发现场。”莫斯特说，“我们挤在大量记者当中。”为了应对潮水般的媒体，有关部门将媒体带到几百米之外的一座山丘上，在那里可以俯瞰整个失事现场。

在那儿，莫斯特和罗恩看到飞机扎进一大片草地的边缘。“爆炸引燃了旁边的树林，但是那里并没有什么……值得看的。”莫斯特回忆。似乎所有的记者都期待看到散落的飞机残骸或者烧焦的尸体被抬出，可是什么都没有。

“就像是个正在燃烧的垃圾焚烧点，”莫斯特描述道，“地上一个V字形坑的末端有一堆黑色的东西。”罗恩用一个长镜头拍下了坠机地点的一张彩色照片，这张照片将会刊登在明天报纸头版的显要位置。

下午3时左右，他们回到报社。当时还没有数码相机，罗恩必须冲到当地的杂货店，对照片进行处理。

第二天，《公报》头版通栏标题是“恐怖袭击家乡”，同时配上两大张美联社发布的双子塔的照片和专题报道。下半个版面就是罗恩拍摄的93号航班坠毁现场的照片和一篇本报记者执笔的本地报道，还有一篇美联社报道，援引了来自贝德福德邻近的萨默塞特小镇马克•斯特尔的话。作为第一批到达现场的人，他向记者描述当时的现场：“地上有一个被飞机撞出的坑，机身已经基本瓦解，除了烤焦的树，现场什么也没留下。”

9月12日《公报》内页全部是关于当地人的反应、本地安保的加强、当地医院和救援人员如何照顾幸存者，当地商户如何给员工开假期让他们看电视报道来应对心灵的冲击（很多居民亲耳听到了爆炸声）的报道。除此之外，报纸上还有一篇关于《公报》前实习生的报道，他原来在五角大楼工作，庆幸的是在这重大的一天到来之前已经离开了五角大楼。

尽管如此，《公报》还得刊登一些相比起来可以说平庸至极的日常报道，比如：一桩本地谋杀案的庭审、一本新书的发行、学校当天开学、本地公民社团的回忆，还有“毫无悬念的体育类报道还在继续”。

当莫斯特和罗恩上午在萨默塞特镇进行“9・11”坠机现场采访时，特写编辑维基•亨利（Vicki Henry）留守报社，因为她“必须维持报社的正常运行。有一段时间大家都很恐慌，必须有人接听电话”。

时间一周一周地过去，莫斯特说：“我们必须弄清现在该怎样进行后续报道。”坠机现场已经不知道去了多少次了，那里已经没有什么新东西。所以报道中心逐渐转向让人们自发地追忆遇难者、烛光守夜和追悼会等主题。

莫斯特说：“如果报道的不是遇难者，就是他们的亲人。永远不变的是，报道的重心是人。”

永远不要说“这里什么都没发生”

事后，《贝德福德公报》的执行编辑克里斯•费尔写下自己的思考。

> 国内最重要的新闻发源地可能就在你的后院。不管你在哪里做新闻，你的报纸已经是或者终将会是国家大事的记录簿。到处问问便知这话的真假。
>
> 9月11日的《贝德福德公报》，让我们再次认识到这句话的正确性。
>
> 当时，我们不知道那架航班是恐怖袭击的最后一班，也不知道乘客们的英勇行径，但是知道它现在是个本地事件。这样的时刻让记者和编辑心头一紧，每个人都像肾上腺激素爆发了一般，我们明白：是时候去

做跟踪报道了。

当天早上的第一个信息是：“一架飞机撞击了双子塔中的一座。”我的第一反应是“一个小错误或因个人导航失误，偏离了航线”。接着我打开电视，看CNN的报道进行确认。像往常一样，看看飞行员和飞机与本社区有没有联系。

看了几分钟后，没听见也没看见什么让人觉得更加严重的东西，我就回去工作了。密切关注突发新闻的人很多，他们会给我最新消息的。

然后我听见有人倒吸了一口凉气，接着传来尖叫声、咒骂声，原来，第二架飞机撞上了第二座塔。

我感觉到一定有重大并且罪恶的行径在蔓延。到底是什么呢？

那段时间，我一直待在电视旁，同其他编辑讨论，并指派记者去找采访线索。我们报道的视角该是什么？镇上有谁正在纽约工作或参观？该联系哪些人？

一个半小时后，五角大楼遭到袭击。一场全面的恐怖主义袭击正在上演。他们还要袭击哪里？袭击还有多少次？每个记者都在到处打听哪里有独特的消息来源，常规版面被换下并重新排版。不久后，报社决定给本期报纸增加版面。

以往做银行抢劫案的报道让我懂得了两个重要的基本点：最快速地到达事发地点；有耐心、花时间确保报道真实性，并关注事件的进一步发展。

接着，社区读者、商人、亲戚、朋友打进了大量电话，提供了很多消息和需要警醒的提醒。电话里和大街上都能听到人们说：“你听说了吗……”社区读者的来电是新闻链条中的一环。人们觉得自己和报社息息相关，所以他们提供消息。对社区报而言，这种情景的发生不仅真实，而且亲切和重要。

有一个电话告诉我们一架飞机在萨默塞特坠毁，只要上了宾夕法尼亚收费公路往西走45分钟就能到达。

到这时我们没有排除任何事件发生的可能性，但是这件事让我们没有一下子缓过神来。萨默塞特的坠机不像是明显预谋的恐怖活动。这到底是随机发生的还是有预谋的坠机事件？

不管怎样，原本是一件国家级的突发新闻现在已经转变成了一个本地现场报道。

我们打电话把刚下班的记者和编辑又叫回来，莫斯特和保罗•罗恩前一晚加班熬夜，只睡了几个小时。他们没有抱怨，都问下一步需要做些什么。这种职业新闻人的敬业让我重新体会到了新闻是一个多么诱人的行业，也让我再次意识到我在和一个多么优秀的团队一起工作。

不过编辑的职能之一是指挥而不是亲临现场。我时不时地感到懊恼，因为任何一个记者都无法抵制能够亲身去现场的“诱惑”。但是在不稳定的形势下，我作为一个告诉大家何时何地有什么新情况发生的人，更重要的是坐镇编辑室而非亲自上前线。

报纸行业与众不同的一点是：不仅对事件做出反应，你也要对竞争对手做出反应。你要先有一个故事去报道，还要比其他人报道得更好。所以，即使是在灾难面前，当人们的普遍反应是共同解决危机时，你也不能忘记竞争对手的存在。当然，这个圈子也有友情，尽管如此，它也是竞争中的一部分。

你必须为这些重大时刻做准备。大多数小报并不会为此专门训练你，就像他们不会专门训练突然断电后的应急反应一样，但是你要做好准备。

伊丽莎白•科伊尔（Elizabeth Coyle）的作品总是饱含热情和正义感。她已经到达现场开始采访，了解人们的反应，并发回报道。

莫斯特对人物和事件的观察很睿智。她对报道谋杀、重大事故、三K党集会和受贿官员都已得心应手，随时准备采访任何突发事件。

保罗是位文字编辑，同时也是最好的摄影师，他自己花钱买长焦镜头并不断自学拍摄提高技术，终成硕果。他现场拍摄的“9·11”当天那张冒烟飞机的照片触动了很多读者的内心。

几个小时过去了，没有进一步的袭击发生，事件的性质变得明朗多了，我们把关注点放在现在称为“尚克斯维尔坠机现场”的地方、93号航班坠毁所造成的影响以及事件的结果上。

还有人说这里什么都没发生，别相信这一种说法了。的确，在美国乡下，你会去写一些关于牲畜或者关于排污系统会议这样的报道。《公报》也有这类报道，这些报道也写得很不错。但是如果93号航班再多飞一分钟，它就会坠落在贝德福德镇。

我们生活在一个“9·11”级别的事件随时都可能发生的时代。当报道的机会降临，你要确保自己准备好了。不管是写讣告、报道新闻发布会还是奶牛展，你都要认真对待每一次任务，就好像世界上的人都会读你的报道一样，你都要为你的报道被全世界人知晓的那一天做好准备。

“9·11”纪念日

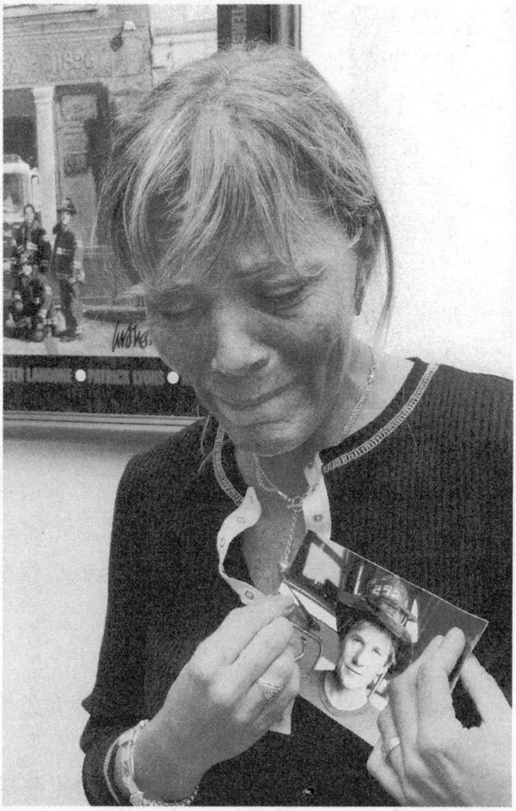

一份开明的社区报处理新闻的方式和众多大报有什么不同呢？

你可以在长岛的《南安普顿报》（*Southampton Press*）的乔（Joe）和德纳（Dana）那里找到最佳答案。乔是编辑，德纳是摄影师。“9·11”一周年纪念日时，他们为一位叫凯西•格尔曼（Kathy Gelman）的女士做了一个特写。凯西的哥哥是纽约的一名消防员，他在双子塔倒塌中丧生。凯西很通情达理地接受了两位记者的采访和拍摄要求。

德纳对照片拍摄过程的回忆如下：

接到这样的任务我当然会紧张。采访对象是一个失去亲人的人，因为报道，她就要被迫回忆失去亲人的痛苦。我告诉她对此我有多么地抱歉。

我注意到，她有一张哥哥和其他消防员站在他们驻扎的布鲁克林消防站前的照片。我问凯西有没有哥哥的单人照，她说有。她把照片拿了出来，那是她哥哥戴着消防帽的一张照片。她看着照片，讲了一点她哥哥的故事，我就开始拍照。

接着，她情绪失控了。

我继续拍照。我觉得展示出失去亲人的痛苦很重要，特别是像经历过“9 · 11”这种永远无法忘记的事件。即使一年时间已经过去，失去哥哥的伤痛仍没有离开她，估计这辈子都不会。我认为我需要把它展示出来。

我还是要向凯西道歉，我再次让她经历了伤痛，我知道说什么也不能让她好受一点。我也对自己在她如此脆弱的时候给她拍照感到很愧疚，但我心里一直坚持一个想法，人们看过这些照片后就不只把

“9·11”当作一场恐怖袭击、一个改变国内生活方式的事件，而是一场人类的惨剧，暴殄天物。这样的惨剧会永久影响受牵连人的一生。

我回到报社告诉我的丈夫乔，我拍到了一张动人的照片。但我有点担心，这照片是不是视觉冲击力过强。

我们最不愿意做的就是利用别人的脆弱让报纸看起来更吸引眼球。那不是我要追求的效果，也不该是报道核心。

当新闻职业与道德出现冲突时，我俩会在家中讨论。我要在读者眼皮底下做正确的事，这是最重要的。即使下班回了家，我也从来没有不是个记者。那晚，乔和我在床上讨论了好久，不能入睡。失眠仅仅是工作的一部分。

乔建议我们打电话问问凯西，告诉她我们的想法，看她愿不愿意让我们刊登那张照片。这是个很不寻常的举动，我们很少这么做，但在现在这样的情况下，只有这样做才是正确的。

乔给凯西打了电话，告诉她我们很想同时刊登报道和照片。凯西同意了。

肖恩夫妇处理这种敏感情形的方式充分展示了一份开明的社区报是如何处理新闻内容的。作家们称之为“仁慈的客观”，是准确、真实、同情和负责的结合体，这也是社区新闻学在美国媒体界如此重要的原因。

全球视角，本地报道

如果你需要一个对社区新闻重要性判断的形象说法，试试下面这句话：

新闻像飓风，离得越近，就变得对你越重要。

每年夏初、秋初，飓风都会袭击美国东海岸：1954年的海泽尔（Hazel）、1992年的安德鲁（Andrew）、1996年的弗兰（Fran）、1999年的弗洛伊德（Floyd）、2003年的伊莎贝尔（Isabel）、2004年的查理（Charley）。历史上最大的一次飓风是1989年的雨果（Hugo）。

《萨默维尔新闻现场》（*Summerville, S.C., Journal-Scene*，以下简称《新闻现场》）是一份南卡罗来纳州萨默维尔市发行量达9000份的周报。1989年9月初，一场加勒比海深处的热带气流扰动成了全国天气新闻的头条。报纸出版人兼编辑比尔•科林斯（Bill Collins）没把它放在心上。但是不到十天，风暴就演变出了历史上从未有过的破坏力。从卫星得到的照片可以看到，被称为“雨果”的飓风像是向美国东南部海岸击出的一记重拳。

位于查尔斯顿市（Charleston）外围的萨默维尔市恰好处在飓风行进的线路上。

在接下来的48小时里，科林斯经历了一场由季风性雨水和狂风组成的噩梦，社区差点被摧毁。气象图上的一个小亮点已经成为最大的头条新闻，那一周，很多报纸窘迫到连付印都很艰难。

暂时住在《新闻现场》编辑部的科林斯说，他清晰地记得自己在办公室看到镇上屋子的顶棚被吹翻，报社屋顶吱呀作响，房子像感到恐惧似的颤抖，镇上的树倒得到处都是，他如何让当周的《新闻现场》保持正常出版？“萨默维尔像是个战争中被轰炸过的地方。”柯林斯回忆道，“但是谢天谢地，镇上没人丧生。”

再次强调：是我们镇上。

对于社区报来说，这就是新闻的特性。新闻就像飓风，离得越近，对你，对镇子，对报纸就越重要。

深入“雨果”飓风

“雨果”飓风余威还未散去，国家级的新闻机构，从大电视台到大报，都把队伍派到了南卡罗来纳州的各个地方，特别是查尔斯顿周边地区。这些每遇灾难事件时就从天而降的大报记者以第一时间发出消息，然后匆匆离去，在美国社区新闻圈中，我们管他们叫“降落伞记者”。

比尔•科林斯留了下来，因为他住在这里，因为他在乎，萨默维尔是他的镇子。

这就是社区新闻和大型媒体的主要区别。大型媒体仅仅是因为灾难才会在你的镇上出现，当灾难结束，他们就回家了。但对于像《新闻现场》、《古斯克里克公报》（*Goose Creek Gazette*）、《沿海时代》（*Coastal Times*）、《麦朵沙滩太阳报》（*Myrtle Beach Sun-News*）这样的当地社区报来说，他们的报道会继续，并且在全国性媒体的聚光灯转向别处后，报道还会延续好几年。社区报采集、报道、处理、写作还有包装新闻的方式都与其他新闻媒介不同，因为他们是不离不弃的家乡新闻团队。

请大家记住在那个黑夜里，在《新闻现场》编辑部坚守，为“他的”镇子祈祷的比尔•科林斯。

对我们来说，新闻并非置身于度外、没有人情味、无名氏的消息，不是孤立的、不关己的。“信源”是个多么无情的词。朋友，进入人的世界吧，我们这里谈论的是真真切切的人。

在社区报里，新闻并不是发生在无生命事物上的事件。新闻就是写人，写当地人，还写变化的世界如何影响当地人的日常生活。新闻是主人翁被牵连进了事件里。我们的工作不仅是准确、公正地记录事件，展示社区精神、给社区带来正能量是我们的使命。

再拿“雨果”飓风做个例子，除了报道，伟大的社区报应该为社区提供一个分享、疗伤、发展的平台。读《萨默维尔新闻现场》成为了一种群体性的仪式，报纸也成了一本可靠的剪辑簿。它们向社区表明：“看，你还在这里，你还读着报纸，你活了下来。我们（包括报纸）可能很渺小，但是我们依然屹立着。”一旦社区和社区报因这种经历相联系，你们就能形成真正的长久的联系。

阐释社区新闻

离家越近越重要。在社区新闻里，我们不讨论“市场”，不讨论“主要覆盖区域”。我们讨论的是居住的镇子。我们同镇子进行对话，我们在镇上生活，我们报道新闻，我们还住在这里。

简明地说，社区新闻属于“三A”俱乐部：我们目标是准确（Accurate）、平易近人（Accessible）、有责任感（Accountable）。

我们和大城市媒体降落伞式风格很不相同。如果你是个受害者或者是个消息源，有时你会觉得那些大城市媒体像游击队。

《塞姆勒晚间新闻》[*Salem (M.A.) Evening News*]是马萨诸塞州一份发行量在38000份的报纸，编辑戴夫•马库斯（Dave Marcus）说，做社区报比做大报更难，难就难在“准确性对社区报比对大报更为重要，假如你说错了公园的位置，很多人立马就会知道你错了，想想那些不满的读者会说些什么，‘写这个的笨蛋是谁？他们竟然不知道博登斯丁公园在哪里’”！

戴夫坚持认为：“准确性非常重要，所以你必须用大报的标准要求自己，同时你也需要同小镇读者建立联系。”

转出，转入

让我们用图来重复以上的主旨，或许这个模型有助于帮你抓住社区报新闻定义的核心概念，这张图可能会让你想起飓风。假如你作为编辑处于飓风中心，那么什么报道对你的社区最重要？越近越重要。

不过，别的飓风也可能“转”到你这里。有时全国性和全球性新闻会“转入”并触及你所在的社区。如果你足够幸运（你的读者要喜欢并且信任社区报和你个人），你可以发掘出一个当日“大事”的绝佳的本地视角。你要做的，正如老话所说：帮读者把报道带回家。

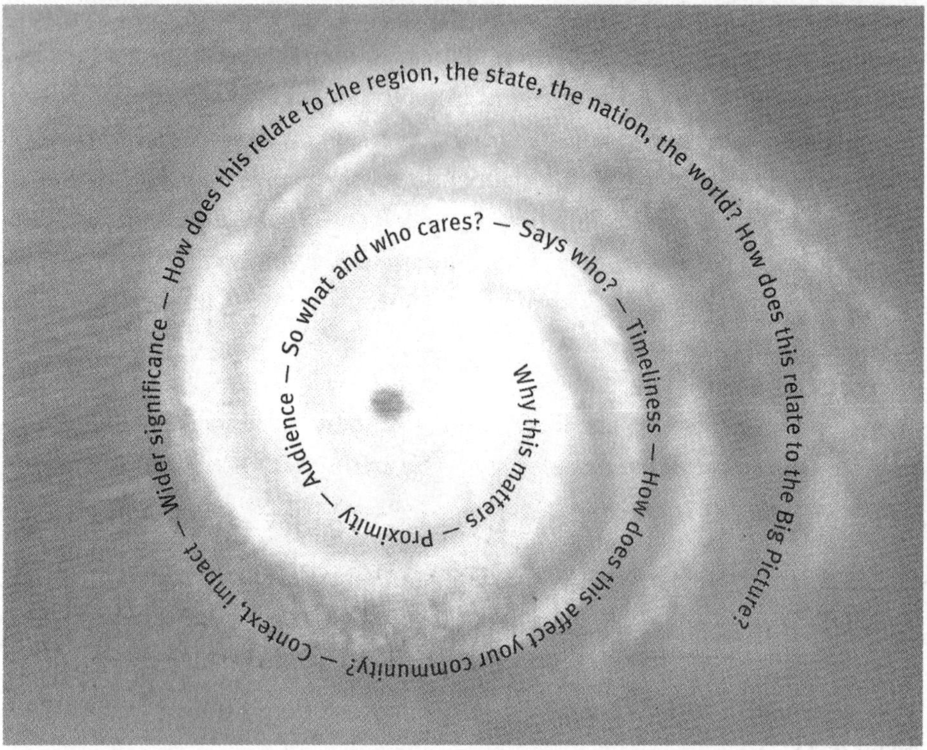

在1999年科罗拉多州立托镇（Littleton）高中大屠杀的守灵中，位于纽约中心的雅芳镇（Avon）的居民注意到，《人物》杂志封面上祈祷的一个少年是以前镇上的居民，他刚刚搬家去了西部。《利文斯顿郡新闻》（*Livingston County News*）是一份发行量不到6000份的周报，体育版资深编辑杰克•海利（Jack Haley）发现了这个线索，为了让报道与本地更相关，报纸从美联社和《人物》杂志那里得到了给自己的报道配上美联社原图的许可。

这就把一个全国性故事拉到家乡来了。本•卡尔森（Ben Carlson）是报道的主笔。他对这个想法很是得意，一张本地非著名人物的脸孔使这篇报道相关性大增，相比之下，相邻的大城市罗切斯特市（Rochester）的大报则缺少这样的亮点，一个不忘进取的小报员工打了他们一个措手不及。

社区新闻议程设置

最好的社区报是无可置辩的全心全意的本地化。一份社区报的新闻议程设置是社区生活的真实反映，他应该像是美国上空同步卫星照的照片一样，从太空拉近到距离你的镇子非常近的距离，一切都栩栩如生，真实而生动。所有在摄像框里发生的东西应该是：

不同的，
有趣的，
可敬的，
古怪的，
吸引人的，
有意义的，
令人火冒三丈的，
有争议的，
迷糊的，
让人好奇的，
搞笑的，
高尚的……
这才是：新闻。

新闻是什么？

新闻可以被广义地定义为具有以下给出的特征之一或者全部的事件。下面这个历史悠久的列表被称为“新闻视角的几个要素”,你可以凭此来评估一个报道或者故事想法的新闻价值。

- 时效性
- 受众
- 接近性和影响力
- 重要性
- 量级
- 凸显性
- 灾难和悲剧
- 古怪或者稀奇
- 矛盾和争议
- 人情味
- 幽默

从《CBS晚间新闻》到《萨默维尔新闻现场》，虽然有时候是按直觉行事，但通常我们都用这张表单来做决定：

- 导语是什么?
- 这篇报道真正关心的是什么?
- 谁会关注?
- 最重要的事是什么?
- 拿什么做标题?
- 我们该怎么展示和定位这个故事?

记住，社区新闻对新闻的反应和大城市日报有天壤之别。再次重申，不一定说哪个更好，仅仅是两个不同的种类。下面将介绍构成社区新闻的元素是如何让社区新闻“转”起来的。

社区新闻学的视角

时效性。人们都说媒体是做“新”生意而不是“老”生意的。新闻——即“新”的“闻”。CNN将之奉为圭臬，他们有24小时不间断的“数据流”。

在社区新闻里，形式服从于功能。如果你的报纸是周报，这会是一种情形，而如果它是一周两刊或者一周三刊，那又是另一种情况。如果你的报纸是日报，那么它就能报道突发新闻。出版的频率越低，报纸就该更有深度，解释性更强。我们和新闻事件发生间隔的时间越长，越应该将事件放到本地环境中，给读者提供更多背景信息。

这就是我们相对于大型日报和电视的优势。临近的电视台或许给你镇上发生的事30秒钟的报道，大型日报或许给你10厘米的版面。但在社区报，你可以用50到100厘米的版面来报道。如果你是握有决定权的编辑，甚至可以用上整个版面。

受众。当你要买一所房子时，一句老话说得好：你要找的东西有三样——地址，地址，还是地址。这在社区新闻学中也一样。地址就是你的受众，而你的受众就在你面前，非常具体。受众从新闻编辑室开始一直延伸到报道所能触及的地方，或许还可以延伸到郡的边界。

如果郡里什么人出事儿了，那就是新闻。同样，郡里的任何人都可以成为新闻并且触发新闻报道（或是特写，或是体育报道，或是社论，或是专栏，或是……你明白我的意思就好）。

用地质学家的话说，我们的受众处于“特定区域”。每一个社区都有自己的特色。位于海边的萨默维尔非裔社区和宾夕法尼亚州的乡村社区有巨大差异，记者和社区对话的前提是要了解当地方言、文化和历史背景，而后者你需要知道，那里多受日耳曼文化的熏陶，没有一点非洲裔美国文化的影子。

接近性和影响力。2004年夏天，美国政府重新部署海外7万个军人提案的消息传开了。尽管这是个全国性报道，对美国本土没有军事基地的地区或许不会造成什么影响，但是你可以肯定的是，这在萨默维尔是个大新闻。当地的经济主要是靠外来人口和查尔斯顿海军基地的补给拉动。如果政府要调回成千上万的军队，他们会被安排驻守在哪里？这就是本地的新闻题材，本地的新闻报道。

做我们这一行要考虑到，影响社区的任何事情都有可能影响到报纸。如果查尔斯顿海军基地人口大量增加，就会影响到萨默维尔的方方面面，包括《萨默维尔新闻现场》，因为很有可能发行量和广告商都会增多。涓滴效应告诉我们：如果你在报纸是个新手记者，你的工资可能要涨了。

底线。社区报与社区有其固有的紧密联系，其他的大都市日报或者某地电视台都无法与之比拟，不管他们离得多近或者他们在镜头里显得多么平易近人。他们的生存并不依靠和社区的联系。而与社区的联系却是社区报的生命线。正因为报纸在意、关心社区发展，在新闻报道方面就会对自己提出更高的要求。报道中流露的关切是与社区关联的自然反应，装腔作势读者一眼就能识破。

量级。更多人出现在圣诞节游行上，更多人观看橄榄球季后赛，更多的选民投票，公益组织筹到了更多的钱，主街道上的车开得更快了——社区新闻对这些新闻视角的反应和其他媒体很相似，不同之处在于我们会尽量把这些事放在本地环境下报道。

凸显性。重要的人总是新闻的焦点。但是在社区新闻里，“重要”意味着大青蛙或者小池塘，这些都是相对的概念。如果郡理事会主席被怀疑醉酒驾驶，那就是镇子极其轰动的新闻。报纸如何报道这件事将会产生比报道本身更深远的影响。比如说你粉饰了他的行为或者根本不进行报道，报纸就有可能失去公信力，因为大家口口相传都知道了这件事，报纸装聋作哑于事无补。想想那句老话：我早就知道这条新闻了，只是想看看报纸到底有没有胆量把它登出来。另一方面，如果你真的把醉酒驾驶的报道印出来，但过度渲染，耸人听闻，你也需要承担不良后果。

灾难和悲剧。像其他媒体一样，社区报必须报道灾难和悲剧，像犯罪、事故、火灾等等。但再次重申，社区新闻对人间苦难的反应和其他媒体具有本质上的差异。对我们来说，这是一个平衡问题。该怎么描述或者用图片展示血案呢？是否要公布强奸的受害者和犯罪嫌疑人的名字呢？是否要刊登死尸的图片？人们在火灾废墟前哭泣的画面能登吗？对于大城市报纸和电视来说，这是标准做法。为什么我们不同呢？如果无法决定是否刊登一张你认为有可能给他人造成伤害的照片，用这条准则问问自己：“如果被报道者是我家庭里的一员呢？如果这是我女儿的尸体躺在人行道上呢？如果强奸的受害者里有我祖母的名字呢？如果在烧毁的房子前失声痛哭的人是我父亲呢？”三思而后行。这是你的镇子，读者是你的邻居。刊登具有轰动效应的人们受苦的照片或者在硬新闻报道里用耸人听闻的描述会有什么后果呢？想想德纳和乔是怎么处理凯西哭泣的照片的吧。

这些是每家社区报都必须抓住、弄清的基本的新闻道德问题。好的报纸在这些方面有很明确的条规，年轻的记者和摄影师在适当的时候会学到这些智慧的处置方法。比如说，《快讯报》不刊登尸体的照片。这就意味着如果你到达某个出人命的事故现场，拍照的角度要谨慎。是的，我们会报出审判强奸案法庭上嫌疑人的名字，但不会报出受害者的名字。当到了为悲剧中遇难者或者在车祸中受伤的人哀悼的时候，尽你所能给他们最大的尊重。在一个事故现场，不要问受害者“你觉得失去你的儿子/房子/妻子是什么感受”。

当你拿起相机时，最好去征求别人的许可。如果你的出现会显得不礼貌，那就从远处用长焦镜头照下来，然后在照片登出前和你的编辑好好商量用哪张最合适。拍照时，最好聚焦于正能量的点，比如突出消防员、警察等处理突发事件的努力，我们卖报纸不是靠低级趣味报道和血淋淋的图片。

是否能划一条红线标明禁区呢？其实这条线一直因个人判断不同而上下浮动，是个灰色地带，而且它需要不断地调整，没有一个绝对正确或者错误的答案。不过“早餐桌上规则”仍然是个好的尺度。如果读者无法读下去，就算读的话吃的荷包蛋都会吐出来，那么你的“品位”就有点问题了。

公众的知情权不是由报纸头版某人母亲血淋淋的尸体来满足的。如果你刊登了这样的照片，你就等着受害者家人来报社强烈抗议吧。记住，因为我们是社区报，被激怒的读者可以直接走进编辑室把你打昏，打你八成是你活该。

让受害者的二次伤害最小化

以下的内容摘选自格伦•斯科特（Glenn Scott）的一份报告。他曾是北卡大学教堂山分校新闻与大众媒体学院的博士生。

> 南达科他州（South Dakota）《自由人通讯》[*Freeman (S.D.) Courier*]周报出版人蒂姆•沃特纳（Tim Waltner）认为学新闻的学生应该像他和他的同龄人那样，体验一下经营小镇周报的生活。他预测，读者对社区报那些负责任的、体现善意的报道的高评价会让他们印象深刻。这些报道往往被对社区没有情感投入的大城市日报或电视节目所忽视。
>
> 沃特纳讲述了他和一对父母伤痛但必要的谈话。
>
> 他们的儿子保罗在“超级碗”派对的当天，意外射杀了一位叫伍迪的好朋友。保罗开车去取比萨，刚好在一个便携的保温器里找到一把枪。沃特纳说他不知道这件悲剧后面的事实真相，他只知道这是场意

外。但是，沃特纳知道自己必须很好地处理报道。沃特纳认识当事家庭，事实上，案发时，他的女儿距离现场很近。这是发生在朋友之间的悲剧，这个事件影响了小镇很多人。尽管沃特纳知道读者可以接受一个直面事实的报道，但他担心大电视台和地区日报会渲染这个事件。作为社区报主编，他首先要为当事人考虑，沃特纳说："在报纸出版前两个小时，我心里突然感觉很不对。"为了让保罗父母对报道有心理准备，他打电话解释，希望他们能理解把保罗的名字登出来是报纸的责任。处于悲伤中的父亲并没有责怪报纸。

"你们的责任是报道真相，"沃特纳记得那位父亲是这么说的，"真相是，保罗冲伍迪开了枪。"

最后的结果是，沃特纳的担心并没有成为现实。大媒体几乎忽视了他的报道，因为当沃特纳的周报出版时，这个事件对大媒体的出版来说已经是"旧新闻"了。

保罗没有因这次意外而遭到起诉。从那以后，这个小伙子知耻而后勇，后来他还帮忙设计了《自由人通讯》的网页。

这就是真实报道收获的结局。

新闻视角的其他几个要素

冲突和争议。由于你的退路十分有限，社区报的记者和编辑，甚至是出版人经常会发现自己处于一个两难境地。抱歉，年轻人，这是你做这一行会碰到的情形。本地政客、政府公共事务、执法机关、公共学校都和纳税人的钱有关联，因此要对他们进行严格的监督。首要法则就是"报道要尽可能地公正、客观"。当报道一件有争议的事件时，确保自己从尽可能多的角度来展示这个故事，也要确保你不会偏袒任何一方。这在社区新闻学里非常重要，因为镇上的人们对你的个人生活非常了解，任何可能被理解为偏袒的东西（不管到底是不是真的）或者利益的冲突都会破坏报道的可信度。如果你的确有愚弄他人的地方，就应立即承认错误并且尽快退出报道。当年轻记者做敏感报道时，一定要让编辑参与修订终稿。如果你和编辑正在筹划写一篇尖锐的社论，要记住：不要愤怒地写，而应小心地选择你斗争的对象。你的论点是公正理智的，还是刻薄刺耳的？

稀奇古怪的事件。在一个咖啡店的大冒险游戏中，一个本地人决定一头扎进镇子广场上的喷泉里；一位老妇人养了一只叫罗斯科的土拨鼠，这只土拨鼠已经在老人被闲置的洗衣机里生活了16年；社区学院的校长必须当众亲猪屁股，因为他承诺如果足球队保持全胜他就会这样做；一辆卡车在主街翻了车，把巧克力糖浆撒了一地；一位女士装作心脏病突发吓走了盗贼；五个罪犯仅仅用指甲刀就从郡监狱挖地道逃了出来。成千上万的类似小故事都归到“稀奇古怪的事件”的新闻标题下。人们要从单调的日常生活中寻求解脱，对新事物甚至是有些古怪的事情的求知欲是很强的。在早先特别慢节奏的新闻时代里，一些报纸因刊登农民拿着像狗状的土豆、人脸样的西红柿而出名。这有什么错吗？没什么错，除非你整张报纸刊登的都是这些东西。

人情味。广义上理解，人情味这个词指那些有一点触动心弦的故事和照片。一个精神上有障碍的男孩失踪一天后被发现住在下水管道里。他被本地救援队伍发现是因为尽管他不会说话，但他脖子上戴了只银铃。这就是个有很浓人情味的好新闻。一位报纸编辑听说本地高中的守门人退休了，这听起来没什么特别，直到校长告诉编辑这位老人家喜欢一边照看锅炉一边弹五弦琴。看，现在我们就有了一个有人情味儿的故事，照片也有着落了。

幽默。一些人认为，媒体的工作就是广而告之和娱乐。幽默是娱乐的最佳形式，但是幽默并不是那么好表现，需要记者、摄影师和编辑都有幽默感。首要原则：不要以捉弄他人来制造幽默。“取笑别人”与“和别人一起笑”之间是泾渭分明的。在新闻和特写报道中，要避免使用讽刺、反语，直到你有些经验了并且社区都了解你的笔法后才可以用。反语会被一些人直接从字面理解，他们根本不会感觉好笑。把这种东西留给社论版、个人专栏和评论版这些可以明显带幽默痕迹的版面。

三巨头：新闻、特写、评论

报纸上除了广告，其他内容不外乎以下三种：新闻、特写、评论。怎么区分呢？他们最显著的不同是什么？乔伊•富兰克林（Joy Franklin）是北卡州大型日报《阿什维尔公民时代》[*Asheville (N.C.) Citizen-Times*]的社论版编辑，他用以下的列表来帮助年轻记者和学生理解三样东西的形式和特征。

新闻

导语：一般是综述性的（包含5W和HOW的其中几个）。

风格：报道的风格通常是倒金字塔式的。

时效性：报道几乎都是时效性强的。

目的：新闻是用来说明事实的。

角度：记者应当保持客观。

位置：大多数都在第一版，但也有在其他版的。

特写

导语：可以用很多种形式。

风格：叙事性的经常会用到轶闻，还有其他风格。

时效性：可强可弱。新闻引子可有可无。

目的：娱乐和讲事实。

角度：主观也可，客观也可。

位置：经常在各叠头版。

评论

导语：形式不拘。

风格：很多种形式和结构都可以使用。

时效性：可以有也可以没有时间制约。

目的：可能是说明事实，但多数是用来说服的。

角度：社论作家个人观点或者是编辑部的观点。

位置：被放置于社论版。如果是个人评论的话，在特稿、体育、生活方式版面的某个固定位置。

所有政治事关本地；所有政治皆成报道

如果新闻像飓风，那么当地政府事务的报道就可以被称为“真正的旋风”，当然，它不是“茶杯里的旋风”，这就是我们被称为新闻人的原因。还会有谁对镇议会、学校理事会、计划委员会、区议会、城市规划委员会、郡理事召开的市政厅活动和会议进行深入全面不间断的报道呢？

社区报报道中没有什么比这更重要的了。对本地政府的报道事关读者切身利益。他们可能不能立即了解情况，他们也可能不能都了解情况，但是记者作为“公众监督员”代表那些不会或者不能出席会议的人旁听各种可能直接影响到读者生活质量的会议是报纸存在的最根本意义之一。

如果郡理事们想要提高税率，从新闻要素看，这篇报道直接关系到读者的钱包，普通老百姓（或许他这辈子都未读过一篇关于郡理事的报道）想知道为什么。“我要多付多少钱？为什么税率要提升？收取的税金用于哪里？”或许你在听证会上会听到这样不满的叫声。“这样的会议什么时候再次召开？我看的那份《号角报》在哪里？我记得上面写着召开的时间。”

切记76厘米长、从第一点到第五点挨个罗列议题的报道没人看得下去。要解读对读者有关的重要细则。

带上相机到现场

在一个没有一家报纸认为值得报道的议会会议上，委员会通过并签署了一项严格的、影响范围大的条例。直到条例开始实施，人们才开始愤怒地做出回应。“为什么我们对此一无所知？”他们哀嚎道。

如果本地社区报没有对政府工作进行必要监督，基本上就没有其他人或组织会去监督了。从历史上看，美国大报和每一份社区报都要承担作为监督者的角色。有些人认为，看门狗角色才使新闻成为几乎是最神圣的职业。

在一个镇子里，选民们正准备投票决定该镇是否能合法地出售啤酒。议会由年长的保守白人男性把持，他们举办了一场听证会。一位著名的自由派公民站起来，称议会人员是一群木偶，已完全被教堂的保守派给控制了。为了突出这种联系，他把一个线球的一端绑在议会的一张桌子上，接着就走出了屋子，边走边放线。

他走一路放一路，他要去哪里？当时只有一位社区报记者在屋子里，他和几位好奇的旁观者尾随那个走出会场的人，一直到被他指认的那个教堂前。在教堂前，那个人把绳子的另一头系在前门上。“这就是他们的联系。”他强调说，“教堂这边拉一下这条线，议会那里的人就会跳舞。你要引用我说的这句话。”

你说得太对了，我们会引用你的话。这是个很棒的材料。人们多么希望我们的记者当时随身带一台相机。因此，早些时候新闻界始终都在喊：“拿上相机到现场！”用另外一种方式说，新闻人的目标就是带着相机在现场亲眼目睹事件。你是如何调整相机光圈进行拍摄，相对于“你在那里拍摄”的事实来说并不重要。

新闻报道要奉行缇普•奥尼尔（Tip O’Neill）的那句著名格言——“所有政治都是当地的。”就报业来讲，还应该加上一句：“所有政治皆成报道。”国家级的、州级的政治性报道同样也会影响到我们的读者。当联邦政府实施“不让一个孩子掉队”的教育法案时，它会影响到这片土地上的每一所学校。社区新闻的任务就是向社区解读这些国家和州级报道的内涵，展示这样的法案会如何直接影响到我们的社区。

会议报道：不怎么诱人，但必须有人去报道

小报的很多年轻记者发现他们第一次报道镇议会会议、学校理事会会议、计划委员会会议或郡理事会议时手足无措，他们很少甚至没有受过训练。

暂且把下面要说的东西称为“傻瓜式的公共事务报道”。这个成果应该归功于里士满大学（University of Richmond）新闻学导师汤姆•穆勒（Tom Mullen），是他化繁为简，整理出了这样一个和“猜猜看游戏”一样简单的新手手册。我们

把其称为：

汤姆会议报道绝招

● 弄清你应该去哪里。这听起来很傻，但很关键。召开会议的大楼是哪一座？在哪个房间？停车场在哪里？要多久才能到现场？

● 早到现场。这是对会议的尊重。当然也是个很实际的问题，早到的话你可以找到一个视野开阔并且能听到会议桌上所有人讲话的位置。没有什么比一个新手冒冒失失闯入正在进行中的议会大厅更糟糕的了。如果当时进行的是场小型会议，你是极少观众中的一位，或者你是唯一的记者，这会凸显出你的不敬业。如果会议级别很高而你又迟到了，你就会冒着被堵在屋子后面什么也听不见、看不见的风险。记住：进不去，你就拿不出报道。

● 着装得体。又一个看起来很白痴的提示。但是看到那么多媒体人报道较为正式的公共事务活动时，穿的却像是刚刚结束后院烧烤回来似的，总会让人感到惊讶。记住，要想变得不受人关注，就要用穿着来伪装自己。男士们，在你的公文包里放一条领带，总有一天它会救你于水火。另一种情况，如果整个议会里的人都穿着高尔夫短衫，松松垮垮，那么你也不必穿得正式。只要睁开双眼用你的常识判断就知道该穿什么了。

● 提前做好功课。提前拿到会议议程，一条一条阅读。不要一头雾水就扎进会议厅。

● 打电话联系。这点很重要，尤其当你是镇里的新面孔时，跟你的采访对象打电话，这样介绍你自己：“我是《号角报》的记者，我注意到了本次的议程安排。这点如何理解？这样的话我就能给读者更好的解释了……”不要害怕用你的无知来作为敲门砖。

● 该报道什么？在会议之前弄清楚你想写些什么，但不要低估新东西出现的可能性。

● 记住，你在人们的目光下。你不仅仅代表自己，还代表报纸，展示出自己最好的状态。看在上帝的份上，保持清醒，千万别睡着！

● 多拿几支笔。这是个人们都瞧不起的规则，经常把它忘掉。没有什么比一个写手没有笔可写更愚蠢的了。

● 给你的笔记标上序号。边记录边整理条目。荧光笔对你会有帮助。

● 认真听可以直接引用的好句子。不要只关注耸人听闻的话，而要关注任何你能直接引用的生动的句子。这样的做法使报道有人味儿，把令人昏昏欲睡的会议报道激活起来。

● 为RP报道。也就是为“Real People（真人）”报道，同样也可以叫作

PYR，即“Picture Your Reader（想象你的读者正在阅读）”。你可以问自己几个问题：“有谁在乎呢？”“有谁需要了解我写的内容呢？”“为什么他们需要知道这些？”并且尝试着想象眼前浮现出你的莎蒂阿姨正在读你的报道，哪个地方她会看不明白呢？

● 不使用行话。当议会在讨论“污水回流监管”时，你需要告诉读者他们在讨论污水的控制。说人们能听懂的话。

如果你准备好写报道了，还有一些要点：

穆勒的建议

● 避免使用官方导语。不要这么说：“市议会投标决定增税……”帮读者处理信息，给读者一个直观的说法，比如说：“每位住房自有者今年都要多交2000美元的税款……”

● 用影响检验法。发生的事情对我的读者重要到什么程度？想想你的莎蒂阿姨吧。

● 用“你会读它吗？”检验法。如果你不是作者，你会读这篇报道吗？

● 用“要么行动，要么闭嘴”检验法。如果会议上的东西你自己都搞不懂，那读者也不会明白你的报道。你的工作是要让事情变得明朗。会议结束后，不要怕去问一位议员“当你说到……时，你的意思是什么”这样的问题。这会显现你对准确的高要求。

讣告不一定要沉闷无味

这是个很多年轻记者都没有意识到的平凡的事实：人年纪越大，他们就越多关注讣告。很讽刺的是，许多年轻记者却被派去写讣告。

许多编辑的逻辑是这样的：这样的事枯燥而又沉重，看看他或她能不能清晰而又准确地写好一个死人。

然而这也是一次测试，考验你的准确性、谦逊程度、进取心和文笔。很遗憾地说，许多讣告都是无聊、刻板或者套话堆砌的。

但是讣告不一定非得“死气沉沉”不可。

我已经写好自己的讣告。读一读，看看你能不能对我这个“已经逝去的人”产生些感觉。

赵克，经验丰富的摄影师、大学老师，热爱他的工作，开玩笑说自己想死在暗室里。周六，他终于如愿以偿。

89岁坚持不退休的赵克，周六早晨被发现死在教堂山阿拉亚路122号家中暗室里。验尸官认定其死因为心脏衰竭。

赵克著书15部，曾在其联合创立的北卡州西部的两份报纸当出版人兼编辑。他在那里工作了15年。赵克在宾夕法尼亚州教了10年的新闻摄影课程。

赵克的遗孀琳妮•弗农•菲尔根斯（Lynne Vernon-Feagans）说："当他再次在大学拿起教鞭时，他好像获得了新生。"赵克还留下一儿一女。

告别仪式将会在3月21日周日下午2点举行，地点在皮尔福伊路105号的社区教堂里，查理•卡斯特牧师将会主持仪式。

葬礼上不需要鲜花，赵克的家人希望人们能把所有的捐助都由北卡大学教堂山分校新闻与大众传媒学院转交给赵克奖学金基金。

通常来说，讣告的作者应该在报道中体现这几个元素：

- 姓名、年龄、住址、职业。
- 时间、地点、死因。
- 出生日期和出生地。
- 成就和所获荣誉。
- 教育程度。
- 服兵役情况。
- 逸事及亲朋好友的回忆。
- 所剩亲属（直系亲属加上孙辈）。
- 葬礼或者悼念会的信息，出葬安排。
- 鲜花，还有为向逝者表示敬意的特别基金或捐助。

讣告的作者从下述的至少一个地方得到他要的材料。

- 太平间、殡仪馆。
- 亲戚朋友。
- 新闻剪报。
- 有参考的文献（比如说《名人录》）。
- 警察、验尸官。
- 医院。
- 主治医师。

让讣告“活”起来

“极不像话，目光短浅。”这是退休的科罗拉多州州立大学（Colorado State University）新闻学教授加勒特•W.雷（Garrett W. Ray）对那些草率而无聊的讣告写作的形容。他和很多精明的报纸编辑都知道，讣告版是整个报纸最先和阅读最多的版面之一。

堪萨斯州立大学和全国报纸协会每年定期举办以“社区报纸和社区建设”为主题的研讨会，有一年雷参与了“让讣告‘活’起来”的小组讨论，他说：

> “地方报纸都在找对读者有用并让他们感到有趣的方法来建立与社区的纽带，同时也为了在竞争愈发激烈的媒介市场中获得更多份额。优秀的本地讣告可以帮助你实现这些目标，但它总没有得到足够重视。”

他认为，编辑应该记住“我们用不寻常的方式触及普通人的生活”。以下这些观点，都是用一种新颖的角度来看待讣告写作的。

● 把讣告像特写一样，当作人物专访来做。

● 提高讣告的地位，把它交给最好的记者来写。

● 每期至少刊登一篇写得特别好的讣告。

● 重点关注“普通人”。

● 做好功课（寻找报纸以前对逝者和逝者亲属的报道）。

● 多和一些消息源聊天。注意倾听可引用的真情流露的话，注意收集可以突出性格的事例。

● 寻觅其生活中的“标志性事件”，具有决定性的时刻。他们在乎什么？愿意为什么付出时间？他们因什么而骄傲？什么给他们带来快乐？

● 倾听“小”故事，即动人的小片段。讲故事才是我们的主业。

● 用特写导语。

● 最重要的是，要准确，不能出错。

● 以一个包括日期和报纸名字的标志结束文章。这对家属很重要，他们可以把文章剪下来保存。

“常规的讣告不能展示出一个人的独特之处。”雷说。伊利诺伊《先驱新闻》（*Herald-News*）意识到了这点，他们对待每一个讣告都像对待特写一样，把它放在一个叫“平凡人”的连载中。“平凡人”是“可能并不出名，但展示了没有‘普通人’这一说”的人群，每一个个体都是无价的，都不普通。

水牛比尔会感到骄傲的

怀俄明州《科迪进取报》（*Cody and Progress Report*）是一份发行量在6000份、已有100多年历史的一周两刊的社区报。谈到绝佳的讣告，这份报纸个性化的写作方式可算典范。你看记者劳里•奎德（Laurie Quaid）在第一次提到逝者时用了全名，以后的段落里都只使用名，亲密感油然而生。

> 从科迪高中毕业后，鲍勃参加了海军，在那里度过了六年时光。他回到科迪镇娶了杰里•里德（Jerry Read），跟他的挚爱一起度过了53年充满美好回忆的人生。
>
> 鲍勃的生命和许多爱他的人一起共有。他喜爱户外运动和钓鱼，尤其是和他的兄弟们一起钓鱼；家人真切缅怀一起度过的美妙光阴；护理中心的人不会忘记他送去的歌声。

《科迪进取报》刊登了一篇有关一个建筑工人的讣告：

> 他是机械高手，他因对所有设备的熟练掌握，以及可靠、诚实的品质而受到人们的高度评价。
>
> 他的第二爱人是业余无线电。他经常会全身心投入到雪松山无线电俱乐部里。在那里他与有共同爱好的人快乐地交流。
>
> 他也喜爱打猎，去世的时候还在和儿子一起打猎。

作为《科迪进取报》的社会版编辑，奎德同时还负责警察局和医院的新闻、摄影，以及写专栏、写出生通告还有讣告。“我从生写到死。”奎德自嘲道。

奎德在写讣告方面有明确的原则。“这是给逝者的一份礼物。”她说，“这是最后有人为他们喝彩，也是他们最后一次上报。我认为他们的生命意义用‘她出生了，她活过，她死了’这样的概括根本无法表达。看到这样的讣告我觉得很难过。”

奎德认为讣告多数是写给逝者留下的亲朋好友看的。“当我们把讣告挪到报纸的最后部分，并且削减里面的形容词使文字干巴巴，还让人们为之付钱时，我感到很难过。我认为讣告很重要，特别是对社区报。”

第 8 章

社区报的社论：利剑而非重锤

敬爱的中国读者：

尽管你可能得下一番功夫才能在美国报纸上找到一页典型的社论专版（因为社论经常处于报纸的内层），但在出色的社区报中，社论却是最为重要的一部分。正如获过奖的社论员兼社区报拥有人肯•里普利所言：“如果说新闻是报纸的心脏，那么社论就是报纸的灵魂。”

——作者

社区报就像热腾腾的厨房

直言不讳的高中生物老师碰到了刚从当地邮局出来的年轻记者，这位老师就像教训一个没头脑的学生一样，对记者不停地指指点点，好像在教给她无上的智慧："你这周的社论……唉，你怎么不坚持写点儿你在行的特写啊？"

没人在新闻学院里告诉你现实会是这样，对吧？

社区层面上的社论完全不像大报社论。大报里，社论会贯彻报纸的编辑方针，写社论的人一般都是匿名，不被读者所认知。社区报就不同。人们都认识我们，他们也知道怎么找到并且盘问我们。如果你说了让当地人不舒服的话，很快就能听到他们当面的质问。社区报所有读者都认为他们有权利对你所说的任何一句话批评上两句，他们都是这么做的，而且他们会一直这样做下去。

干我们这一行唯一最奇特的一点是：我们轻轻敲击键盘或者按下快门，就可以触及社区中的每个人。这种影响力不是没有代价的——你若触及民众，就要付出受到街谈巷议的代价。

这并不意味着你要回避大胆的社论立场，而是要坚守社区新闻学最基本的要求——带着职业责任感去写作，而且你要给其他人与你交流的机会。

该出手时就出手，但要想好对手是谁，因为一个社区就像一座玻璃屋，你随随便便地开炮会震坏许多窗子。

为什么社论版这么重要

没有什么能比社论版更能区分出色的社区报、一般的社区报和差劲的社区报了。出色的社区报的社论版应该是本地化的，真实的，及时的，贴近生活的，而不是尖刻的，刺耳的，仇恨的。社论版内容会在政治观点、个人看法、社论、评论、漫画和读者来信间做出平衡。关于社论版最重要的一点是，它从不回避社区重大事件。不同意见在此碰撞是社会自由的关键。

宾夕法尼亚州布鲁斯伯格的《新闻进取报》（*Press-Enterprise*）是一份发行量达22000份的日报，编辑吉姆•萨切蒂（Jim Sachetti）说："社论板块是报纸的灵魂，它可以反映出报纸真正在乎的是质量还是卖广告赚钱。"

萨切蒂煞有介事地问自己工作的这份日报的社论有什么重要性？"往大了说，这些社论算什么？我们只是一份在宾夕法尼亚的中心小镇的小报而已。"紧接着，他就回答了自己："美国是世界上最宜居的国家，如果没有报纸上公开争辩的存在，它就不会是今天这个样子！"

社区报出版过成千上万的社论，它们被萨切蒂称为"一本美国历史的蓝皮书"。他强调："不管它多小，你必须认识到它的重要性。"

就像沃尔特•李普曼说的那样："一份自由的报纸是一个伟大社会的必需品，而不是奢侈品。"

回到萨切蒂，他认为："社论需要鼓动人们来到社论版发言分享意见，进行交流。公众意见的对话质量是成就优秀社论版的关键。"萨切蒂相信"民众发表自己的见解对历史记录很重要，对国家未来的发展同样重要"。

关于有争议类社论的写作

《公民主张》（*Citizen Advocate*）是得克萨斯州科佩尔市的一份发行量为5000份的周报，它的出版人兼编辑珍•墨菲（Jean Murph）表示，她在美军2003年入侵伊拉克前写了一篇反对伊战的社论，"我有责任去写，这就像我过去20年每周都带着责任感去写作一样"。墨菲说，在保守派居多的社区里，仅有五个人因为这篇社论退订报纸。但她怀疑那五个不满的人现在要么从超市报架上还在买《公民主张》，要么很快就会继续订阅。

使用现成的社论是一种逃避

一些编辑和出版商出于胆小怕事、精力不足、懒惰或者就是不在乎，用没有当地内容的辛迪加稿件或者把其他报纸的内容直接拷贝过来。这些社论简直像是美军军用的即食口粮——味道像没法消化的饲料。这样的报纸，不会有人买，不会有人在乎，也不会有人写信给编辑，因为当地居民没有理由去读与己无关的社论版面。

比尔•梅耶是堪萨斯州一位备受赞誉的周报出版人兼编辑，他强烈斥责那些"从来不表明自己立场"的社区报编辑，他说："他们只能发表这些"阉割"过的社论，根本看不到'论'！要不然他们就只会发些老好人写的文章，跟木薯淀粉做的布丁一样无味，力道跟棉花糖砸在身上没什么两样。"

社区新闻的领袖们承认这种"僵尸社论版"的存在，但实际情况比他们承认的还要严重得多。有关这种社论版最最糟糕的是，它们给社区传递了这样的信号：

- 我觉得没有必要给你提供一个贴近生活的本地社论版面。
- 我很懒，但对此，我骄傲。
- 我不在乎你。

拉撒路[1]重新起身前行！

如果你想让“僵尸社论版”像圣经中的死人拉撒路那样，重新站起来焕发生机，就要动员每个人进行彻底革新。

编辑必须承诺定期写出新鲜的社论。

在某个话题上，请相关的社区领袖担任专栏作者，他们写出的社论要加上本人的头像照片。如果必须发工资的话，给他们小部分酬金或者提供免费的报纸订阅。但大多数情况下，有社区意识的作家都不为钱写作，而是为了自己的灵感能被分享而写，同时也为了造福社区而写。

把每周的专栏任务分派给手下的每个员工，包括摄影师。你会惊喜地发现这招是多么有效。记着，每个专栏都要附上负责人好看的头像照片。

鼓励读者给编辑写信。

社论何时成型

报纸最能让读者血脉喷张的就是社论上出现的不同观点。其实，在早餐桌上大骂报纸是美国光荣的传统。看看美国的新闻史，最早的报纸都具有鲜明的党派倾向，社论观点非常明确，甚至连追求客观的新闻报道也会夹杂毫无顾忌的评论。

直到20世纪早期，报纸开始接纳客观报道概念，并从此把评论和客观报道分开。如今，人们视这条准则如《圣经》般神圣。报纸对社论的使用已经有了明确的界限。

让我们来快速复习一下社论写作的要点：

- 导语：很多东西可被用作导语。
- 形式：可以使用多种形式和结构。
- 时效性：有的强，有的不强。
- 目的：不仅告知，同时说服大众。
- 基调：主观，立场鲜明。
- 位置：大多数情况下固定发表在社论版。

---

①圣经中人物，被耶稣从坟墓中复活。

社论写作和社区新闻学的解读

有些社论用来提供事实，解释缘由，教化大众，有的甚至是用来娱乐的，但大多数社论是为了说服而生。主观的写法加上鲜明的观点是区别社论和新闻写作的重要标志。

要是在以前，如果没钱上大学，通过读报你依然能受到良好的社会教育，因而在美国报纸又被称为“穷人的大学”，而报纸社论被当作影响“公众意见的模子”。很多青年人不看报，从社交媒体获知新闻，网站是一个并不缺少观点的地方，所以一点不奇怪，多数大城市日报社论版的影响力日渐衰落。

但是就社区新闻而言，社论不会因此而停滞不前。因为，每个社区都需要在本地议题上有坚定的声音（电视显然没有时间和精力来做这些事），需要有人对本地和外界事件进行充分反思，需要无畏的勇士去做一些虽不起眼也许要失败，但对社区发展有意义的事。

为什么要写社论？目标是什么？北卡罗来纳州布里瓦德的《特兰西瓦尼亚时代》（*Transylvania Time of Brevard, N.C.*）的报头能告诉你答案：“只要能使特兰西瓦尼亚郡受益，我们就会不停为之奋斗。”这意味着如果对本郡不利，报纸会坚决地说“不”！

一个优秀的社区报社论作家知道社论写作能引起的反响有五个层次：

1. 注意它：读者眼球被社论吸引。或许是被标题，或许是被文采吸引，但最有可能是你写的东西触及了他关注的话题。

2. 理解它：读者读完社论全篇并记住它。

3. 化合它：读者读完后会思考，或者可以这么说，他们的大脑会“处理”刚读到的信息、数据、观点和论证。

4. 采取行动：更理想的状态是，读者会感觉社论激起了渴望，这种渴望让他想做些实事来改变现状。

5. 产生互动：我们现在来看看最好的一面。当读者告诉你，你的社论让他从椅子上一跃而起、撸胳膊挽袖子要找你理论时，你完全有理由跟自己说声“干得漂亮”。他们可以不把自己心中的“普利策奖”颁给你，但你一天的工作已经圆满完成了。相比于大城市同行，社区报社论作家更可能直接得到读者的真实反馈。

KISS原则

社论通常被放在社论版的左上角，它会有一个坚定的立场、一种明确的导向、一种可预料的态度。社论版在报纸中位置通常固定不变，如果你把社论瞎排一气，读者就可能放弃你的报纸，人们习惯于这种固定的版式安排。

很多媒体专家都对“头版刊登社论”这一做法感到不满，但当编辑要鼓吹一个理念时，这一招就经常被拿来使用。把本该用来传达客观事实的版面用作观点宣传，这种行为本身就有极大的误导性和危险性。不能把社论放在头版也有其他的原因：这样做有哗众取宠之嫌。这也就意味着，你对凭社论版吸引读者其实没什么信心。

谁来写社论？这取决于报纸规模的大小。中型日报规模以上的报纸，由发行人、高级主编还有社论版编辑组成的社论版编委会确定报纸对特定事件的观点。在很多小型日报和周报中，社论基本由一位编辑完成。

社论版委员会实在是个奢侈品，多数小报都负担不起。在大多社区报里，社论就是编辑个人的观点，就这么简单，社论不是报纸的观点。报纸没有观点，人才有观点。

如果一家小报有多人发表社论，而他们的观点又各不相同，该怎么办？解决办法就是让社论作者署名。这样的话，社论版就可以很自然地容纳和反映不同的社论观点了。这样做不仅让读者知道到底是谁写的社论，而且同时突出了社区新闻笃信的原则——个人为言论负责。

社论立场通常在写作之前就被定下来了，不管是集体决议，还是个人观点，镇上居民通常都知道报纸对特定事件的立场。比如说，读者都知道《号角报》是支持环保的，因为《号角报》的社论一直都是这个基调。

沃尔特大叔的建议

备受爱戴的沃尔特•斯皮尔曼（Walter Spearman）是教堂山北卡罗来纳大学多年的新闻学教授。40多年来，他仁慈的精神和包容的视角影响了无数未来的报纸编辑。在他极受欢迎的社论写作课上，已故的沃尔特大叔给出了如下一些建议：

● 社论是利剑，而不是大锤。当你做一个观点陈述时，一定要准确，聪明，不露声色。不要对问题迎头棒喝，那会使你像一个毫无感情的机器人。

● 对事不对人。把精力放到你要处理的问题上，永远不要去做人身攻击。如果你要写一名郡里的行政人员贪污，你只能说这是他作为政府人员的过失，是对公众信任的背叛，而不能说你觉得这个人多么混蛋。

● 不要带着愤怒写作。大多数的新手觉得，当他们受伤失望时更容易写出社论（歌曲、诗歌也一样）。如果你气急败坏，无法理智地看问题，你想写社论并非不可，不过写完就把文章扔了吧。坐下来冷静一下，或许再等上一段时间，抛开你的偏激，重写一遍。

● 避免讽刺。讽刺要出效果靠的是声音的表现，也就是说，报纸天生就有“声音”这一障碍。因为读者无法读出语调，一部分人可能只理解字面的意思，完全误解你的意图。讽刺是最容易被没有幽默感的人所误解的一种。所以，最好不要用讥讽的评论、诙谐的表达和过“冷”的幽默。

独木不难支

《春泉希望行动报》[*Spring Hope (N.C) Enterprise*]的肯•里普利是一位有经验的出版人兼编辑。他是“独木不难支”的最佳案例。发行量2500份，每周8—12版的报纸几乎由他一手运营。尽管如此，肯还是获得了无数奖状，全是嘉奖他所撰写的优秀社论。肯是个不惧硬茬儿的人，他说：“新闻是报纸的灵魂，社论是报纸的灵魂，而报纸是社区的脊髓。”

因为有了他，《春泉希望行动报》很有风格。不管多晚多累，肯每周都会敲出一篇社论，只因为这对他十分重要。肯把自己描述为“有节制的发飙”，他说：“要做报纸，你必须有自己的脊梁。我为自己能够行使领导才能，发表自己的观点而感到骄傲。我们可以告诉人们什么是重要的，什么是不重要的。社论版是一个社区自我反省的论坛，我能做的就是让人们独立思考。我的角色是形成看法，塑造能影响行为的态度，表达自己的立场。”

肯说自己写社论的第一原则是：“我的第一格言和希波克拉底氏誓言相同，‘第一，不要伤害’。”此外，另一个准则是：“社论的意义在于它能带来积极的改变。”

社论所评说的事件并不总是区分黑白那么简单，事实上，大多事情都不是黑白分明的。“我活的年岁越长，看事件时，‘灰色’会越多。”他这么说。

肯的社论或是解释事件，或是对一个事件提出相关指导，或是向读者解读政府某机构举动的意图，或是鼓励生者，或是缅怀逝者。

肯把自己最有效的意见称为“制导导弹”，这种“杀伤”范围集中、目标明确的“聪明炸弹”可能仅仅指向某个事件，更有可能指向某位公职人员，比如说某个市议员。

最后，如果社论没起效果，让肯义愤填膺的时候，他还可能抛出“原子弹社论”。他承认，这种社论最有趣，但是只会在他对某种局面或某位政客彻底失去信心的时候才会用到。

肯被认为是人口约1200人的春泉镇的一个强大人物。他说：“我有能力去说服别人。这是我仅有的能力。我的葬礼肯定是镇上最隆重的，镇上一半人会来吊唁我，另一半人要确认我是否真死了。”

报纸的力量

特里•卡尔霍恩（Terry Calhoun）是北卡州绍斯波特周报《州港领航员报》的新闻编辑。他曾经这样对社区新闻学的学生劳伦•里皮（Lauren Rippey）说：“我在社区报的第一篇社论是批评一个城市规划者，当我知道那个规划者在社论出来后立即递交了辞呈，我震惊了。我早先是在一份中型日报工作，大多数的被采访对象甚至都不承认读过社论版。我列了一份单子，是我为改变社区所做的十条最重要的贡献。比如说，现在郡里已经有非赢利的老年人理事会了，政府援助因为我的社论而逐步去政治化了，我做到这些不只靠批评别人的过失，而是靠提出解决方案。我的前任曾经被问到为什么不去竞选政府职位，他回答道：‘因为我无法忍受失去在社区里的影响力和力量。’”

表演秀：专栏和评论

拥有固定专栏需要长期投入，一周又一周，你要惦记着它，时刻在想自己下周该写些什么，或者琢磨上次写的专栏是否换个写法会更好。

有人说，写专栏就像在大庭广众下脱衣服。开始，你会觉得颜面扫尽，但最终你会习惯于别人的注视。在“脱”了几次后，你会知道怎么一个扣子一个扣子别致地“脱”，有节制地展示自己，展示的时间长一点。要想做好专栏，你得有点自我暴露的精神，还要加上些许表演成分。

社区报里，没有什么比专栏写作更排斥新手，时不时让新手摸不着头脑的了。只有少数年轻写手天生善于评论，更少人能写出幽默感来。确实，评论不是一种教得会的技能，而要靠多年积淀。除非有非凡的天赋或独特的视角，通常情况下，年轻写手或因为生活经验不足，不能给读者传达有意义的故事和观点，或因不够成熟，没法提炼出人生经验，更没法或清楚，或幽默，或委婉、或智慧地写出来。

尽管这样，在最优秀的社区报里，新闻编辑室的每个人，不论职业经历或是否受过训练，都被要求写一篇专栏文章。尽管这些文章质量很多只能算C+，但让每人每周都写仍是个很正确的选择，至于为什么，听我解释。

大城市的报纸都有出色的专栏作家，他们写的都是上品。在社区报里，如果你想把版面搞得生活味儿十足，编辑室里每个人或许都要参与进来。相对于大报，社区报的专栏文章不必振聋发聩。因为文章是第一人称写的，加上有作者固定的大头照，报纸就被注入了人情味儿，带有作者的个人特质。这才是社区报专栏真正潜在的价值。

在社区新闻层面上，“我们代表社区”是专栏要传达的理念。如果能做出活色生香的社论版，报纸就把这一理念展现得淋漓尽致了。

密西西比州的《麦库布行动日报》[*McComb (M.S.) Enterprise-Journal*]是一份发行量为13000份的日报，在它的报头下面有这么一行字——“全世界对本社区最感兴趣的报纸”。

专栏让报纸更有人情味。如果你有机会主持专栏，也许是向读者展示作为普通人一面的好机会。比如说这周你把衣服和孩子的红色蜡笔一起放进洗衣机，结果全家的衣服都一片红，你只能向网络或者有经验的人求助，结果得到一个妙方。这样的专栏故事虽家长里短很琐碎，但很真实，更容易拉近报纸和读者的距离。

专栏能向读者传达很多信息，比如：我们在一起，你从不孤单；我们很相似；有很多人和你想法一致；个人的声音也有价值；我们不妄自尊大，不是因为我是记者或者编辑，我就比你强到哪儿去；我们的生活在此时此地多么美好。

北卡威克福里斯特（Wake Forest, N.C.）的《维克周报》（*The Wake Weekly*）前出版人鲍勃•艾伦（Bob Allen）曾经因为繁忙，一周没写专栏。几天后，他被前台一位愤怒的女士叫出印刷间。“啊……额……”鲍勃回忆道，“我看到她的表情，我知道我摊上大事儿了……”

那位女士对鲍勃指指点点：“年轻人，你要是这周还不写专栏，就别把报纸给我送来了！”

给编辑的信

《奥兰多哨兵报》[*Orlando (F.L.) Sentinel*]日发行量在297000份，像这样的大型都市报的编辑平均一天收到400封读者来信，而他只能刊登四到六封。其他的394封都不会见报，寄信人也不会收到回复，这会让寄信人怎么想?

《号角报》一周收到四至六封信，每封信都会见报，这又会让寄信人怎么想?

社区报再次体现出它受众少的优势。在这里，最令人满意的是读者和报纸之间的互动效果。人们是作为个体被认知，而不是按群体划分。对待来信，编辑的第一准则应该是：如果可以的话，发表所有来信。如果《号角报》收到一封不适宜发表的来信，编辑通常会找时间给来信读者打电话交流。

当受众人数超过了一定限度，这种情形就不可能出现了。报纸没有那么多版面刊登来信，编辑也没那么多时间给每个人回信。

一份有负责感的社区报社论版会为人们提供一个对话平台。当亨德森维尔镇（Hendersonville, N.C.）因暴风雪停电，《时代新闻》（*Times-News*）用备用发电机印出的报纸接连不断地给小镇提供唯一的当地信息，包括新闻和社区范围的天气预报（此时没有电视播出），这种情况持续了一周。当时，社论版登满了来信。前报纸编辑乔•富兰克林（Joy Franklin）回忆道："社区通过报纸进行自我交流。"危机之中保持信息畅通对灾难受害者有着极大的激励作用。

报纸如何对待读者来信可以用来检视社区是否有活力。如果你一封信都没收到，要不是因为你的社论版形同"僵尸"，要不就是你没给读者写信的机会，要不就是你根本不知道怎么激发读者来信，应定期在社论版下方写上温馨提示，比如，报纸欢迎并感谢有关本地话题的来稿，列出电邮和电话等。

大多数来信出现的问题是匿名、恶意人身攻击或诽谤。因为报纸要对版面上出现的诽谤负责，编辑一定要小心潜在的诽谤内容。大多数报纸是不会刊发出语伤人的信和匿名信的。

未署名信件或者匿名电话都是一颗定时炸弹。如果笔者或者打电话的人都没有勇气署上自己的名字，他怎么能被给予隐藏在报纸身后发言的特权呢？

那么，难道要把所有匿名信都扔了吗？也不是。如果你收到一封非常吸引人的信，作者签上了名但要求发表时不署名，你应当给他打个电话，如果真实性有保障，可以就来信主题做一个新闻特写或者调查报道。

读者来信的要求

你的报纸有没有一个简明的、充分为读者考虑的来信刊登细则？下面是一个很好的例子。比尔•瑞德（Bill Reader）现在是俄亥俄大学的一名助理教授，曾任《中心时代日报》（*Centre Daily Times*）社论版编辑，这份报纸现隶属于麦克拉奇报团，是宾州一份发行量达29400份的日报，被简称为CDT。

CDT欢迎有关本地话题的原创来信。优先刊登能激发新颖讨论的来信。我们希望来信者能遵从以下提示：

● 文笔简练。最好不要超过500字。长信可能会被删减，或被拒绝，被要求发回重新编辑。长信也可能会被部分摘录到报纸上，但它会被全文发表在CDT的网站（www.centredaily.com）上。

● 不要过度频繁来信。报纸只允许读者每30天来信一次。CDT希望尽可能让更多人有机会在这个平台上亮相。

● 来信需署名。CDT只发表署名评论。匿名信将被扔进垃圾桶，未填写完整姓名、地址和电话号码的信件也会被扔掉。来信发表时只会显示作者的名字和其所处的区或者镇。

● 避免人身攻击。可以表达对观点的不满，但不要对其作者大发脾气。这个平台是用来交流观点和想法，而不是用来人身攻击的。如果你发现自己稿子里有类似于“他就是怎么怎么样的一个人”或者“像他这种人的问题就是……”之类的话，请先回去把这些人身攻击的文字划掉再把信寄过来。

● 我们保留拒绝的权利。CDT保留不发表来信的权利。通常来说，我们只拒绝含有诽谤、脏话、不实消息和字迹模糊的来信。我们从不拒绝和CDT社论意见不一致的信件，事实上，我们鼓励意见相左，我们一直都在刊发这样的来信。

● 请事先做好校对工作。有大量拼写错误或排版错误的来信可能不会及时刊发，也可能不会刊发。所以，请您寄信前自行校对。

● 我们不接受二次投稿。通常，我们拒绝刊登一稿多投的来信，我们也不接受曾向其他机构或人员寄出过的信件的复印件。

● 欢迎寄来感谢信。CDT很乐意发表你对社区团体或个人的服务和善举的感谢信。每周四，这些感谢信都会在“在中心”版面上发表。

● 请保持耐心。CDT会尽可能在收信、核实、修改完成后，按接收信件的先后顺序刊登。报纸将尽可能地多发信件，根据来信多少，一封信或许要等两周才能被发表。简短的来信或者与现实话题连接紧密的来信可能会更快发表。因为如下变量存在我们无法保证来信发表的固定周期：手中未发表的信件（通常有20到30封）；一些特殊的项目需要某类特定的信件（比如选举）；联系作者证实和澄清某些点所用的时间；来信所述新闻发生了变化。

但是，另一方面……

怎么看待匿名来电？有人第一反应就是“无礼的”。或许事实不像你想象的那样。比尔•瑞德思考了社区新闻中的伦理难题：

发表匿名来稿的理由在于以下事实。

> 一些报纸设有邀请观众匿名打电话的专题栏目，读者可以通过一个自助语音系统宣泄自己的观点，最后挂电话结束，然后报纸发表这些评论，看起来很简单。
>
> 但事实上，这里显然充满了问题。至少有以下这些。
>
> 当这些匿名电话平台在全美蔓延的时候，新闻职业道德标准在哪

里？看到那些下流不堪的论坛令人瞠目结舌，我们痛批这是公众言论质量的下降，是恶意中伤的企图，是言论自由的滥用，也是对新闻业这片已被污染土地的更严重的玷污。

这些都是合理的担心，请让我解释为何匿名是新闻业的一个重要传统。

我也是个伪君子，因为在对待匿名的态度上，我经常变换立场。我现在的工作是社论版编辑，当然拒绝未署名信件和匿名电话。我的上份工作是现场采访记者，当报社开启了自己的“发泄平台”，我成了反对者中声音最大的那个。

但是作为一个对公众话语感兴趣的媒体学者，不管工作上我多么厌恶这些平台上的言论，私下里我会被这样的言论所吸引，因为在这些简短的话中，不管它们对公务人员、公共政策和公共舆论做出怎样的抨击，我都能看到宪法第一修正案以它最原始、最纯粹的形式出现。

尽管匿名平台对每个人开放，它迎合的还是愤世嫉俗的人群。没错，美国是个自由的国家，但不是每个人都习惯于大声说出自己的观点。在华盛顿，记者们认识到了这一点，他们给那些有影响力的人匿名发言的特权。

但是，穷乡僻壤的普通人没有这样的特殊待遇。因为在这些地方无权无势的人们无处藏身，他们常常不敢发声。

来看看下面的情况，研究“谁给编辑写信”的无数调查者都得出一样的结论：白人、中年、保守、富裕的男性。实质上一开始，都是这些特定的人群在发声，这些人从来不怕说出自己的想法，也不怕签上自己的名字。

这样的人群恰好也是运营报纸的人群，而且报纸在他们手中已经有一阵子了，可以说是物以类聚，人以群分。多年下来，报纸和它最应该为之服务的人群之间已经垒起了一堵高墙。

裁缝害怕揭发自己血汗工厂的老板，老夫妇不敢举报对邻居滥用权力的警察，遭老师性侵的早孕少女不敢告诉公众真相，这些弱势群体被无形的一堵墙隔开了，这堵墙使我们屏蔽了很多真正有话要说的人的声音。

邀请观众匿名打进电话的做法似乎推倒了这堵墙，但同时一群乌合之众也混入公共言论中，他们有的懦弱，有的精于算计，有的尖酸刻薄。但看看所有的署名读者来信，会发现一个共性，不管匿名与否，信件大多都是消极的，甚至常常是恶毒的。

反对匿名平台的一个常有的论调是害怕有人恶意中伤。这种论调完全站不住脚，匿名和恶意中伤之间没有必然联系，你可以看到，署名信件也有恶意中伤。美国最高法院也对此表了态，他们支持宪法第一修正案中对匿名评论的保护。最著名的“塔利诉加州案”（Tally v. California）中，大法官雨果•布莱克（Hugo L. Black）写道：“匿名有时被认为是最能用于建设性的目的。身份认证和对报复的恐惧都会阻碍公共大事的本应心平气和的讨论。”看看宪法第一修正案的历史，不承认匿名评论价值的编辑最好读读卡托（Cato）（约翰•特伦查德和托马斯•戈登曾用的假名）的信，赛琳丝•都古德太太（Mrs. Silence Dogood，美国之父本杰明•富兰克林曾用的假名）的文章和宾夕法尼亚农民（约翰•迪克森曾用的假名）的来信。我们现在知道是谁写出这些重要的为言论自由而斗争的启蒙文件，但在当时革命的年代，自由并不是靠这些人的名字来拥护，而是靠他们的观察和思考。

历史上，即使不那么有意义的匿名信也一直在被发表。你找几卷微缩胶卷，看看以前的读者来信，就会发现有多少人的署名都是“一名军人”“一位公民”“一名当地妇女”，或者是“一位纳税人”。

实际上，社论版允许发表匿名文章是由来已久的传统，可它已经因现代新闻价值观而逐步衰落，在法律层面无可靠依据，道德上对“匿名对社会有害”的绝对认定并不符合历史，同时也不符合当代报道的实例。

经过用心编辑，发表不管是来自电话、信件、传真或者电邮的匿名评论都可以给报纸的社论版增色不少。当公共言论平台向有话要说而不只是有胆量署名的人开放时，匿名意见肯定会提升公共交流平台的质量。

另一些声音，另一些编辑室

当三K党来到小镇

作为记者，我们应该尽己所能保持中立对吧？但也有非常中立的报纸为了社区利益，做出一些“一边倒”的报道。宾夕法尼亚州波茨维尔的《共和先驱晚报》（*Republic & Evening Herald*）是一份发行量达36000份的报纸，1996年，《共和先驱晚报》买下了北斯库尔吉尔郡的《雪伦多先驱晚报》（*Shenandoah Evening Herald*）。雪伦多镇盛产无烟煤，这里曾被称为“东部最剽悍小镇”。报纸主编吉姆•凯弗林（Jim Kevlin）说：“你要是在这样的乡村担任社区报编辑，意志必须足够坚强。”

当三K党把在法院前游行的日期定为1998年9月26日时，《共和先驱晚报》编辑室的第一反应是无助，因为这种活动会激起任何一个社区居民内心深处的仇恨。

然后，编辑们问自己一个问题：“如果阿道夫•希特勒来到镇上，我们该怎么做？”全面报道就此展开。

采访这些种族主义者，然后采访另一些非种族主义者比如牧师来平衡观点，这是新闻的惯用手法，但我们觉得还不够。于是，我们向社区抵抗仇恨组织委员会求助，用他们的指导原则策划报道。

如果读者愿意抵制三K党，报纸的社论、新闻、新媒体互动语音系统、网络报道就引导并鼓励读者，并提供抵制三K党的方法：

● 按照委员会建议，报纸第一天发出了对三K党的强烈抗议，敦促其尽快离开，并给读者一个互动语音平台，读者可以打电话来发出与报纸观点一致的声音。进一步的社论中，报纸鼓励大家当天去参加别的活动来避开三K党集会。

● 为应对此事专门成立的“团结日”委员会为此制定了当天可供选择的其他活动项目，作为配合，报纸全面报道这些活动项目，以消除三K党活动影响。头版“活动指南”里有一张可供读者签名并寄出的“团结宣言”券、一张全版彩页“支持团结日”海报，还有一条可以让人们别在身上的紫色丝带（委员会希望人们当天穿象征慈悲的紫色衣服）。

● 人们可以在“团结日”官网上看到一个故事档案馆、反仇恨网站的链接，一封方便人们签署的“团结宣言”电邮，还有让孩子们可以随意涂色和打印的支持“团结日”的标志。

● 关于三K党集会的日常新闻中，报纸探讨了三K党的宗旨和行为方式，采访那些受三K党蛊惑的人并报道他们的现状，强调本郡种族的多样性，报道正在进行的反三K党活动。

● 游行当天，头版的大标题为“合众为一”，整版报道当天反仇恨游行的情况，并对不同种族的人们在这里建立家庭、繁衍生息的故事做了特写报道。

三K党游行当天有一场守夜祈祷音乐会，由全国知名的反仇恨音乐家出演。此外，还有无数的反仇恨活动。为了让人们避开三K党的游行，波茨维尔和贝里克的足球比赛也被专门调整到游行当天。

最终，大约有500人被三K党活动吸引，这是无法避免的。但为了给三K党点颜色看看，当25个带白色头罩的人进入小镇时，他们接连遇到的都是装饰成紫色的住宅和商铺。在三K党集会现场，法院三楼扯起了“支持团结日”大标语，紫色蝴蝶结装点了所有办公室。

当受警察保护的90分钟游行时间结束后，三K党成员赶紧钻进车里并逃离了小镇，他们希望在小镇动点手脚的计划落空了。

原本一个危机事件最终成了小镇发展的机遇。乐观的成果有很多，而且这些成果很有希望一直在小镇延续。“团结日”委员会逐渐发展为一个全郡范围的永久性的“团结联盟”。次年，为了推进各种族间的理解和友谊，人们筹划了整整一周的活动。州议会宣布了一个新的纪念日：9月的第四个星期六为“宾夕法尼亚团结日”。

委员会认为，是小镇做出的种种活动挫败了三K党在本地以后的活动计划。这里发生的一切，包括其快速的应对、多样的活动、永久性团结联盟的形成等，都可以当作其他社区的典范。相比之下，邻郡一个社区选择不去理会三K党的一次相似的集会，一次得逞，结果三K党以后每周都去游行。仇恨活动一旦播种就很难铲除。

在一次团结日委员会的会议上，一位本地商人讲述了他在欧洲游行时，在德国的一段经历：当穿过毒气室时，有人问导游“德国人都到哪里去了（意指为什么他们不做些什么呢）”。导游回答道：“当他们能做些什么的时候，他们没有去做；当他们该做些什么的时候，他们就做不到了。”

如果这样的问题在波茨维尔被提出，《共和先驱晚报》可以骄傲地说：“能做的时候，我们做了！”

第 9 章

社区体育：难道只是场比赛吗？

敬爱的中国读者：

据我所知，体育赛事报道在中国并非主流，但它在美国一直是社区报纸报道的重大组成部分。本章节中，我会向大家展示这个对你们看似神秘的东西，如果本地媒体能找出一种合适的报道本地体育赛事（如乒乓球、体操、篮球、网球、羽毛球）的方式，你也许会觉得本章节很有启发性。当我去年夏天在重庆的西南财经政法大学讲课时，我亲历了一场没有任何本地媒体来报道的激烈的校内锦标赛，尽管当时有成百上千的学生在场观看，尽管大家都对比赛结果有显而易见的兴趣。也许对中国社区报而言，挖掘本地体育赛事报道，是未来的努力方向之一。

——作者

这也叫比赛？

比赛地点并不是新到《号角报》的摄影师乔脑海中的那样，不是金莺公园[①]也不是扬基体育场[②]。

桑迪•鲁恩学校棒球场中央的草足能埋住脚踝，记分员坐在折叠椅上，靠在一张可拆卸的小桌子上记录比分。

体育场里没有大灯，没有球员休息室，没有广告牌。这是孩子们玩的沙地的边缘。露天看台（如果你觉得能叫看台的话）就是一个长满草的土坡，现在坐满了裹着被褥和毯子的家长，他们在为一场桑迪•鲁恩海盗队（Sandy Run Pirates）和怡心花园费城人队（Pleasant Gardens Phillies）的比赛加油鼓劲。

从一家重点传媒大学毕业后，这是乔在《号角报》的第一份差事。他深知自己很优秀，曾经获得过赫斯特奖（Hearst Award）。[③]为什么今天他要来拍摄美国少年棒球联盟的比赛呢？难道他们不知道他是谁吗？最后让他感到羞辱的是——他的编辑甚至希望他写出这场比赛的报道！这是开玩笑吧！

乔怀疑自己选择这份发行量为8000份的一周两刊的报纸来开始自己的职业生涯是否正确。这是他现在能找到的最好工作了。乔的设想是，把自己现在做的事情权当“乡村采风”，只要一有机会他就跳槽去一家知名的大城市日报。然后他就可以忘掉自己在这个无名小镇做过什么了。

乔盘算的同时，比赛开始了。第一名击球手已经上垒，现在正准备盗垒。他已经感到厌倦，注视着脖子上挂的同样无精打采的高档数码相机。这时击跑员已经安全上了二垒，不过好笑的是，投手扔出的曲线球直接砸中他的脑门儿然后弹飞。

乔必须忍着不让自己笑得太放肆，心想：这些小家伙根本不懂怎么打棒球。如果这是场真正的球赛，兴许我还能抓拍到一些挺好的体育新闻照片。

不久，一场夏日的倾盆大雨光临了这座小球场。记分员躲在小桌子底下避雨并给报社文娱部打了电话，告诉他们比赛暂时被延后了。乔急着收好自己的相机，根本没注意发生了什么。“天！来这里真是浪费时间。”他嘟嘟囔囔地走向汽车。

---

①金莺公园：美国职业棒球大联盟巴尔的摩金莺队主场。

②扬基体育场：美国职业棒球大联盟杨吉队主场。

③赫斯特奖：由美国记者和大众传媒教育委员会颁发的年度新闻教育奖项。

该做事时就做事

古人有一句智慧的谚语，大概意思是这样的："该吃饭时就吃饭；该呼吸时就呼吸；该离开人世时就离开。"乔恩•卡巴•金（Jon Kabat-Zinn）的书名《此心只在当下》（*Wherever You Go*，*There You Are*）就抓住了这层禅意。它意味着生活不是活在记忆中的过去，也不是想象中的未来，而就在当下，也可以说成"该做事时就做事"。

就在乔的眼皮底下，他有拍出极具人情味的照片和写出令人欢乐的、有价值的报道的机会。但是态度成了绊脚石，他心中的镜头盖合上了。只要这种"糟态"持续，不管是尼康、佳能，还是任何人造出的先进设备都无法让乔在社区报层面看到体育报道的价值。

多么大的浪费啊！

再次重申：在你去《体育画报》这样顶级的媒体工作之前，你必须在《巴特勒鹰报》（*Butler Eagle*）或者《卡里新闻》（*Cary News*）这样的小报锻炼提高技能。或许你从未听说过这些"小"报，但你去问问任何一位现任《体育画报》的记者或者摄影师，他们都会告诉你：他们就是在做社区体育报道中尽心尽力才一步步走向成熟的。

学会在社区层次工作，学会以己度人，学会根据社区事务来写报道——这些都是你在社区报工作时可以获得的技能——不管你是报道体育，还是摄影，抑或是写讣告。

"我把自己今天能达到的成就归功于在社区周报工作时打下的基础，它们帮我养成负责任的态度。"《奥马哈世界先驱报》（*World-Herald, Omaha*）优秀的摄影师杰夫•卡尼（Jeff Carney）如是说。高中时，他就开始为父母的销量为4000份的社区报《瓦呼市报》（*The Newspaper of Wahoo, N.E.*）进行摄影。

"在大报工作，我们突然闯入别人的生活然后迅速撤离。但社区报环境教我学会'如何和人打交道时给他们尊严'。"

对摄影师而言，《国家地理杂志》就是梦想高地，作者曾有幸获得每年夏天该杂志颁发给新闻摄影教授的工作奖金。在杂志工作时，与伟大的摄影师路易斯•马扎滕塔（Louis Mazzatenta）交流时，他就将他职业生涯的起点定于在社区报的实习。

"那是我出发的地方——印第安纳州秘鲁市发行量为8000份的《秘鲁市每日论坛报》（*Daily Tribune*）。"马扎滕塔笑着说，"当时我什么都做，我爱死那里了！我回忆起当时的日子就很欢喜。我要去摄影，写插图说明，写报道，做排版，感觉自己不可或缺。当我走进校董事会会议厅时，他们都把我当个重要人物。那时我才21岁，受宠若惊啊。"

第一次做社区新闻报道时，年轻的记者或者摄影师就会发现社区报与大城市报纸最为显著的区别。总编辑让你第一次去报道高中比赛并希望你拍照片回来，或者如果你是个摄影师，总编又会叫你在摄影之外做个报道。在社区报这些都是再正常不过的事了。

需要的是责任心，责任心，还是责任心

优秀的本地体育新闻报道可以也理应是报纸最正面的力量。这甚至不需要你具备高超的写作水准或摄影技巧，只需要你对全面、详尽、持续的报道负起责任。

“对我来说，责任心就是为我在乎的工作起早贪黑。”《自由长矛之星报》的苏珊娜•凯尔这么说，“我不在意起早贪黑，因为我爱我所做。”

这是你的地盘。在这里没人可以打败你。电视给周五晚的高中足球比赛的时间不超过20秒，而且是在晚上11点的新闻中。你做的远比大城市日报（假设他们决定来报道）做得好，因为你就聚焦于报道范围内的社区学校。此外，大城市日报的摄像师还有其他五场比赛要报道，而且今晚就要截稿，通常在第一节比赛结

束后就离场了。

对你来说，你不用像电视台或者大型日报的摄影师一样在第一节就离场，你可以看完整场比赛，用注重细节的描写完成比赛报道。因为你被社区的人们熟知、信任，你可以在替补席后面游走，可以进入中场休息室和赛后教练办公室。如果你有在大报工作的朋友，他们会羡慕地告诉你，你所得到的机会是一种“奢侈”。

为父母周报工作的杰夫•卡尼热爱“做社区报的事”。他说，高中体育赛最为纯粹，没有球员罢工，没有中途退赛，没有劳资纠纷。对于记者和摄影师来说，这是一份幸事。“你就身处比赛之中。那里没有那么多媒体记者。你可以从多个角度和位置尝试拍摄效果。在大型比赛中，你经常被其他人推来挤去，无法拍摄报道。”

接下来，你花了必要的时间写好稿件后，一份优秀的社区报会在版面上给你的作品预留足够的空间。你的报道刊登出来时，也许长达76厘米，里面配上大量的比赛照片。记住：有的学生家长会剪下这篇比赛报道并贴到冰箱上，或者夹在家庭相册里，甚至会夹在《圣经》里面。

寻找平衡，定下基调，有所强调

眼看本地的大专足球队就要力不从心，大败于客场的强队。突然间，主队教练唐•士嘉堡（Don Scarborough）跳下场边的长凳，一边沿着场边跑着，一边将手围拢在嘴边，挨个叫着队员们的名字：

“乔治，我相信你有能力做到！”

“比利，我相信你能行！”

“戴维，我相信你！”

鼓励与肯定的话语从场边飘来，在队员们耳中微弱却又清晰地响起，这份贴心的关怀会成为他们每一个人的美好回忆。

在场地另一边的观众们也被教练为队员们加油的呐喊所感动了。这既不是什么场面话，也不是什么需要说给所有人听的宣言，更不是什么战略或诡计——仅仅是一个教练的心声而已。

主队仍然败北，但从长远来看，分数会被遗忘，而教练情不自禁的情绪表达会被一直记住。唐教练的行为已经表明了他的态度——不论输赢，他都对自己的男孩们怀有信心。

如果说社区报的体育报道有什么使命的话，使命正在于此。在报道本地体育新闻时，社区报应当满怀欣赏地观看本地选手的表现，并为他们加油呐喊，多数时候应表现出积极乐观的报道动力、语气和视角。

正面报道无疑会给社区报与社区带来双赢。首先，社区报得到了构建社区自豪感的机会。更重要的是，社区报会教给学生选手将受用一生的观念——比如说个人人格的不可侵犯性，以及重在参与的内在价值观——而不是不惜一切手段去赢得比赛。唐教练曾经这样告诉他的球队："从失败中取得的人格历练，可比从胜利中得到的更多。"

在体育方面，媒体如何处理失败这个话题将会从根本上影响青年人。当我们让孩子不惜一切代价去取胜时，可能会带来糟糕的后果，人们会成为胜利的奴隶。读一读下面两段来自社区新闻记者笔记本的内容吧：

> 少棒联盟的教练看着对方的击球手向本队左外野手——他的儿子，击出了一个高飞球。小男孩漏接了这个球。全场观众都听见教练像疯子一样向他的儿子怒吼："你到底在干吗啊！"
>
> 有六名参赛者参加了残奥会的100米赛跑。当比赛结束后，最后一名参赛者在场上欢呼雀跃起来，开心地宣告："我得了第六名！我是第六名！"

以上两条报道，哪一条会让你砸了饭碗，哪一条又会让你感到振奋？哪一条具有建设性，哪一条又具有破坏性？我们所做的，不是靠伤害别人来成全自己的生意，我们所要做的，是通过客观公正积极向上的报道来建设社区。

这并不意味着你在撰写社区体育报道时要无底线地退让。你不用把所有内容都写成"阳光普照，充满了抱抱熊和彩虹"；你也不用去拍本地队伍的马屁，或者充当给他们戴高帽的托儿。社区报不同于主流大报的地方在于它的个性化。

"个性化"意味着你要建立首要的评判标准：如果这份报道，或这张图片写的是我、我的孩子或某位亲人，应该如何下笔？

这种处理体育报道的方式，意味着我们应该更加关注，更认真，更准确，更精益求精，也更加客观。一句话，报道社区体育赛事，也要把握尺度，不能过度消费他人的故事。当然，有时候这会很难——尤其是在本地队伍总落败的时候。

在客观地报道与轻佻地吹捧之间有一条分界线。假设有位社区报记者，在本地队败了个落花流水之后，仍然写出了这样浮夸的报道："虽然输给了南端角队（South Point）60分，可这对东部高中骑士队（East High Cavaliers）来说是因祸得福。"

这听起来就像一篇厚颜无耻的公关文稿，而非报道。现在你知道，什么是越界了。

批还是不批？限度在哪里？

社区报该如何把握体育报道中批评的度？对此，我们有一条百试不爽的原则：一支球队或一个运动员的层次愈高——从儿童棒球到美国橄榄球大联盟，报纸就可以做出愈多负面评论。媒体应该以与之相应的眼光，看待那些已经上升到专业层次的体育赛事。这样做的理由是，那些为赛事埋单的人期望看到对赛事中运动员表现的准确专业的评价。在实际操作中还会有一种难以处理的情况，就是如何评价那些领着运动员奖学金的大学生选手们——他们应该被算作是从赛事中领取报酬的选手吗？另一条不成文的原则是：学校愈大，报道就应愈全面深入。即使有了如上两条原则，社区报仍应该在体育评论方面多加谨慎。

如果不能确定批评尺度，那就宁可别发表评论，针对高中生个人进行批评性、判断性报道就被算作超出了尺度，这对非专业的体育报道来说尤其重要。要记住，你周三在报纸上批评的那个孩子，可能下周末你在超市购物时会遇见他，你还能直视他的眼睛吗？

当然你也可以直言不讳，在不伤害那个在比赛中失手的孩子的前提下，对赛事做出公正而客观的评价，这样做的关键就是要在报道中取得平衡。当然，取得平衡并不简单，因为在体育赛事中所能表现出来的只有胜与败两极。业余爱好者总是为比分所左右，但经验丰富的社区体育记者会另辟蹊径，淡化失手的年轻人在比赛中的过失。因为对于这个年纪的人来说，报道背后的指责意味可能是毁灭性的。一方面，纸质出版物将会被长久留存；另一方面，批评过度的报道会使读者觉得报纸不近人情又吹毛求疵。如果在报道中有所批评，那也应该是恰当的话语。这样的话语也应来自于权威人士，例如教练，而非记者自己。

情景伦理和本能判断

早在几年前，当安德里亚•赫尔利（Andrea Hurley）还在每周拥有2700份销量的《摩尔西斯堡新闻报》[*Mercersburg (P.A.) Journal*]当编辑的时候，某一天，她带着相机去报道周五晚上一场当地球队的橄榄球比赛，没想到，却撞见了以下这个场面。让我们跟她一起回到那天晚上（她是唯一在场见证的记者和摄影师）。她这样说道：

> 星期五晚上是高年级家长日。比赛开始前，一个初中男孩和另一个这个夏天在车祸中丧生的孩子的家人一起走上赛场。他们为这个男孩（儿子生前最好的朋友）呈上了他们儿子的外套……然后一起下场回到

赛场边的长椅那儿，与其他家长坐在一起。男孩手中仍紧紧拿着那件外套……接着他脱下自己的外套，换上了好友的外套。

他开始失控地抽泣，渐渐的，几乎所有队里的孩子都围了过来拥抱他，一起哭了出来。这个场景非常令人动容。你是要拍摄照片，还是留给这些孩子们一点时间去释放情绪呢？毫无疑问这个场景能拍出绝佳的照片。

如果赫尔利真的按下了快门，她不是就擅自侵入了一个非常私人的时刻吗？如果这份周刊发表了这幅每个人都哭得不能自控的照片，难道不会对这群高中男孩带来不必要的尴尬吗？报纸也有可能被再次诟病为不择手段追求销量的冷血动物。

但从另一个方面看，如果她决定不拍照片，算不算失职呢？作为记者，她为什么不能用一个无闪光的长焦镜头从远处拍摄一张充满人情温暖的照片呢？为什么不能对这个事件撰写一些充满同情的评论呢？

第三种选择是不拍照片，而是通过书写充满同情的评论，让画面从文字中浮现出来。

第四种选择是什么都不做。

你认为赫尔利应该怎么做？

防止厚此薄彼的处理

如果你的报道覆盖范围之内有好几支队伍，而他们之间，尤其是队伍所属的学校之间，处于紧张的竞争关系，作为一位通过私人途径与他们接触的记者，要如何实现公正公平的报道呢？

一家新兴的社区报解决了这个问题。它所在的郡有三所互为竞争对手的高中，它给每所高中指派了一名固定编辑，每周给每所高中一个整版，报道分量非常大。大容量报道带来的新鲜感过去之后，人们充满猜疑地关注每间学校得到的份额区别，但最终发现没有哪间学校被额外分得更多版面。这份报纸甚至轮流安排三所学校的版面放置次序，以杜绝任何报道不公的指责。

“处好关系=打通渠道=实现成功”的等式在体育报道中尤为适用。迈克尔•C.L.汤普森（Michael C.L. Thompson）是一位老教师兼作家，他说：“成功来源于不断积累。”在体育报道中，最好由同一位编辑、记者或是摄影师固定负责整个赛场、整支队伍或是整个赛季的报道，这样教练、运动员和父母们，周复一周地与同一位记者接触，关系变得更私人化之后就可以为记者提供一些幕后轶事以及照片，而一个风风火火提枪上阵的巡回体育记者是无法获得这些内幕资源的。

给社区体育记者的忠告

● 如果你刚开始接触体育报道，就应该先尽可能地增加自己对每种体育活动的认识，再尝试报道某场具体比赛。反其道而行会让你看上去像个什么情况都不了解就闯进郡委员会会议的傻瓜。

● 如果社区里有社区大学或者综合性大学，他们的体育信息员会给你提供故事、照片以及想法。让自己的报道能够脱颖而出的捷径是：本土化、个性化、视觉化。

● 高中校园是许多社区体育活动开展的主要场所，因此经常会引起当地社区报纸的注意。每个地区流行的运动都不一样。有些地方流行橄榄球，有些地方流行摔跤，有些地方流行篮球。不管是什么运动——你的报纸都应该包罗万象，搜集每个人的故事，挖掘当地角度，当周最佳比赛、最佳运动员、教练的故事，赛前、赛后的故事，还有一切你可以挖出来的花边新闻。

● 如果小镇上某支队伍赢得一场巨大胜利，你的报纸应该和粉丝们一起追着它不放。这是一个让社区报大放光芒的好机会，出版周期在此时都可以忽略不计。当一个社区明星小联队全国闻名时，具有创新性的社区报会跨越半个国家把他们的体育编辑紧急调来抢报故事和照片。随之而来载满凯旋学生的双层大巴会为这个社区带来巨大商机、高度的读者关注以及前所未有的销量。除此之外，轰炸式报道也会让原本没有任何关注度的比赛声名鹊起。

● 为了打出最佳水准，运动员们赛前必须使自己进入最佳状态。他们能这样做，作为记者的我们为什么不能呢？最好的体育记者或者摄影师往往会为每一场比赛打起十二分精神。每个人都有自己的方式。有的记者比赛前会在办公室里做几组引体向上。另一个没那么耗费体力的方法是提前到达比赛场地，将自己沉浸入赛场气氛中，借此促使自己进入状态。

● 布鲁克林道基队（Brooklyn Dodgers）富有远见的经理人布兰奇•里基（Branch Rickey）说过：“好运会随谋划不期而至。”借用童子军的话来说，就是“时刻准备着”。比赛开始前，先去比赛项目管理处拿一张比赛队员的名单。在关键球员的名字底下做好标记。带上一支备用钢笔。你在雨中能工作吗？以防万一为你的相机带一个透明塑料袋。你随身带着万能的强力胶带了吗？

● 记大量的笔记。无论是体育报道还是其他类型的报道，笔记都能决定记者的生死。如果你同时需要拍摄和报道，拍下比赛，然后在你拴在皮带上的笔记本上把你看到的东西写下来。通过这种方式，你很快就会发明自己的一套缩写方法。比如说“45 OLT 4/50”的意思就是“45号球员绕过了左侧的阻截球员向着球场的50码线跑了4码。

● 或许还有更好的办法。你可以培训一个高中生志愿者，让他为你把每场比赛拍下来。许多富有激情的学生都会愿意免费为你工作，在这个过程中他们能收获经验，也能在球场边线近距离感受火热的气氛。这是一个双赢选择。

● 你的报纸想要进行更多的体育报道，却又无力再聘请一位记者吗？建立一个社区体育通讯员的关系网吧。教练、父母、妻子、丈夫，任何人都可以为你提供比赛结果和详细比分表。你只要在年末带他们到牛排馆去聚聚餐，或者免除他们的报刊订阅费就可以了。

● 打破常规思维。有一位年轻的体育编辑，在报道一个常规的季前高中橄榄球赛时，说服了球队教练，让自己穿上了队服，与其他队员们一起训练了一些日子。报社摄影师跟踪拍下了这件好玩的事，用了一整个版面，用第一人称讲述了“噢，那个后卫是一名体育编辑”的故事。这个报道赢得巨大反响，还获得了全美报刊协会专题写作比赛的第一名。

《南松镇领航员报》编辑部的故事：当社区报遇上国际体育赛事，小报纸亦有大作为

当一项国际体育赛事和众多“大媒体”光临小镇时，以小为美的社区报应该如何作为？

1999年，北卡罗来纳州，美国男子高尔夫球公开赛第一次将比赛场地选定在南松镇。当年的《南松镇领航员报》，一份发行量达到15000份、一周两刊、已在当地牢牢站稳脚跟的社区报，不但没有被国际比赛和媒体同行们的阵势吓倒，反而借此脱颖而出。

在公开赛举行的一周里，从1999年的6月14日到20日，《南松镇领航员报》从一周两刊的周报变为每天新鲜出街的日报。

这场改变的背后不能忽略一个重要的时间节点。1996年，年轻的大卫•沃伦洛夫（公开赛举行那年他34岁）从这份报纸的传奇性人物山姆•拉根（Sam Ragan）手中接过了出版人的接力棒。充满干劲的大卫瞄准了两年后即将举行的美国高尔夫公开赛，并将这场公开赛视为《南松镇领航员报》进行变革的一次契机。

两年的潜心准备没有白费。大卫与另外四个搭档一起，将《南松镇领航员报》带到了一个新高度。他们不仅重新装修了位于小镇闹市区的办公室，而且还购置了一台高性能印刷机。在公开赛举行期间，彩色图片贯穿整份报纸。

大卫认为：“小镇特色不会因为一场比赛而改变，但是报纸可以借此机会扩大影响。尽管我们是一份小报，但这丝毫不妨碍我们像大报一样追求质量与品质。”

事实的确如此。这份逢周一和周四出版的宽幅报纸，100%本地内容。周一至少40个版，而周四版还要厚得多，至少80个版，每期报纸平均6叠，需要5台印刷机同时开工。

在公开赛期间，精力旺盛的编辑史蒂夫•伯萨（Steve Bouser）带领团队，每天增加一份56个版面的窄幅日报，其中32个版面的内容早在5月份就已准备就绪。报纸上所有稿件和照片都由报社记者拍摄或社区居民提供，完全看不到来自通讯社的通稿和图片。

为了按时完成报道任务，沃伦洛夫雇用了被他自己称为“全明星”的外援团队，分别支援《南松镇领航员报》的体育新闻部、摄影部和发行部，于是每个部门各多了两名精兵强将。

有意思的是，《南松镇领航员报》在公开赛期间出版的日报不用邮差投递，而是通过特意穿着旧时报童衣服的当地孩子们在街头巷尾进行零售，所有零售所得都被捐给了当地的男孩女孩俱乐部①。

在公开赛期间，由网站编辑约翰•查普尔（John Chappell）管理的“南松镇领航员报网站”（www.thepilot.com）平均每周点击量达到6000到7000次，比赛期间的总点击量达到637000次。大卫高兴地说：“幸好我们的网站没有崩溃。”

编辑部布局

摩尔郡，位于北卡罗来纳州南面中部的桑德希尔地带（Sandhills Region），拥有常住人口72000名，其中包括聚居在派恩斯特（Pinehurst Village）的高收入者、南松镇的中产阶级，还有居住在松林活动板房里的贫困人口。

从1998到1999年，位于宾夕法尼亚大道上的《南松镇领航员报》编辑部经历了持续整整一年的改造和装修。重装后的编辑部淡化了办公区域的划分，部门与部门之间不设隔断，每个人都可以在不同部门之间自由穿梭。这样的布局设计当然是有心为之，大卫解释说：“这是一个社区报编辑部应有的布局。我们可以看见彼此，直接呼喊彼此，我们还可以将东西扔来扔去。甚至一个人使用洗手间时，都需要经过其余每个人的办公桌……这一切都使得整个编辑部更加开放和更有活力。”

布局的改变带来的不仅仅是空间的改变。有人对此印象深刻：“这是一种氛围，在这里，每一个人都会非常真诚地去欣赏和尊重他人的工作，并且懂得团结协作的重要性。”在广告部办公室一面墙上，则有这样一句话：“广告成就自由的新闻界。”

前台直接面对大门，一张厨房吧台样式的桌子代替了传统的用来间隔的屏风，这样读者和广告客户一进门就能看见笑脸盈盈的接待人员。重新铺装的松树木质地板发出油亮的光泽，4米高的锡质天花板营造出一种温馨。每一处细节的

①男孩女孩俱乐部：Boys and Girls Clubs，为儿童或青少年提供娱乐项目。

设计都在彰显“读者至上”的原则。大卫骄傲地说，我们的读者与广告客户只要站在这里，就能看到整个编辑部忙碌的状态。而且他将前任出版人兼主编的办公室保留下来，并将朝向社区主街的一面墙改造成一扇凸窗，这样经过的每个人都能看见他，大家戏称他为“透明鱼缸里的一条鱼”。

工作节奏

“地狱般的一个星期就要开始了。”老编辑露出一副苦涩的笑容。

周日晚上，编辑、记者、摄影师齐聚编辑部，开始为十几个小时后即将出版的首期日报做准备。编辑史蒂夫带领大家讨论经费预算。

专门负责报道高尔夫的记者霍华德•沃德（Howard Ward）是整个报道计划的统筹，史蒂夫解释说：“霍华德在这个报道领域就好比是施瓦茨科普夫[①]，而我就像是重返五角大楼的鲍威尔[②]。”“那大卫就是比尔•克林顿了。”有人打趣地说道。

一则幽默的段子常常会成为大家一周工作的快乐源泉。如果编辑部成了一间供应快乐的商店，则无论做什么，每一个人都因为在这里工作而感到骄傲和自豪。公开赛期间，两名摄影记者、两名高尔夫记者和两名发行行家加入了报社队伍。干起活来时，每个人都冲在前头。大卫特别强调，是每个人。这是《南松镇领航员报》与生俱来的团队精神。

在这特殊的一周里，报社财务科、前台和后勤女职员们也出动了——悉心地为加班的人们制作早餐。编辑部冰箱里塞满足够的三明治和各种食物，似乎随时都能捧出一顿周日教堂大餐。

从周报变为日报的激动与兴奋在编辑部里传递，然而，过了几天，大家开始变得有些疲倦，因为遭遇了一些小插曲。

● 预先印好的报纸由于堆得太高，压坏了底下的货盘。货盘损坏导致一大摞报纸随即“摔倒”在地，沾染上污迹。出版人为此感到十分恼火。

● 赛场边临时搭建的工作帐篷由于下雨天漏水，使得记者史蒂夫•威廉姆斯（Steve Williams）和编辑亨特•蔡斯（Hunter Chase）根本无法使用笔记本电脑办公。

● 资深新闻编辑克拉克•考克斯（Clark Cox）因为突然病倒而不得不暂时离开编辑部。尽管史蒂夫及时换上了替补人选，但不得不承认，对主编而言，克拉克的缺席相当于失去了右手。

---

①施瓦茨科普夫：Schwarzkopf，美国1991年把伊拉克50多万军队从科威特赶出去的总司令。

②鲍威尔：Colin Powell，2001年1月至2005年1月任美国国务卿，是美国历史上第一位黑人国务卿。

- 因为莫名其妙的原因，印刷机的蓝色油墨竟然用完了。
- 报纸的打包生产线在最需要它的时候偏偏出了故障。

尽管遇到了各种困难，但是所有人还是咬牙继续坚持。周三出版的日报由于得到高度认可，让大家又重振信心。

到了周日，所有人都已精疲力竭。在过去的6天里，文字记者们紧张地为稿件忙碌，摄影记者们则扛着机子在雨中拍摄，走过的路程总计超过6千米。报社每一个人都在挑战自己的极限，并出色地完成工作。

决赛在周日开幕。运动员佩恩•斯图尔特（Payne Stewart）和菲尔•米克尔森（Phil Mickelson）进入到最后一洞的较量。如果今天之内还不能决出胜负，大家还要做好继续报道的准备。然而，当天下午，佩恩•斯图尔特的关键一击，直接将自己送上了冠军宝座。

比赛终于结束了，编辑部顿时沸腾。冠军是谁并不重要，因为大家已经时刻做好了迎接冠军的准备。

收杆之日花絮

已经是晚上九点一刻了。一名自愿来帮忙的摄影记者坐在特约撰稿人马乔里•道奇里奇（Marjorie Daughtridge）的位置上，吃着三天前的蘑菇鸡片。他从早上7点半就开始工作，到现在已经超过12个小时了。面前的桌子上放着电话机、笔记本、笔、便利贴、字典和一本《美联社写作手册》，还有几张道奇里奇的丈夫和宠物狗的照片、一株无精打采的小植物、一罐榛果巧克力以及一块咬剩一半的动物饼干。

坐在这名摄影记者旁边的是美术编辑布伦达•伯杰（Brenda Berger）。她已经耗费了几个小时设计一个用于公布比赛成绩的版面，突然设计软件崩溃了。“幸好只有一页需要重新做。”富有经验的她显得十分冷静。编辑部中的每一个人都被视为这份报纸的财富和支柱。

比赛收杆之日也意味着这次公开赛特别报道宣告一个段落。当最后一个版面“出炉”时，史蒂夫突然从桌子后面起身，向大家欢呼：“嗨，伙计们！我们总算大功告成了！”

小结

这一切就像是一部舞台作品，夹杂着愉悦、激动、困惑、沮丧和欢快的情绪，有时让人欣喜若狂，有时让人黯然神伤。

当一切结束再回过头看时，史蒂夫说的话直指核心："我并不认为这份报纸会一成不变。尽管我们还会做回原来一周两期的《南松镇领航员报》，但我们永远不会停止改变。这就好比是一场持久战，要时刻保持忧患和团队意识。作为一个编辑部，我们在一起经历了太多事情，以至于改变了对彼此的看法，也改变了《南松镇领航员报》这份报纸。"

如果有人认为，《南松镇领航员报》会借机从周报变成日报，那就大错特错了。如果真是这样，编辑部就要有人罢工或是不干了。正像记者梅丽莎•布瑞德洛夫（Melissa Breedlove）所说："那可不是个明智的决定。"

大卫的总结是："在公开赛举行的一周里，《南松镇领航员报》关于这项赛事的报道比周边几个城市的主要日报的总和都要多。事实证明，社区小报可以与大型日报展开竞争。更为重要的是，社区小报在这场竞争中大获全胜。"

公开赛期间的日报特刊不仅为《南松镇领航员报》赢得了声誉，也为其带来了赢利。大卫慷慨地抽出赢利的15%，根据每个人的贡献大小发放奖金。

第10章

社区报的采写技巧、设计及摄影

敬爱的中国读者:

在我的国家，出色的写作常出现在小地方或发行量较少的报纸上，可以说，报纸的规模大小和质量优劣没有必然联系。另外，优秀的报道几乎总是源自于出色的采访。此外，社区报报道所涉及的“社会新闻”——订婚、结婚通告、周年纪念、生日、俱乐部消息，以及邻里消息——对读者而言关系重大，是每一份成功社区报的核心内容。当然报纸版面空间的设计也非常重要，它可以成为锦上添花的神来之笔。

——作者

采写技巧

优秀的新闻采写过程可以分为三个阶段：收集资料，撰写文章，编辑修订。

让我们从收集资料开始说起。在社区报业务中，采访是最关键阶段，我们对某个主题感到好奇，之后通过采访收集第一手资料。很多新手往往忽略了采访，认为真正重要的是写作。信息丰富的采访能诞生出强有力的报道，而薄弱的采访只会产生苍白无力的报道。

采访的第一要务是获取信任。这是一个重要而严肃的任务，再怎么强调也不为过。我们是记者，而不是小说家。我们写的不是小说，我们不创造角色，我们也不杜撰话语。只要我们有熟练的采访技巧，肯用心工作并花费一定时间去赢得采访对象的信任，他们自然会乐意分享故事、闪光的话语与灵光的思考。社区报人可以说是挖掘生活中闪光点的矿工。一言以蔽之，在社区新闻中，近距离=与采访对象融洽的关系=成功的报道。

第一个问题为采访定调。

甲：“你好，你最近好吗？”

乙：“还行吧，你呢？”

甲：“好到不能再好啦，再见！”

乙：“嗯，拜拜！”

这个对话看似简单，但仔细审视就可以发现，甲先发起了一个友好的问候，询问乙的近况。乙回答了，并反之询问甲的情况。问题往来之后，两人恰当地告别。甲乙之间的对话形成了一个完整的圆，一个漂亮而又紧凑的小采访。

现在考虑余下这种情况下会发生什么：甲仅仅只说了一个字“嘿”。这时，乙大概也只会简单地回一句“你好”了。

如果甲没有发起问题，乙就无须回答，因此第一个问题为整个采访定下基调。

如果你问采访对象，一位著名的本地钢琴演奏家：“请问，您是在哪里出生的？”这个问题暗示了你对她一无所知，对方也许会想：“哦，天哪，这个记者根本就没有做过功课。这样下去，这一下午都得和他耗在这里。”

及时地控制场面

无论你喜欢与否，承认与否，采访就是控制场面的过程。如果你不控制场面，由着话题和事件乱走的话，报道也会天马行空，不知所云。老练的社区报记者知道如何礼貌地转移话题。采访就像温柔地用缰绳驾驭骏马，如果放弃控制，骏马便会漫无目地地乱走。

采访的底线就是：你的采访你控制，别说什么从心随性了，及时去采访！

寻找受访者熟悉的环境

采访目标是得到从受访者出发的内部视角。当受访者处于他们自在的环境中时，你能得到关于他们最清晰、最准确的描述。

因此，选择采访地点的准则是选取受访者最熟悉的场所——家中或者工作场合。比如在大街上采访警察，在排练房里采访舞者，在钢琴边采访演奏家，在书斋里采访作家。

社区新闻中，编辑部和采访地点之间的距离往往非常短，你有更多时间投入到采访中来。尽量避免在编辑部办公室里，或者通过电话和电子邮件去采访。（有些情况例外，比如你的采访对象和你很熟，或者是长期的线人，或者是公职人员等。）

受访者熟悉的环境不仅会给你深入的视角，而且会使你的受访者更加舒适，有利于你挖掘更多细节。与其建立良好的关系，成功会随之而来。

“灶边闲谈”式的提问

米契尔社区学院（Mitchell Community College）的民族学家罗克珊•牛顿（Roxanne Newton）有一个巧妙的采访技巧——一切从“灶边闲谈”开始。“‘你知道我对妇女在劳工运动中的故事很感兴趣，给我说说你的故事吧’，这么一说，你就等着受访者打开话匣子吧。”

变敏感一点

可能你很快就会发现，你的大部分采访对象从未有过面对媒体的经验。对许多人来说，这是他们第一次也许是仅有的一次接受媒体采访的机会，记者对他们来说就好像外星人。因此，你不用去重复那些常见的新闻主题，你的视角越新颖，你的故事就越抓人眼球。

了解背景

《国家地理杂志》的记者和摄影师们要花费数周时间，为每篇报道做背景调查。当然，社区新闻无需那么多视角，但背景调查的要求也不能被轻视。一方面，在小型社区中，大家彼此知根知底，若你是第一次做某方面的报道，你得好好去了解采访对象，否则只能写出一些路人皆知的内容。另一方面，充分的背景调查有利于节约时间，不至于在采访过程中问出大量愚蠢、业余的问题。

如果情况不允许，迫使你在开始之前完全没做准备，请向对方道歉，并承认这一点，可以在采访后用电子邮件或电话跟进，完成你的背景调查。

拜访

请记住自己的角色：首先是“人”，然后才是记者。先去拜访采访对象，不带笔和笔记本，不要把录音笔和相机包放在地板上。和对方谈谈照片墙、家里的装修、花园。赞美你所看到的，礼貌地展示你的好奇。在谈话中提问，而不是从笔记本上寻找罗列好的问题。

不要抢戏

虽然以上这种交谈应该是推动采访的动力，但不要总谈论你自己，这不是单口相声，而是两个人的采访。

营造舒适的空间

桌子把你和采访对象隔开，形成一种情感障碍。老板使用桌子是想让雇员感到自己有多么渺小。但采访时，请尽量保持你们之间适当的空间，营造一个开放随意的环境。

记录详细信息

实际上你可以观察所有的东西：办公桌上的摆设、墙壁上的装饰、房间的格局。每个人的个性都可以从这些小“窗口”中反映出来。

你去采访一位德高望重的老教授，在书房里看到三个时钟并排放在电脑上方的书架上。如果你好奇地提出问题，也许你会得到这样一个神奇的答案：“因为太忙了，我只能这样安排时间。第一个是教学时间，第二个是研究时间，第三个是写作时间。”

依赖电话或电子邮件，你绝不可能洞察到这一细节。

记住采访的时间

良好的开端是成功的一半。迟到会给采访对象留下你很轻率的印象，影响采访的友好氛围。

自己去体会

说到时间，你得给自己留下充裕的时间。一个优秀的一对一采访需要花费一到两个小时。之后你可以根据第一稿再做一次采访，或者打电话给相关人士获取更多信息。但没有什么比面对面的交流更有效——这就是社区新闻的特色。

宽以待人

给受访者留出宽裕的空间和时间。一方面，无论你何等心急火燎，也不要催促对方回答；另一方面，尊重对方的时间安排，了解他们有多少时间可以用来接受采访。重要人士通常有满满当当的时间表。

引用对方的话

你也该引用对方在采访中的话。引用可以使报道更准确，更真实。引用时必须加引号，一字不差地引用。引用值得引用的那些话。

着装得体与入乡随俗

什么场合穿什么衣服是记者的常识。采访市长时你需要的是衬衫和领带、正式的西装。采访一个酿蜂蜜的农家时，你需要的是牛仔裤、T恤和靴子。不要穿着高跟鞋去报道玉米去壳，也别穿着破洞牛仔裤去报道市议会新闻。着装的规则是入乡随俗。穿着不当，会使你格格不入，采访对象也会感到不舒服，你们之间难以建立融洽的关系。

做笔记

规则一：找到一支你喜欢的笔，带着你的笔到处走。它应该是一支实用的签字笔，避免铅笔、钢笔和圆珠笔——这些笔迹可能会褪色，或者不能在某些表面上书写（如手掌）。

规则二（同样简单、同样重要）：找到一个适合你的手掌大小，你觉得舒服的笔记本，或者用笔记本电脑。笔记是能保存多年的原始资料，也许有一天这些笔记就会变成一本书。

人们通常会在交谈过程中看着对方，这样会令你很难分心去做笔记。你应该尽可能地训练自己一心两用的能力。

- 用缩写或者代码写特定词汇，提高书写速度。
- 创造性地倾听对方，记下关键词，代词或介词，可以待以后补充。

● 不要问“是”或者“否”这种封闭性问题。

● 记录细节。

● 学习如何去“结束”一个采访，而不是“终止”一个采访。告诉采访对象报道会在何时刊登，留下后续联系的电子邮件或电话，递上一张名片以示你是个平易近人的、可靠的专业人士。最后，感谢对方花时间接受采访。如果你的采访对象要求发表前审查照片或报道，请礼貌地解释这不符合报社规定——除非是技术性的报道，或者编辑要求让受访者检查是否有错漏（不能修改内容）。

● 结束采访后回头复习笔记，在第一时间补上空格和简写的内容。

● 用荧光笔标记整理笔记，用同一种颜色表示同一主题，这样开写的时候就能方便地找到材料。

● 结束采访后的第一时间撰写报道，间隔的时间越长，报道就越无力。笔记的存在是为了唤起你的记忆，而不是替代报道。

不要忘记你为谁而写作

虽然“人情味”这个词在新闻中已经被用滥了。在社区新闻中，如果一篇报道、特写，甚至社论都没有人情味的话，它也就失去了与读者之间的关键联系。

社区报的设计

米勒的经验之谈，哈特尔的九条小建议

我们都喜欢好的设计。一份精心设计过的版面往往可以在不知不觉中引导读者轻松阅读页面上的内容。如果是一份设计粗糙的版面摆在面前，我们便不知所措了——紧接着注意力就会被其他事情吸引过去。

一篇优秀的报道若是缺少与之相配的图片，就会让读者觉得单调。一张美丽的照片若是配了一篇乏味的报道，就好似鲜花插在了牛粪上。一份天才做出来的设计，若是配上了没有说服力的照片与草草写就的故事，就好像二手车推销员在天花乱坠地夸夸其谈，试图把劣等品说成珍宝。

来自佛罗里达州波因特媒体研究学院（Poynter Institute for Media Studies）的肯尼•厄比（Kenny Irby）认为，设计的终极功能是解决问题。设计师面临着三种挑战：文字的排版、图片的摆放以及留白的位置——这一切都需要精心地进行规划。平心而论，我们也看到了许多虽然设计欠佳，但仍然非常值得一读的报纸。作为居民获取社区信息的唯一途径，它们长相平平，却在社区公共生活和建设中发挥着重要作用。但一些经验之谈和小技巧能使社区报更上一层楼。

90年代中期，《中心时代日报》这份宾夕法尼亚州立学院发行量达到29400份的日报，经历了一次复杂的重新设计。自重生以来，报纸的发行量上升至49000份，并多次夺得世界性的设计大奖。当年的执行主编和副总裁约翰•温•米勒（John Winn Miller）告诉笔者："荣誉不仅归功于我们的整体设计，而且还归功于报纸的实用性，我们用报道和照片反映着社区。"以下是米勒关于设计和排版的一些技巧：

● 抬头：在体育和特写版面上方列出本周主题与专栏作家。在最下方则有一个报道索引，重点强调第二天的重头报道。

● 读者频道：在特写中罗列出如何获取报道中所提到的商品，有时也会做一个罗列了包括学校颁奖、婚礼安排等等事件的日历。在日历的最下方，我们欢迎读者投稿，并附上编辑记者的联系方式。除此之外，我们也为读者提供娱乐信息，包括电影、演唱会、音乐会和电影时刻表，读者不用再费心思在广告的缝隙里寻找它们。

● 简讯：报纸报道区域很大，包括36个市政区域及5个学区，我们使用各式各样的简讯使读者的阅读更便捷。例如，"当下议程"告诉读者关于政府会议的消息；周六做一个本周政府会议综述，包括谁参加、如何投票、讨论了什么问题、下一次会议的时间等内容。

● 快速查找：在网上，每一篇报道都附带更多信息选项，比如记者的署名后带有电子邮件和电话号码，以方便读者直接与我们交流。

● 高效地留白：报道首要重点是本地新闻。为给读者提供"一站式服务"，我们在A2版上开设了《早餐简讯》栏目，简要报道国内外大事。我们并不像《华尔街日报》那样用大篇幅报道新闻内幕，因此可以节约版面用以增加报道数量，留出的版面可用于刊载商业彩票号码、人物专栏，还有漫画等。

● 聚焦深入报道：为了平衡那些短小肤浅的报道，我们在A3版开设了一个《聚光灯》栏目。该栏目专门聚焦一个主题做一篇或多篇报道，并配以照片和图形。

● 更多快报：刊登不适合放在A1版的本地新闻，比如说关于警察、法院、大学或者本州附近的新闻。

有着131年历史的《福斯特民主党人日报》（*Foster's Daily Democrat of Dover, N.H.*），拥有24000份的发行量。其周日刊助理编辑莫莉•哈特尔（Molly Hartle）列出了以下九条小建议：

● 简单就好：你没有时间处理需要三个不同软件的复杂设计。只用一个软件，并避免耗时的任务。

● 提高工作效率：了解自己的极限，快速设计版面是必不可缺的技能。早早就艺术元素和字体之类的东西做出决定，避免回头。良好的设计并不一定非要花费几个小时不可。

● 坚持只用一个字体：你没有时间浏览字体目录表或者尝试100种不同字体。尝试用一种字体发挥不同创意，试试不同的尺寸、大小和颜色。

● 避免花钱：大多数小报没有购买通讯社图片的预算。你可以寻求价格低廉的图片元素或者使用剪贴画。

● 团队协作：不要忘了，如果没有记者、摄影师和编辑，设计师的工作毫无意义。

● 寻求帮助：为一家小报社做设计，最大的缺点之一是没有同行能给予专业上的反馈和评价。加强横向交流，把设计好的报纸给其他报纸同行过目，征求他们的专业意见。

● 读别的出版物：读别的报纸、杂志、书籍。你不订《波士顿环球报》并不意味着你不可以把《波士顿环球报》优秀的设计版面钉在墙上作为每日参考。

● 阅读：许多小报没有预算送设计师去参加研讨会或短期课程。设计师需要通过阅读来提升自我。搜索亚马逊上“报纸设计”类别下的最新书籍，或在当地图书馆翻阅经典设计书。

社区报的摄影

“即使明天就会遭致失明，每个人还是应该去学学摄影，相机会成为诉说世界之美的工具：‘事物是这样的。看看吧，看看它。’”

——多罗西娅•兰格（Dorothea Lange）

视觉的力量，用照片来讲故事

打开家乡报纸的第一版，读读这周的《时代周刊》《滚石》或是《国家问询者》（*National Enquirer*），它们的头版都有什么共同点？头版配图是内容的引导，它应该是充满诱惑、夺人眼球的，它吸引着你翻开内页。图片是最原始的语言，也是通用的交流方式。认真对待你的照片吧。读者喜欢图片，一直、永远是这样的。

对于社区报来说，要让故事和页面变得更具吸引力，摄影是最简单，也是最便宜的方式。但通常情况下，刚从新闻学院毕业的新手往往没有拍摄新闻图片的经验，大部分人可能只拍过度假或派对照片。虽然图片不是必需品，但大部分社区报都有使用图片的需求。曾经，社区报往往难以为图片支付高昂的费用，编辑和出版人也更强调用文字描述而不是用图片——图片往往在社区报中被草率对待。

与此同时，大报却越来越重视图片和设计的作用。精明的出版人会把图片作为一种新的营销工具，一种提高报纸身价的方式——社区报应该更多地关注这一点。

社区报的摄影是什么？

“报纸的使命是为社区提供书面和视觉的记录。”迈克尔•塞勒特（Michael Sellett），发行量达5000份的《杰克逊霍尔新闻及指南报》周刊（*Jackson Hole News and Guide*）的出版人说，“图像具有引导读者深入普通人生活的力量。从某种意义上说，我们用镜头捕捉杰克逊霍尔的灵魂。这便是真正的社区新闻。”

已故的伟大战地摄影师罗伯特•卡帕（Robert Capa）有一句名言也正适合社区报摄影。卡帕说：“如果照片不够好，就是你靠得不够近。”

社区报的摄影师：先做人，再摄影

任何一位曾经为小报拍过照片的人都知道，相对于接近并快速与他人建立信任来说，相机的好坏并不是那么重要。

“你有大约5分钟的时间成为采访对象的至交。”宾夕法尼亚州的摄影老手格雷格•格里耶科（Greg Grieco）说：“如果你能赢得他们的信任，你就能拍出一幅很好的作品。”

在国家级报纸杂志都享有盛名的普利策奖获得者比尔•斯特罗德（Bill Strode）说：“与人交往是极其重要的。首先做一个人，然后做一名记者，最后再做一名摄影师。”

听听，斯特罗德说得就像他深谙社区报这行似的。他说：“听到国家媒体的摄影师们一直在抱怨、发牢骚，我真的很厌烦。摄影师们，是时候发自内心地去挖掘些好照片了，是时候尽力去做些更有意义的事情了……如果你能通过拍摄更好的照片来帮助所在地的公益基金……如果我们能有这样的态度……你的照片可能正好帮上忙。这将会改变你对于自己工作的整个态度。”

年复一年，日复一日

社区报记者必须报道那些年度盛事、年度集市、当地节日庆典、高中毕业典礼、圣诞游行，一年又一年，这是一个巨大的挑战，报道总是一而再地重复着，缺乏想象力或脑子烧坏了的记者无法从中看到新意。

这里有一些提示：尝试从个人角度去观察这些事件。跟随个体去深入这个事件，通过事件和个人视角，做一个深度特写报道——现在不是正时髦“某某某一生中的一天”这样的形式吗？在一个年度集市上，你可以跟随一个小女孩去采集她的宠物小羊比赛，或是跟随那些幕后的人——一个场地管理员、支帐篷的人或厨师，或是计划参加今年拖拉机大赛的农民们。保持创新精神和敏锐头脑，你的好奇心会带你去任何想去的地方。

第11章

社区报伦理：换一种方式看事物

敬爱的中国读者：

这一章的任务是构建一个实用的道德框架，给社区报记者提供一种解决日常道德困境的思维方式，希望能帮助你们从满是道德伦理挑战的丛林中寻找到自己的出路——不管是重庆，还是教堂山；不管是北京，还是波士顿，在这一问题上，我们都应态度一致。

请记住，我们的工作不只是报道新闻，更是为了服务社区！“服务社区”这点很重要！这意味着我们永远要将社区利益置于首位。

——作者

社区报伦理

无论你怎么称呼它——社区新闻、公民新闻、公共新闻，或者高度当地报道——它并不是一种新事物，早在美国成为一个国家之前，第一份社区报纸就已开始密切关注当地政治。它的存在说明民主社会的运转离不开高度地方化报纸。

如今人们重新聚焦于社区报，源于其难以替代的作用。在20世纪90年代，大城市规模失控促使我们思考适合人的尺度是什么，邻里又意味着什么，社区的运转使人的个性化在某种程度上得以更好地保留。于是暗流涌动，大的团体开始分裂，其实它们从未真正联结在一起。

尽管和大城市报一样，社区报也要承担看门狗的角色，但两者在伦理方面有着很大差异，霍夫斯特拉大学（Hofstra University）的史蒂芬•R.诺尔顿（Steven R. Knowlton）认为：

“当一个坏家伙当场被公众抓住，大城市报纸的报道几乎带有一种胜利者的喜悦感，但对于社区报，同样的情形发生时，它还是会报道，不过一定是用悲伤的笔触。”

生活在同一个社区，记者和读者都生活在有所重合的社会网络中，社区报人与被告或者有罪一方的关系不可能是抽象、割裂的，他可能是某位邻居，或者在教堂、俱乐部、某个协会打过照面。

梅本（Mebane）是北卡州《进取》（*Enterprise*）周报的编辑，当地阿尔杰农•普瑞姆高中（Algernon Primm）一位有望进入顶尖大学、前景美好的篮球特长生因为和其他46个同学一起贩卖毒品而被捕，她坦率地说：“那些日子心灵备受煎熬，真的不想做记者。但是你又必须做你要做的。”

这正是社区报的独特之处：它无法与那些社论或者新闻拉开距离，它身处其中。当需要艰难地做出道德伦理判断时，社区报编辑最好有一个能牢牢锁定指向北方的“道德罗盘”，稍有不慎，各种问题将纷至沓来。

因为他们了解你

责任之石可能对每一位社区记者来说都是最巨大的重负，但它也是可以拥有的最丰富的宝藏。用得恰到好处的话，它可以帮你获取一生的满足感。

比如说，社区居民了解你（你在食品店购物，参加卫理教会，你的小孩代表校队比赛，或者你的报道总是平衡而公正），他们就会自然地倾向于相信你的文字和你在报纸上展现的形象。你要清楚这是一种信任的托付，并非轻轻松松就能获取。试想，你的读者是某个好邻居或者最好的朋友，某个你永远也不会故意欺骗的人，如果你在报道上犯了错误，就会想立刻修正它，当错误已经铸成时，可用相同字体立即更正。当头版报道出现明显错误时，更正就应该大大方方地在这里登出，否则把更正淹没在众多内页分类广告之中，读者们就会认为报纸道歉诚意不足。

一句话概括社区新闻伦理的核心：绝不明知故骗。

公共服务/公共利益

社区报在社区中扮演了怎样的角色?

首先，你必须承认并遵守社区新闻的第一定律：报纸和它所在的城镇间存在着互惠关系。社区报以积极的、支持的、滋养的方式关心社区，社区发展了，有更多的报道内容，更多的商家投放广告，当然社区报也会受益。

社区报不单是一份信息纸，更是一张服务纸。

当涉及公共服务时，社区报并不贬低大城市报，但后者确实是一个相对简单的角色：因为与读者距离相对疏离，笔触可以毫不留情，孤傲且愤世嫉俗，而且处处流露出精英式的傲慢。

社区报所扮演的角色，远远比大城市报更加复杂，难度更高。它既要保证公正而平衡的新闻，同时，又要促进社区保持发展动力，为具有正能量的事件鼓与呼。有时其扮演的角色相互矛盾，在其中找到平衡实在不是一件容易的事。

社区报既是社区的建言者、支持者、呼吁者，也是反映社区生活的镜子。确切地说，我们必须保持态度果敢，但又不失仁慈。有时候，社区报必须做一名具有“严厉之爱”的顾问指导，它必须展现一些社区居民或许并不想知道但是必须被曝光的事情。这就是真金火炼的地方。

戴夫•马库斯是发行量达38000份的《塞勒姆晚报》（*Salem Evening News*）的编辑，他认为：“很少有人理解社区新闻的难能可贵。大城市报和社区报的区别就是大城市报没有机会把每一个读者都当作一个有血有肉有情感的个体。大城市报眼中只有重大事件和问题，看到的只是一个个人口统计学意义上的群体。但是生活在社区中，我们能零距离接触到每个人，我们用自己平时使用的手机接听电话。我们很清楚读者是谁，他们希望从这里获取什么，只有了解他们的快乐和烦恼，我们才能有目的地去帮助他们。”

社区新闻工作者介入社区生活的方方面面。记者可能属于美国退伍军人协会，体育编辑可能在教堂垒球队打球，新闻编辑可能是少年棒球队教练，主编可能活跃在当地的艺术协会，执行主编可能受托担任社区大学的董事会成员，出版人可能还在扶轮社或者社区发展协会工作。

在这么小的范围内，一旦产生利益冲突怎么办？比如报道不公正，或者当员工在社区的生活角色与报道角色有冲突时怎么办？那样是否会产生报道不公平的嫌疑？

你能怎么办？把员工的活动范围限制在新闻编辑部吗？如果你生活在小城镇，你不可能不融入丰富多彩、充实且有意义的社区生活。

致力于服务社区的社区报角色非常复杂，千变万化，当涉及怎样服务社区，怎样掌握新闻评论的度等伦理问题时，除了“人是最重要的”这么一条铁律，似乎没有以不变应万变的万灵答案。

坚持你的基本原则

有一套适用的策略能帮助我们在高压状态下做出符合伦理的决定。社区新闻专业的学生克里斯蒂娜•琥珀（Christina Rexrode）说阿什伯勒的《阿什伯勒消息论坛》，史蒂芬传媒集团（Stephens Media Group）旗下发行量达163000份的日报有一条原则：不刊登“裸露的或毁容的尸体”照片，因为“它剥夺了生命的尊严”。

一位当地副警长在执勤时被开枪射杀，尽管尸体被盖上了，《快递论坛报》决定不采用这张聚焦于尸体的照片，相反，报纸刊登了一张警官用手铐逮捕枪击嫌疑人的照片，照片的角落里是被模糊处理的盖着白布的尸体。邻近大城市日报选登的现场照片为了追求视觉和情感冲击，不惜让尸体成为卖点。编辑鲍勃•威廉姆斯说：“关键是我们住在这里，和读者的关系完全不同……不应该因为可以做，就这么做。”尽管社区报如此谨慎，但依然收到了一位愤怒读者的投诉，编辑为这位读者提出了一个针对性的比较：“不知道你有没有看大城市报的新闻图片？那才会是你愤怒的理由。”

棘手问题

学校可以有消防演习，那报纸为什么不可以有道德演习？这样当坏事发生时，我们就能更好地有所准备。

在日常工作中，社区报编辑最可能遇到哪些道德困境呢？

死尸，写还是不写？

在一家一周两刊的报社里，还有两小时就到提交照片的截稿期限了，突然传来消息，春耕时一辆拖拉机把正在劳作的人撞了，情况听起来很糟。主编艾德（Ed）抓起相机就跑出了办公室前往事故现场。这会是谁呢？他思索着。等他到了现场，迎接他的是最令人不安的场景。没有人像以往一样四处奔走救人，急救人员要么神情沮丧漫无目的地乱转，要么兀然地站在拖拉机周围，低着头。艾德怀疑情况相当糟糕，他慢慢走近事故中心，黯然发现了一位以前认识的邮政工作人员，于是向他询问受害者的身份，结果着实让人惊讶，那是郡委会主席。

正当艾德思索如何拍摄照片和处理报道时，现场出现了一位竞争对手报社的记者，没有任何先兆，这位记者粗暴地穿过救援人员，径直走到拖拉机车下的遇难者尸体旁开始拍照。快速地询问了几个问题后，他离开了现场，回到报社开始编写这条独家新闻。离开之前，有人听到他说："不错，这是个好新闻。"

一位记者认为这场事故是个"精彩的故事"，而另一位记者认为这是一个悲剧，同时也意识到社区的重要政治领导意外死亡的长远影响。艾德的新闻配图没有使用尸体残损的照片，遵守了报社不用尸体画面的规定，只拍摄了翻倒在一边的拖拉机和站在周围的工作人员绝望的表情。报道重点放在更有意义更加理性地阐释这件悲剧的角度上，它既关系到受害者的家庭，又关系到全郡的政治动态。而竞争对手把重点放在对死亡现场的表现上，采用了耸人听闻的标题和大幅具有视觉冲击力的照片。不需要火箭设计科学家，任何一个人都知道谁家的报纸在报摊上卖得更快。

如果涉及你的家人呢？

德维恩•高瀚（Dewaine Gahan）和他的妻子波比（Bobbie）拥有并运营内布拉斯加州一份发行量达18000份的周报《奥克兰独立报》（*Oakland Independent*）。数年来，他们一直在拍摄和刊登车祸现场车体残骸的照片。德维恩说当有人向他们抱怨这样的图片具有侵犯性，令人反感时，他们从不会多加考虑。

后来有一天，他们刊登了一张相当严重的车祸照片。你甚至分辨不出受害者还被困在车中，但是道路上的血迹在彩色照片中清晰地暴露出来。

等到第二天，当报纸已经开始售卖时，这位受害者的身份才被证实，此人是波比的兄弟。

德维恩说："从此，我们再也不刊登车祸残骸的照片，以后也绝对不会。这实在太伤人了，并且这样的伤害大于别的好处。"

先报道还是先救人?

波因特传媒研究学院的肯尼•厄比回忆起他早年职业生涯中一件重要的事。当时他在密歇根州的一家社区报社任职，他跑去报道一起交通意外事故。

在别人到达现场之前，厄比发现车的残骸中紧紧卡着一位女士。他不假思索地拿了一条自己车上的毯子出来搭在这位女士身上，并且不断地安抚她跟她说话，以防她进入休克状态，直到最后救护车到达现场实施救援。

等到那个时候，厄比才开始一名摄影记者的工作，拍摄救护人员把这位女士从破碎的车体中营救出来的照片。而直到那个时候，别的摄影记者也才抵达，开始拍摄同样的现场。

回到新闻编辑室，编辑对营救内容的照片不感兴趣，他愤怒地嚷道：“你是第一个到那的人啊！你现在拍回来的都是些什么呀！那些独家照片呢？”

厄比回答道：“没有那些照片，因为我没有拍。”

之后，厄比认为：“我做了必须做的，在那里我就做出了自己的决定，我那么做是对的。”

使用单薄的战术来获取报道吗?

有时候，你会被要求做一些和你自己想法相去甚远的报道。想想“贝基”的故事，他是宾夕法尼亚州中部一份社区报的记者。

1996年夏天，环球航空公司800号航班在一团火焰中急降到宾夕法尼亚州的蒙托斯维尔（Montoursville, Pa），16个当地高中生、1位老师和4位监护人丧生。这21个人都来自这个人口只有4937人的小镇，这对该社区的冲击可想而知。国家媒体蜂拥而至，这些渲染悲情的照片引起了当地居民的怒火，在这种情况下，居民的愤怒是合理的。

贝基也在现场，自从这个小镇被纳入她所在报社的报道范围，她也算半个小镇成员，当地人都慢慢和她熟识起来。她并不是特别想接这次报道任务，但无法推脱。直到事发四五天后，报道的主题仍然是：蒙托斯维尔悼念……蒙托斯维尔仍然处在悲痛中。贝基开始拒绝继续这样做，她强烈地质疑：“我们还需要刊登人们抽泣悲痛的照片？还要登载以此为主要内容的报道说蒙托斯维尔仍然处在悲痛中吗？”

最后的导火索是她被分配去报道最后的葬礼，她拒绝了。她曾经目睹过有些大报记者为了进入教堂而假扮成哀悼者。

“我去了蒙托斯维尔，但是只坐在车里没走出去。”她回忆道。她回到办公室的时候，写了一篇个人评论：实际上，所有事都应该适可而止，我们应当让蒙托斯维尔有自己的空间来为逝者哀悼。

编辑相当不高兴，并因此扣了她一天的工资。

“噢，如果事情再来一遍，我还是会这么做。”她坚决地说。

什么时候需要爆粗口？

玛吉（Marge）是《号角报》的摄影记者，她带着笔记本和相机包中记录的内容满怀欣喜地回到编辑部，这将是一篇完整的报道。

图片已经下载并编辑好，一位年轻的排版编辑突然问道：“嘿，我们有什么可用的好的引语吗？”

“让我想想，”玛吉大笑着，指着她图片中的一位渔船船长说，“这个人跟我说，今天早晨他妈的一直在卖鱼屎。”

编辑很得意：“嘿！这是一条超棒的引述！绝对能够抓人眼球。”

于是玛吉把这句话写进了照片说明中，但随后又有点动摇：“你真的认为我们可以让这个人在报纸上谩骂吗？”

“噢，没关系的，”编辑回答道，“他的确那么说了，不是么？并且，他也知道你在《号角报》工作，对吧？”

“可我还是认为最好问一问主编的意见。”玛吉说。

“那我也不反对，”编辑耸耸肩，“但这条引述确实很棒。”

主编布伦达并没有想太久。“你们真的想这么做吗？在这个社区中，这个人不需要靠这条引语出名。如果报纸上登出他骂人的话，那么他会被教会责骂，他的小孩在学校会被同学们戏弄，他的妻子会成为被嘲笑的对象，他自己在公共场合也会非常尴尬。除非有什么必要的理由，否则我们不应该把这种不太文明的话直接放在引述里。”

“您说得对，不过有了这条引述，整个页面和故事都会更加出彩。”编辑怂恿道。

但是主编一锤定音地说道：“听着，我也知道你说的是对的。但是，社区新闻不是舞台剧，我们是在和生活在这里的人打交道，而不是和一群我们想象出来的虚拟的人。这些人必须遵循社区的某些标准而生活。如果我们为了刊登一条吸引人的引语就到处去宣扬他们言语上的不谨慎，那我们一方面会因为损害了别人在社区中的身份而伤害了自己的信息来源，另一方面我们会得罪很多读者，最终将没有人愿意和我们交流。”

社区标准

当谈到好恶问题时，每个社区对于什么是可接受的，什么是超过底线的，都有着共同的感觉。裸体、咒骂和浴室幽默可能在一些出版物中占有一席之地，但在社区新闻中却不然——除非有强制性的理由来使用这些让人反感的东西。

虽然渔船船长的故事提供了报纸无理由印刷冒犯性引述的案例，但是接下来呢？在一个气氛动荡的公开听证会上，郡委会主席对一位发表长篇大论的公民怒吼道："快点坐下，先生！你已经开始惹毛我了。"

一位当选官员在公开会议上辱骂他所在选区的一名成员，我们就有必要登出这句话。报纸怎么能不用这样的引语呢？

但是，这对社区报来说并非易事。这并不仅仅是印不印刷的问题，还牵涉到如何处理随之而来的后果。由于主席的失态，一位通晓社区情况的编辑或许会借机写一篇解释性社论阐述报纸的方针，解释为什么要直接引用其具有攻击性的语言，为什么在这种情况下报纸选择将它逐字印刷出来。

当涉及良好的品味和社区标准时，大多数社区报认为自己，从广泛意义上讲，是一种"家庭报"。这种古老的措辞表明社区报对每个读者来说都是"可靠的"，从年幼的孩童一直到外婆级的人物。但是不同的社区有不同的标准，因此服务于不同社区的社区报也体现出不同的社区标准。

美国东北部聚集着很多负有盛名的大学，有一名艺术系大学生设计了一款海报，吸引眼球的是画面上用过的避孕套提醒众人加强防艾意识，校园里所有人都在谈论这个新颖的设计。想不到社区报刊登这条新闻后，很快收到一封言辞激烈的读者来信，一位居住在农村地区的家长说她被报道内容冒犯了。

回信中，编辑在某种程度上解释道：

> 感谢您的坦诚以及您对"毕业生使用避孕套创造艺术"报道的回馈。我非常赞同您的意见，这篇报道确实包含了一些有争议的内容。然而，我认为这完全在读者的承受范围内。我们对新闻编辑的判断都是基于所有读者的感受。这些读者主要都是学生。社区的标准在大学城和别的地方是不同的，更加宽容，也不大容易为他们所见、所听和所读而感到震惊和冒犯。即使如此，我们还是仔细地权衡了是否发表这篇报道。我们认为主要的读者，尽管认为部分内容令人不快，但他们会想要了解这篇报道。同时，我们的报纸只是报道了这个富有争议的公共展览——其他地区报纸也同样进行了报道，并不是我们创造了在您看来令人不快的这种艺术。
>
> 确实，同样的事件根据不同社区的不同标准，会有不同的报道方式。如果是另一家报社，也许会以另一种方式来出版。

搞砸了，怎么办？

当所有工作都已经完成，有时候记者为了逗乐会故意编写一个矫揉造作或者庸俗粗鄙的标题，当然在报纸正式印刷前，需要用真正的标题把它替换掉。

但正如比尔•荷马所说，当这个纯属好玩的标题意外地刊登到了报纸上时，它就成了灾难。北卡州《桑福德先驱报》的出版人最熟悉这类糟糕事件的发展情节了。从积极的一面看，荷马已经成为这类危机管理的专家，他开了一个叫作"当你在词句上搞砸时，怎么办？"的讲习班。起因是这样的：

某一天早上，在《桑福德先驱报》头版的最上部分，高于报刊名的地方，一则体育广告的标题全部用大写字母写着：

"JACKETS BLOW IT OUT THE ASS①."

当荷马看到这则标题时，他立马打电话给编辑："你看过今天的报纸了吗？"

"噢，天哪！"对方回应道。

荷马说，他立马决定报社对此应该"迎头而上，坦言失误，不求借口"，首先在报纸网站上写了一篇致歉公告，回复了每一通电话，并且在第二天的纸质版上再次发表致歉：

> 《桑福德先驱报》一直以成为优秀的当地家庭报纸为目标。但周三的报纸让我们栽了大跟头。头版顶部的促销广告标题涉及西部哈尼特高中篮球比赛，其中包含了猥亵的内容。这是编辑的失误以及对报纸出版的监管缺失，简直令人难以置信。这样的语言在我们的报纸中根本不应有立足之地。这使我感到十分窘迫。这是十分令人不快的、不合适的并且绝不应该发生的失误。相信我们以后会做得更好，这个社区也配得上一份更好的报纸。

荷马继续向当地两所高中的读者、学生、全体教员和行政人员致歉，并许诺："我们已经采取了适当的措施，确保此类不像话的错误不再发生。"编辑的致歉说明如下：

> 由于《桑福德先驱报》周三头版上可怕的错误，我真心希望能够单独向每一位读者致歉。许多人打电话质疑这种事情怎么可能发生。作为头版编辑，我希望能够把西部哈尼特高中篮球比赛的新闻作为重头戏，

①带有性含义的俗语，意为肛交内射。

因为这对我们的读者而言是一场重要的比赛。一般情况下，头版先于体育版制作完毕，但如果有比赛，我会把头版顶部原本是广告的位置留给体育版。这时，我会写一些如同“夹克促销在这”来提醒体育编辑填补这个位置。但周二晚上，我写了一些非常粗鲁的话，其实就是和体育部员工们逗趣而已，但我从没想到，一不小心它居然被印刷出来了。对读者、西部哈尼特学校，我深感歉意。我保证这种事再也不会发生。非常感激许多打电话来的读者，感激您对错误的容忍、理解和支持。你们的善意帮助我度过了职业生涯中最糟糕的一天。

荷马说，读者的反应各种各样，有人说反感我们，有人说爱我们，也有人说原谅我们，也有人不原谅。在可预见的“震惊和惊骇”“难道你疯了吗？”甚至包括要求开除编辑的电话、信件和邮件后，荷马说他很惊讶于许多读者的支持：

“我希望不要太为难（编辑）……我笑得太厉害都眼冒金星了。”

“坚持住……这一切都会过去的。”

“我只能想象您正在经历一段艰难的时间吧。”

“我希望桑德福不要这么古板以至于认为我们接受不了这样一点点的监督缺失。笑是好事，任何真正觉得这个标题问题太过于严重的人都应该放松一下。《桑德福先驱报》今天并不比昨天（或者前天）差。你们不需要道歉。坦白地说，上班的时候我们还期望着有这么一场娱乐秀。”

“老兄，我一看到这个错误就知道某人某处失了球……我确信到现在为止，你已经如同被慢火烘烤过一样，可能你自己更加煎熬。但事情已经发生了，你道了歉，对我来说这就足够了。”

有一位读者质疑荷马应对此次公开失态的做法，并要求“以此作为开始改进的机会，还原桑德福回归高质量报纸”。荷马并没有对这条评论置之不理，而是付诸行动，两个直接的结果是“新闻编辑室质量和卓越计划”（类似于长期战略策划）的出台和一系列与社区领导讨论社区未来走向、社区报角色定位会议的召开。

抄袭：源于拉丁语“绑架”一词

露西对新做的深度报道相当满意：她对事件做了全面调查，并且了解到新任足球教练巴布•弗拉华特（Bubba Flushwater）受雇过程的复杂故事，这在下一届州际记者协会比赛上也许将为她赢得赞誉。

为了搜集背景故事，露西煞费苦心地阅读《体育画报》的过刊，这位传奇教练在他长长的职业生涯中被该刊报道了好几次。露西甚至执着地打电话给当地大学的体育赛事主管，以确保趣闻轶事的准确性。

随着交稿期限的接近，这位忙碌的教练仍然没有回复电话，露西也愈加不安。她没有直接从这位教练那里得到可以引用的话，只拿到了他第一次新闻发布会的消息。实在没有更新的信息，她只能将就使用《体育画报》上的那些旧闻了。

直到报道登上《号角报》后，编辑汤姆走到她桌前，说："露西，我们需要谈一谈。到我的办公室来。"气氛十分压抑，她已经觉察到出了什么大事。

"听着，这可能没什么……"汤姆开始讲，"但是《新闻报》的拉尔夫（Ralph）刚刚给我打了个电话。他控告今天的报纸挪用了《体育画报》中关于那个教练的文章。这是真的吗？"

露西的脸刷地红了，结结巴巴地说："我……这个……确实彻底地看过那些文章。"

汤姆扶靠在办公桌边，眼睛都不眨一下地盯着她。"那些报道都是关于那个教练过去的事。那些直接引语，你是自己获取的吗？"

"不是……"露西的声音听起来小而无力，接着她又辩白道，"可是《体育画报》说他们核实过这些事件都真实发生过。"

"也就是说你确实用了《体育画报》的内容。"汤姆长长叹了一口气，向后倒在椅子中，呆呆地盯着天花板。"天哪，露西，大学时候他们都教了你们些什么啊？你不知道这叫抄袭吗？你知不知道你现在可能被辞退？"汤姆顿了顿，自言自语一般接着说，"拉尔夫说如果他是我的话，就会毫不犹豫地辞退你。"

"但是我不知道……"露西的脸上淌着热泪。

"你不知道什么？"汤姆问道，"你不知道剽窃别人的作品是不道德的吗？不知道无论任何时候，你引用别人的作品就必须给他们署名吗？不知道避免抄袭的最佳办法就是标明引用吗？"

"听着，你可能把这次过错粉饰为没有经验。但是无论如何，你已经打破了新闻业的第一条规则：不剽窃。如果使用了不是自己独立调查或报道的内容，就需要完完整整地标明出处。这样有助于信息公开。"汤姆顿了顿，似乎又是自言自语，"……当然我自己也有错，在正式出版前没有读完每个人的稿件副本。但是你也知道，在新闻编辑室，有些时候我不可能百分之百做到这点。"

汤姆双手指尖交叉在脸前，撅着嘴唇沉思，然后说："这么处理吧，你回到你的位置，把所有从《体育画报》'借用'的话用下画线标出。然后你写一封个人道歉信给《体育画报》的记者。当你做完这两件事后，都提交给我过目。同时，我也会写一则道歉声明刊登在明天的报纸上，你可能会不高兴，因为这会使你在公共场合非常尴尬，但是如果你想留在这家报社，我们就必须这么做。顺便说一句，我也希望你留下来。你既然搞砸了事情，现在就必须吃些苦头。你懂了吗？"

露西点点头，忍住呜咽。“谢谢您，这样的事再也不会发生了。”

汤姆勉强挤出一个悔恨的微笑：“社区报才是新闻系毕业生可以学到真东西的地方。”

如下是《号角报》第二天的道歉更正：

> 上期《号角报》发表了一篇体育记者露西关于巴布的报道，名为《坚韧如钉》。其中许多关于巴布的生活轶事都曾在1995年《体育画报》发表，我们应该标明《体育画报》作为这些故事的一手来源。我们已经意识到审查、信息公开和正确引用外部资料的至关重要性。深为《号角报》的错误表示悔过，并向读者致歉。

能对“握紧并微笑”类摆拍说不行吗？

我们都看过这样的照片：两个人握手，一个人同时把一张支票交给另一个人。预先安排的标准动作，这样一张静态照片就称作“握紧并微笑”。摄影师最反感的是当一位政治人物设计了一场活动，希望自己能够上镜好看，就邀请媒体见证这些时刻。报社越大，就越少刊登这种“标准姿势”照片。是这样吗？

如果当地雄狮俱乐部为了帮助贫困家庭孩子能够定期检查眼睛、配新眼镜而筹集了5000美元，难道他们就不值得拍一张“标准照”吗？

如果妇女教会团体为了帮助穷人解决居住问题而举行烧烤派对来筹集资金，难道他们也不能有一张“标准照”吗？

对于这些值得鼓励的事件，你怎么能忍心拒绝？你不需要拒绝，你只需要积极思考一下。你报道事件过程或结果，就可以避免枯燥无味的“握紧并微笑”的照片了。

例如，派一名摄影师到雄狮俱乐部煎饼晚餐会或教会烧烤义卖上，通过报道帮助这些团体筹集资金；或者跟踪一个受资助的孩子进行深度采访，然后尽力挖掘背后资助人的故事。每一张“握紧并微笑”的照片都配得上一个积极正面的报道。无论是每年举办的女童子军的饼干销售还是红十字会的献血动员大会，报道这些重复的故事，关键是要找到时新的角度。

还有些别的办法：让社区俱乐部或企业自拍集体照，报社每月刊登一次，广而告之他们的慈善举动。如果各种团体在广告特刊上购买版面就可以把照片配合登在一起，每个人都愿意看见自己的脸出现在报纸上，这不是两全其美的事吗？

不需要逃避死板不变的庆祝类照片，最简单的办法就是把所有集体照收集起来，定期以整版形式刊登出来，可以叫作“剪贴簿”，并配上不同的主题，例如同学聚会、五代同堂，或者获奖者等等。

“握紧并微笑”和比格超市

当地比格超市的经理来电说希望能够刊登每月优秀员工的照片，这家店有六个独立部门，也就是说她要求登六张大头照。

当你告诉她刊登每月（每周或者每天）优秀员工的做法违反了报社政策时，她可能会变得好斗并且威胁你：“你知道我们投放了多少广告吗？”

这值得争吵吗？你会怎么做？

同样受过压力的社区报同仁提供了解决的办法：

第一，告知这位经理你将会报道她的优秀员工，但仅仅是列出名字。到年终，可以刊登一张年度最佳雇员的照片并配合特写报道。

第二，建议经理给这些优秀员工来一张大合照，并且一个月只能刊登一次。向她解释镇上商店很多，为公平起见，报纸只能提供这么多版面。

第三，如果版面允许，把照片刊登到“剪贴簿”上。

怎样报道自杀事件？

如果社区中有人自杀了，怎么报道？过细地描述自杀行为有美化嫌疑，许多报社设置了一系列政策，比如：

● 不论是新闻报道还是讣告都不列死因。

● 在报道新闻的情况下，死因应采用殡仪馆或隶属于执法机构的警方所列出的死因。例如用“……死于自己造成的枪伤”代替“自杀”一词。

● 编辑一份“干净的讣告”，即不列出死因。这样死者家属可以剪报留存。

马萨诸塞州《南桥》（*The Southbridge*）前主编洛伦•吉廖内（Loren Ghiglione）目前是西北大学新闻学院新闻系主任，他如此强调：

> 无论新闻记者多么希望保持冷酷的自我形象，都需要认识到自杀包裹着愤怒甚至恐怖等情绪。它象征着社会的失败，父母、教会、辅导员和其他安全网都没有奏效。生者的伤痛以及自杀本身有一定的新闻价值，它不会消失，让它悄悄束之于社区的高阁之中吧。
>
> 做这样的报道切记不要充满戏剧性地刻画受害者，也不要用验尸官一句话的定论或者讣告中惯常使用的“突然死亡”一类的词。在社区自杀的年度报告中，把重点放在由自杀而引发的对诸多问题的思考上，而

不要过于煽情地描述自杀行为。希望逝者能够为生者提供一两个教训，就足够了。

另一些声音，另一些编辑室

以下改编自一篇原发表在1998年4月全美新闻摄影家协会（National Press Photographers Association）杂志的文章。

> 尽管戴安娜王妃惨死的事件已经久远，但由于狗仔队的参与，它对摄影记者来说仍然是一个标杆性的事件。
>
> 其实社区记者，包括社区摄影记者也很难免除那种寻求独家新闻的贪婪。对大多数人来讲，1997年巴黎所发生的事和我们对社区新闻的认定是对立的。虽然事情发生在欧洲，但狗仔队的行为常常是美国大城市报纸最糟糕的伎俩。媒体从业者和被报道者的利益往往是冲突的，这些记者太渴求独家新闻，因此很少为采访对象考虑。他们缺失责任感和义务感，采取“打了就跑”“拍了就溜”的模式，完全没有同情心。
>
> 但是我想，巴黎隧道中的那件事如果发生在或者可能发生在我们的城镇中，我们的报纸上，或者在你的城镇，你的报纸上，那会怎么样？请问你的摄影记者会嘲笑司机吗？他会为了独家新闻跳上摩托车去追赶轿车吗？然后当惨祸发生时不提供援助就跑开了？
>
> 出于自卫，把自己和“他们那些坏人”——狗仔队或者那些大城市报的摄影记者——区分开来是无益的，因为绝大部分读者把我们也视为疯狂的同类。所以对社区报记者而言，最好能够清楚“我们是谁”和“我们在做什么”，尤其要思考“受害者的二次伤害”的问题。
>
> 社区报摄影记者是否知道面对灾难性新闻事件时怎样报道？有人教过他们社区新闻该怎么做吗？报社是否提供新闻报道手册？记者在实操前接受过任何训练吗？还是只能通过每一次事故、每一场灾难、每一回新闻工作者临场的蹩脚行为而获得痛苦的教训？

优秀的社区报不需要等到灾难发生才想到设置道德规范，早就应该为记者提供可以参考的行为准则。或许我的亲身经历能够说明这些问题。

周五下午，应两位老朋友——密友塞西尔•宾利（Cecil Bentley），一位相对年轻的执行编辑；伍迪•马歇尔（Woody Marshall），一位更加年轻的图片总编——的邀请，我到佐治亚州梅肯镇（Macon, G.A.）给《电讯报》记者们讲授社区新闻伦理。

这份日报发行量达85000份，覆盖面达到了惊人的39个郡，一位编辑说："但我们仍然追求做一份和读者保持密切联系的社区报。"

大概有十几个摄影师和编辑记者挤在会议室中，我正在那里展示15年来在北卡罗来纳州运营两份社区报的照片合集，谈到如何保有摄影记者的同情心，如何在做记者的同时不忘自己作为一个普通人、社区活跃分子的身份。

接着我拿出有关伦理困境幻灯片的光盘，在两个小时里，探讨的内容涵盖了社区新闻的各种标准。比如早餐规则（你的读者能在看头版时不恶心地把麦片吐出来吗？），何时接近、何时疏离、如何平衡客观陈述与观点，讨论了媒体在处理少数族裔危机报道中毫无同情心的问题，再比如如何处理隐私与公众的知情权等伦理问题，并共同谴责狗仔队不假思索追逐煽情新闻的做法。

《时代》杂志曾发表一封读者来信："一定有必要刊登像萨拉热窝炮击后沾满鲜血的雪和死去的孩子这样的照片吗？我已经厌倦了那种震惊和沮丧，每次都直接跳过这些血腥的版面。我们本可以通过语言来达到相同的效果。"

我们持有不同意见：和文字相比，摄影更能有力地击中读者，虽然报社关于使用灾难类照片的政策肯定会得罪一些读者，但终究这类伦理性的问题可以依据不同情况找到对应的解决办法。

我们在灾难现场的行为以及次日报纸上展现的内容，其实都取决于心中是否有一个"记者的道德指南针"，它能永远指明"正北方"到底在什么地方，即使在暴风雨中都不会迷失方向。

我告诉记者们，当你已经做出决定要使用有争议的照片时，你必须能够向自己和读者解释这样做的理由。是什么促使你使用那张照片？你对潜在的种族问题敏感吗？你的理由能够被接受吗？谁是利益相关者？如果角色互换，你感觉如何？短期和长期后果是什么？波因特媒体研究所的鲍勃•斯蒂尔（Bob Steele）说，这不是在谈论道德，这是在"塑造道德"。

下午4时结束讲课任务之后，作为实操经历，每个人都领到了去各个点为第二天的报纸拍摄照片的任务：一场新闻发布会、一个芭蕾舞团、一家被评为四星级的家庭旅店以及一场篮球比赛。

我们坐着博•卡贝尔（Beau Cabel）的皮卡车，行驶在沿路都是樱花树的梅肯大街上，准备去跟拍芭蕾舞团，摄影师对我说："你看，今天谈论的关于摄影的那些事儿……都很酷，但是在梅肯几乎不可能遇上这些事情。"

下午6时，我和皮尔刚回到报社，伍迪冲进房间，大喊着："大新闻，一宗谋杀兼自杀案。"他冷静地补充道："尼克在现场，他马上就来。"

尼克是一名30多岁的印度籍摄影师，身材瘦长，戴着眼镜，看起来像教授。我注意到在讲座过程中，他似乎一直若有所思，但在分配任务时悄悄溜出房间。

当时他正在梅肯大街上的某个快餐店准备早点把晚饭吃了，突然听到外面一阵骚动。意识到这是一次枪击事件后，他立刻跑回汽车。当周围一片混乱时，尼克从容配备好尼康相机。在警方拉上黄色警戒线之前，他已经拍了40多张照片。

此刻，在编辑部通常贫嘴的尼克一反常态地安静。

“你还好吗，伙计？”伍迪问他。

“是的，我很好。”尼克生硬地回答。显然，他被所看到和拍下的画面震住了。如果让他去拍摄篮球比赛的照片，他会感觉更好些。

伍迪在处理这些照片时，标注批准使用和禁止使用的记号。透过放大镜，他能看到警务人员脸上急切的表情，他正弯腰去为一名俯卧的年轻女子号脉，女子的鲜血溅在附近的车门上。

伍迪、排版师、文案编辑和我展开了一场辩论：

“真是一张非常好的照片！”

“我们不能用。”

“她还活着吗？”

“如果她死了呢？”

“有什么区别呢？”

“区别大着呢！”

“如果她现在还活着，我们决定使用这张照片，但报纸付印前她又死了那怎么办？”

“那又有什么区别呢？”

“区别还是很大！”

“如果不登这张这么棒的照片，那拍了又有什么意义呢？”

“嘿，整个下午不都在谈论这个吗？”

新消息到了：受害者还活着，而行凶者自杀了。他是受害者之前关系不和的男朋友。晚上，他尾随受害者到其大学，当她下车时朝她胸部开了一枪。

编辑、跑警务的记者和其他摄影师围着伍迪，站在电脑旁边，都看着这张照片。

伍迪双臂环抱做思索状：“你看不到她的脸，但有些人会在意轿车门上的血。”我们都认同这一点。

但事件发生在上下班高峰时间，在梅肯大街上一个非常繁忙的公共场所，很多人亲眼目睹这件事的发生，也有很多人被枪火所伤。这使得这篇报道在某种程度上算作一篇新闻报道。

电脑周围的其他员工议论纷纷：对受害者和家人来讲这公平吗？如果受害人是白人呢？我们会给受害者带来二次伤害吗？这是没来由的血腥？我们会利用受

害者的悲苦来提高报纸销量吗？讨论后，他们达成A计划：采用照片。

他们还拿出了B计划，如果受害人死亡，就使用女子在担架上的照片以减少不适感。他们把备用照片也准备好。最后，编辑部把两个版本交给总编辑宾利，让他做出最终的裁定。

当晚，我们在塞西尔家中得知他当时也在枪击案现场。我们安静地聚集在厨房，伍迪带来坏消息：那名年轻女子已经确认死亡。

塞西尔十几岁的未成年小女儿走进厨房，看着照片上血液溅满车门和女子俯卧在停车场快要死亡的照片。“哦，我可不想一大早就看到这个。”她说。

尽管如此，伍迪还想使用这张照片，编辑芭芭拉叹了口气。“好吧。”塞西尔建议，用一张凶手的面部照片来“部分遮住现场”。

“每个人都同意吗？”塞西尔问道。厨房里的人大都慢慢点头。没有人看起来对这个决定特别高兴。他们知道这样会得罪一些读者，但大家都认为这个事件对整个社区来说都太不寻常了。

“责任由我来扛。”主编对着他的橱柜很有信心地说。

短短两个小时，《电讯报》的员工经历了一个质变，从枯燥艰深的伦理空谈到次日头版真刀实枪的操练，这简直是艰难权衡各种利弊的漫长一天。

后续

公众对报社公开此照片的反应是“温和，相对温和”，图片主管伍迪•马歇尔这么形容道。《电讯报》的《实话实说》栏目有三个来电表示反对。第一个打来电话的人说：“如果这是一名白人女子……你们就永远不会把那样的照片搬上头版。”第二位读者被激怒了：“报社的人难道什么都不关心，只关心怎么把报纸卖出去吗？那张照片……实在太过分了。我不相信你会让你的孩子去看这样的照片。”

《电讯报》只收到一封读者来信，那是一名护士写的，受害人死亡时她就在医院的急诊室中，言辞非常激烈：“当我看到那个死去女孩的扭歪尸体倒在一辆溅满鲜血的汽车旁的画面时，我实在难以忍受。我觉得《电讯报》应该考虑到不是每个人，尤其是受害者家庭，都想看到一个垂死的孩子在这个地球上还剩最后一口气的可怕细节。我不明白为什么这类新闻有更大的销售量。我只希望编辑能够有机会见证在急救中心时那个家庭的悲伤，那么在报告死亡细节时，也许你会更加谨慎。”

《电讯报》咨询委员会得到的消息是公众反应好坏参半，但整体非常积极。只有一个人完全反对照片的使用，他认为如果使用照片时能把车门上的血迹去掉就好了。马歇尔回答道："我必须很有礼貌地解释为什么不能这么做。我觉得大多数人是认可这种照片的，因为它表明到底发生了什么……会议结束后董事会的一位成员告诉我，她从不知道《电讯报》选择照片这么谨慎，方方面面的因素都要考虑。我想此后她应该会更加尊重《电讯报》。"马歇尔的结论是，学习如何"塑造道德"使他能够更好地阐明使用这些争议性照片的理由。

在谋杀兼自杀案发生的一周内，《电讯报》连续做了三篇后续报道，进一步把悲剧放到社会大背景下去剖析，因为这关系到社区的未来，与身处其中的每个人都密切相关。

摄影辩论和灰色阴影

编辑兼摄影师杰里米•沃尔特（Jeremy Waltner）给弗里曼（Freeman SD.）的《快递报》（*Courier*）写了如下一篇评论，该报由他的父亲蒂姆•沃尔特（Tim Waltner）所有，是一份发行量达2000份的独立周报。

上周发行的《快递报》第三版上出现两张火灾照片，大火烧毁了一台机器。没有人员死亡，但损失很明显。

三个星期前，一张照片上是三辆装载着粮食但翻了的卡车。一名消防员站在旁边，正伸手帮助受害者。乘客锁骨骨折。

在10月3日发行的《快递报》上，第三版一张照片显示弗里曼的消防员正在拯救受困者，他的汽车与别的汽车迎头相撞。该男子当晚死亡。

回溯近几年，《快递报》同很多别的报纸一样，很传统地刊登火灾、车祸或其他发生在我们社区和周边的悲剧的照片。

这中间隐藏着潜在的冲突。

从全国范围看，受众最大的抱怨之一是，媒体详述坏事，这使得悲剧中的受害者通过图片受到二次伤害。

愤怒的公众或打电话，或威胁，甚至取消订阅或者撤销广告。触及核心的根本问题是记者对职业伦理的愚钝感觉。

我和其他记者一样一直在有关照片的伦理问题上纠结。当我们谈论它时，手心都是汗，太棘手了。

我们质疑自己，质疑动机，质疑职业道德。

因为这个问题是很灰色的。或许有时候读者认为我们发布图片的动机是渲染悲剧。真正的情况是很多时候远非如此，我们不会让东拼西凑而成的文章随意出版，还咯咯笑着："啊，哈哈！又卖出去一份报纸。"

现实中，我们提出了很多问题，但找到的答案令人沮丧，模糊不清。

我们什么时候应该什么时候不应该发布照片？如果有死亡情况发生，怎么办？如果图片上有清楚的血迹，怎么办？如果受害者的脸清晰可见，怎么办？图片有侵犯隐私嫌疑，怎么办？我们存在的意义是做历史的见证吗？我们存在的意义是为了卖报纸吗？我们存在的意义是为了彰显真理吗？火灾警报一响，救护车一动，我们就要紧跟在后面吗？追逐救护车很光荣吗？我们需要改变吗？

如果当相机从最早发明到现在为止有一条书面规则说火灾和事故的现场照片（应该）永远不被拍摄，会怎样？

我们就不会有第二次世界大战图片、“挑战者”号爆炸、费尔南东面南方教堂的大火……

我们该在什么时候开始拍照，什么时候停止？

任何一个地方都没有标准答案。

但大家似乎又都有答案。

有关灾难报道的照片尺度会持续不断辩论下去。

我希望读者明白，大多数报社都在这个问题上小心翼翼，既要牢记读者的敏感点在何处，又不忘记录历史使命，要永远处于最佳平衡点实在不是一件容易的事。

第12章

新闻编辑室管理：人事方向

敬爱的中国读者：

请允许我同你分享一则在美国受到广泛认可的著名法则，商业成功的秘诀：快乐的人工作会更努力。一间和谐的新闻工作室=出色的报纸=利润。尽管也有像股权、地点、竞争等因素影响报纸的成功，但在“员工能够互相欣赏，享受协同工作”这点上，怎么强调都不为过。管理者该怎样促进这一重要的、动态的发展呢？也许这一章会带来启示。

——作者

为什么这对你很重要

宾夕法尼亚州研究商业心理学的副教授大卫•戴（David Day）说："处理人事事务也许是管理者们必须处理的最棘手的事——然而这也是他们最不熟悉的事。"

如果你是一个刚毕业的大学生，或是一个渴望在社区新闻领域闯出一番事业的新手记者，你也许会认为你离成为一位编辑或者一位出版人还很远。但在社区新闻中，这样的事说来就来。你可能会在远未准备好的阶段进入管理层，面临处理人事问题的考验。这种能力有些人与生俱来，有些人则要艰难习得。一般而言，这是一项后天习得的技能。很多报纸无力聘请专门的人事经理，只好由编辑兼任。在透明得如同金鱼缸的社区报纸中，人事工作是一项必要而耗时的任务。

我们的关系出现了问题

凯西热爱她的工作。作为《号角报》的首席摄影师，她可以昼夜不分地工作一整周，因为这份工作给了她实现个人价值以及享受专业成就的机会。

但她的丈夫布莱恩却有点不爽。凯西在家时间很少，回家还不忘工作。她曾在工作一整天后，回到家就躺倒在床，不可避免地开始抱怨工作中的烦心事，甚至控制不住地朝布莱恩发泄。更糟的是，就连5岁的儿子赛斯，也会因为一些小小的过错而引火上身。

布莱恩，这位安静而体贴的会计师，曾努力地维持他们之间的关系。毕竟，大学毕业前，为了支持他完成学业，凯西不也曾选择留在当地为报纸工作吗？现在该他默默地付出了。当凯西外出拍摄晚间比赛、市议会、童子军演练日、农贸集会、艺术节、大学剧团排练等活动时，布莱恩负责照顾赛斯的起居。好像总有没完没了的事将凯西从家带走。

慢慢地，当凯西总是外出报道那些在他看来没有多大意义的小事时，布莱恩开始感觉自己好像正独自运营一家幼儿园。"还好我懂得怎么煮饭。"他越发尖刻地想道。不然他和赛斯早就要挨饿了。他试着回忆：一家三口上一次一起坐在饭桌上吃饭是什么时候。

他开始公开地对凯西的工作安排表示不满，甚至暗示他们该去见见婚姻咨询师。但每次向凯西提到这个问题，她要么发火，要么落泪，最后总是以一句"你知道我忙得根本没时间”否决提议，布莱恩再也没敢提起这个话题。最糟糕的是，小赛斯似乎感觉到了家里的紧张气氛。

在赛斯的课堂表演那天，一切矛盾都爆发了。布莱恩连小家伙的戏服都做好了，那个节目里赛斯扮演一块石头。但凯西还是没能到场观看表演，几个小时后她急匆匆地打来电话，解释缺席是因为公路上发生了一起严重的车祸。布莱恩此时知道，那根长长的导火线终于烧到头了。

他决定将他的不满都写下来。但布莱恩一下笔，就感觉到心中怒火喷薄而出得太快，以致写字的速度完全跟不上。匆忙间，他开始缩短单词，遗漏字母。

当凯西读到这封信时，她无法理解：首先，为什么他会生她的气？其次，那个奇怪的单词“relt”是什么意思。

“它是‘relationship’（关系）的简写！”布莱恩终于爆发了，“我们之间关系就只有那么短！你没发现吗？我们之间的关系是怎么回事？我们甚至没有足够的相处时间来发展关系。我们的关系就是这‘relt’！”

我们在同一艘船上

同样的故事也有可能发生在大都市日报的记者和配偶身上，但当上述场景发生在社区报时，产生的影响要广泛得多。因为一切事物在社区报里都更为集中——相对少的人挤在相对小的空间里工作——人际关系不可避免地会变得高度私人化。无论是同事间、编辑与手下员工间、商业部门和新闻部门间、文字编辑和美术编辑间，还是印刷厂和新闻编辑室间，都是这样。

这可以归结为一句话：我们在同一艘船上。如果这句话听着耳熟，那是因为它也被用来描述报纸与社区之间的关系。许多大型都市报的记者相互之间不一定认识，可以独来独往，但在社区报，员工更像家人一样。在这个大家庭里，大家要与不是自己主动选择的人待在一起，不管你乐意与否，彼此的弱点、优点、私人生活、偶像、害怕的事、宠物、小毛病、饮酒习惯等一目了然，比如咖啡加不加奶、热狗加不加酱。你们也许根本不喜欢彼此，但还要相互忍受各种小毛病和坏习惯，必须学会如何在一起工作。报社的工作氛围取决于个体间相处的友好程度。

再考虑一下人性中的阴暗面。报社可不像鞋店那么简单。秉性各异的人被扔进一个高度紧张、经常被催稿、一举一动引发关注、好像从来没有休假的企业，你觉得会发生什么？这将会变得火药味十足。

人事问题的高发地带有：员工与从事非媒体工作的配偶，共同工作的员工或不同部门的员工，职员与管理层，等等。谨记关于这个行业的一句老话：所有工作都是更加私人化的，人事工作也不例外。

如果社区报首席摄影师的婚姻出现危机，那么整个新闻编辑室都会察觉。一旦布莱恩让凯西直面他们相处时间过少的问题，她的工作必然会受到影响。他们的矛盾不仅会影响凯西本人的工作状态，还有可能波及整份报纸。

这段婚姻还能继续吗?

一位优秀的社区报从业者与一位非媒体从业者要如何共同经营一段良好的婚姻?当你的圈外配偶无法理解你对工作的热情，抱怨你在工作上花费了大量时间时，你要怎么做?

工作永远是第一位的，不是吗?

这……还真不一定。

每对夫妇都得想清楚他们最关心的是什么。这就需要在一堆重要的事物中做出取舍，比如事业、家庭、生活方式、居住地等都可以是选项。

身为媒体工作者一方，必须要让其圈外配偶明白，这份工作的特殊性在于其对时间节点的要求，个人生活各方面很难保证不被工作打断，这会给婚姻生活带来麻烦，但是，仍有二者兼顾的可能，但你必须把握好速度和节奏。

下面是些解决“relt”通用的准则。

新闻人都很自负。他们经常犯的错误就是认为周围的同伴能自动意识到他们从事着一项神圣的工作，但实际上他们的伴侣并不像他们那样对报道市议会或少年棒球联赛充满热情。他们应该试着与伴侣分享工作时的激情，分享对采访中每一个故事的理解和感受，而不是单方面地说教。

给对方和工作同等的时间。你的伴侣最近过得怎么样?仔细倾听，不要听到一半就把对话带回你自己和你的工作。留出能够进行创造性对话的时间，让两人有真正的交流，这段私人时间要把工作彻底排除在外。

回到新闻编辑室里的“relt”这个话题。常言道：“别和同事谈恋爱。”但由于有着相似的兴趣爱好，媒体工作者之间的恋爱并不偶然。尽管如此，这种关系碰到的麻烦似乎并不比媒体从业者和圈外人结合的要少。在一起工作的夫妻间也有数不尽的矛盾冲突，包括作为同行，在新闻头条和署名上不可避免的竞争、职业方向、薪水和升职方面的矛盾、利益冲突，甚至可能还有谁在谁手下工作的问题。有些报社直接禁止办公室恋情。然而也有报社认为这样的结合有益于保证稳定的雇佣关系，不仅允许，实际上还鼓励同一报社的员工发展恋情。

另一些声音，另一些编辑室

家族式报纸

过去25年里，美国社区新闻业一个明显的趋势是家族式报纸的数量下降，而由报团拥有的连锁经营的社区报数量上升。但因此鼓吹家族式报纸的衰亡是完全错误的，实际情况远没有那么严重。美国依然有很多发展良好质量上乘的家族拥有的社区报。在我的家乡北卡州，52%的“非日报”仍然是独立运营的——其中很多是家族式报纸。现在需要探讨的问题是，亲兄弟姐妹间、夫妻间、父母间是如何共同工作的？他们每晚都会把工作带回家吗？他们快乐吗？他们是怎样成为行业竞争中的常胜将军？下面让我们以两份北卡罗来纳州的高质量周刊为例，一窥究竟。

回溯《维克周报》的历史

鲍勃•艾伦和佩吉•艾伦（Bob and Peggy Allen）夫妇从20世纪50年代初期开始出版《维克周报》，花了很长时间才把它做成一份繁盛、成功、受人尊敬的家族式周刊，并使其经常登上美国最佳周报的光荣榜。

20世纪50年代初期，当时只有22岁的鲍勃和哥哥一起买下了发行量不到700份在生死线上挣扎的报纸《维克周报》，到了1956年，周刊变为鲍勃和佩吉夫妻两人拥有。多年来，鲍勃负责销售管理，佩吉则负责新闻事务。佩吉回忆道：“直到第二个儿子格雷格能够帮忙前，鲍勃一直是我们唯一的广告销售员。”新闻报道，包括选题会，都由两人分担，其中一个还因为要照顾孩子而无法出席会议。

当被问及是否会把工作带回家时，你几乎能听见佩吉回答时的轻笑：“这些年我们被工作拖住待在办公室的时间比我们能把工作带回家的时间要多得多。等到孩子们长大一点——我有四个儿子——他们就在办公室开始打扫卫生、印试样等工作了。大多数时候，他们留在办公室做作业，然后在地板上睡到回家时间。这也算是使他们远离电视的一种方法。”

艾伦夫妇为他们拥有四个对这个行业感兴趣的儿子感到幸运。吉米当了很多年的新闻编辑，他的妻子金吉，毕业于北卡罗来纳大学教堂山分校，几年前就开始报道学校和郡政府；鲍勃最大的儿子鲍比在行政部门工作；格雷格从北卡罗来纳大学教堂山分校毕业后，在《维克周报》做了好几年的广告经理，直到他决定到俄亥俄州一间提供报纸复印机的制图公司从事销售工作；鲍勃最小的儿子托德毕业于同一所大学，目前担任《维克周报》的广告经理。

艾伦夫妇已到了该退休的年龄，佩吉说：“家族式报纸中有一点弥足珍贵，

家人会在彼此陷入困境时伸出援手，从社论到广告，你都能得到很及时的建议，报纸把全家人更紧密地连在一起。”她还提到，不管四个儿子走得离维克弗里斯特多远，“你可以把男孩们从报社带走，但你带不走男孩们心中的报纸情结”。

有人说：“不管这个家族的成员承认与否，他们是镇上生来就适合做新闻的人。”但这个名声并非得来毫不费力。多年来这个家庭一直在社区里保持很高的活跃度。佩吉说：“鲍勃和两个儿子都是本镇商会董事会成员，为社区活动几乎事必躬亲。”艾伦夫妇相信从小让孩子们浸淫在社区报环境中，有助于帮男孩们成长为优秀的公民。孩子们始终知道，一旦闯了祸，他们的名字会立刻出现在第二天的报纸上。

佩吉问自己：“如果时光倒流，我们还会这样做吗？当然。其实现在，退休的事让我们感觉不舍。”但毕竟岁月不饶人，想不出还能有什么比由他们的四个儿子或其中的几个来继续经营这份报纸更完美的事了。

传递接力棒

1998年，《维克周报》发生了重大变化。

格雷格是家里的次子。他从三年级到高中一直为《维克周报》工作，大学毕业后返回报社。他干了7年报纸销售工作，1991年离开了《维克周报》，部分原因是“家族的人太多了”，他说时嘴角牵起一丝苦笑。

但到了1997年，鲍勃和佩吉已经将近70岁了，《维克周报》距被出售只有一线之遥，格雷格的弟弟吉米出了一个主意：他们可以而且应该联合起来把《维克周报》从父母手中买下来。

解决了经济上的问题后，他们又被谁当领导的问题困住了。

格雷格不满于50-50的股权平均分配方案，认为在危急情况下，应该由一个人担负全责，格雷格想成为那个人。经过几个星期的反复商量，两兄弟通过一个异乎寻常的方式达成共识，吉米宣布了一个吓倒所有人的决定："我们只差一点就达成协定了，但是我受到了上帝的感召，我要成为神职人员。"

于是格雷格独自买下了《维克周报》，在1998年1月1日成了独立出版人。如果有机会和这位出版人一起在镇上四处走走，看到镇上的居民们和他之间的互动，你一定会发现居民们对格雷格的欣赏以及对《维克周报》能作为一份独立、本地化的社区报纸继续运营的喜悦。

他说："只有自己拥有它，才能幸运地不受一堆主管的限制，不用被要求去追求永无止境的高利润。"

在兄弟共同度过报纸的过渡期后，吉米于夏天离职到坎贝尔大学（Campbell University）攻读神学博士学位，后来他担任一份由北卡罗来纳州浸信会发行的《圣经记录者》（*Bible Recorder*）的助理编辑，可以说他仍在做着社区新闻的工作，这本小型刊物每周发行48000份。"它就像一个大型社区报纸"，他当时这样认为，因为"你仍然在和社区打交道，只不过形式更加丰富了"。

快速发展的五年

如果非要用一个词来形容所有权变更五年后《维克周报》与小镇的不同，那就是"壮大"。

由于附近规划的高尔夫球场形成两个新社区，镇上的人口翻了一番。除此之外，报纸覆盖范围内的邻近小镇罗斯威尔（Rolesville），今年多了1500户新住户，简直算是"爆炸性"增长。

8500份的发行量已经跟不上人口增长的速度，格雷格打算通过细分目标读者的方式大胆争取那些新市民。

格雷格和担任董事长兼联合出版人的妻子珍妮特•罗斯（Janet Rose）聘请了一组企业顾问。"这就像在5周里读完MBA学位。"格雷格郑重地说。企业重组带来了一些新东西，管理团队的带头人每周与出版人会面进行一次规划会议，所有部门每月一起用餐一次讨论报社面临的问题。

《维克周报》内部有着坚实的团队意识。格雷格说："我一直确信，我们就像一群大雁。在V形队里，由一只头雁在前面带领，剩下的大雁则在后面叽叽喳喳地叫，直到另一只大雁挺身而出，给之前那只头雁歇口气的机会。"

重组计划的成果之一是沟通、效率和产出得到了提升，利润也有所增加。这是非常重要的，自2001年和随后的经济衰退以来，经营一份报纸要比之前难得多，社区报的管理者们必须更加精于业务，但对于《维克周报》的员工们来说，之前的调整发挥效果了。“我从来不知道提前计划会那么有趣。”格雷格笑着说。

艾伦家庭后记

按格雷格所说，他非常欣赏妻子珍妮特的运营和管理能力，她的加入让报纸变得更加强大。“她是个精力充沛的人。”因此格雷格将会计、人事工作、应缴款项这种躲不开的重担全部移交给她。

鲍勃和佩吉退休后生活过得丰富多彩，佩吉在减肥中心锻炼塑身，鲍勃游泳，看起来身体棒极了，当然，他仍然会像以前一样挑《维克周报》的毛病。

而那个像大人一样沉着地接听前台电话的小孩是谁？那是格雷格能干的14岁儿子戴维斯，同时他还是一个熟练的摄影记者。他显然是《维克周报》下一任的继承人。真是个幸运的小子。从编辑转行成为神职人员的吉米也回家了，成了赫利蒂奇地方浸信会的牧师。他和金吉现在有了4个孩子。

格雷格不是一个恋旧的人，他说：“我们取得了很多出色的成果……但要在当今世界生存下去，你不能止步不前。”

格雷格展望未来

“我仍相信社区报有着无限广阔的未来——因为你可以在社区报上看到不可能在其他报纸上看到的熟悉的人名和照片。”

举个例子，《维克周报》用了连续四个版面报道镇上每年一度的独立日焰火晚会，发布了45张图片，在这些图片里你至少能辨别出221张熟悉的脸。当然，有几张群像人数实在太多，难以一一辨认，但大多数的照片里每人的脸都清晰可辨。《维克周报》力图让每张照片都“能辨认出每个人”。格雷格摊开一叠报纸，大声说出这个事实：“一个名字都没有漏！”

这就是《维克周报》对本地化报道的不懈追求。

成功的社区报是否共有一个模式？

艾德•哈珀“血管里流淌着墨水”，这是一位编辑的说法，意在表明艾德的生活中连呼吸、进食甚至睡觉都离不开报纸。

北卡州的南港无疑是个迷人的滨海小镇，哈珀坐在他最爱的海边咖啡厅里谈起了他热爱的两件不可分割的事物：他的小镇和家族经营的报纸。“我爱这工作！”他坚决地说。（整个对话里，他会把这话说至少三次。）

做同样的工作32年以后还能每天早上醒来都像哈珀一样说出“我爱这工作”，是不是很棒？

谈及每周发行量9103份的《州港领航员报》的成功业绩，哈珀首先将其“归功于我的家庭”。他的父亲，已故的詹姆斯•哈珀（James Harper），早在1935年就对报业产生了兴趣，与妻子玛格丽特一起将《州港领航员报》办成了一份持续赢利的周刊，并将报纸建设成为社区内部深受喜爱的一家机构。

“我父亲在报社和社区之间建立起一种奇妙的关系。”艾德说，“报纸成功的原因就在于他深爱这片土地。我也真心实意地热爱南港。”

50岁左右的艾德•哈珀，从体形上看似乎大学时曾是橄榄球队的跑卫，说起《州港领航员报》的员工时，他的口吻就像一位出色的主教练。他说：“我们的团队既能干又有才华。大家都认为推出一件优秀的产品靠的是合作。”

这件产品就是《州港领航员报》，报纸与小镇同名。南港位于通航量巨大的开普费尔河（Cape Fear River）上，通向港口城市威明顿（Wilmington）。

《州港领航员报》的成功模式大致包括以下几个关键要素：

1. 本地，本地，还是本地。南港位于北卡罗来纳州南部海岸，高尔夫球场、度假区和海滩不断扩展，对游客、退休者和高尔夫爱好者的吸引力越来越大。房地产和汽车广告是报纸重要的利润来源。古董和特色商店、饭店和旅游者大大推动了小镇的经济发展。艾德认为，即使一家即将开业的沃尔玛超市，也不会对小镇的稳定有切实影响。“过去五年《州港领航员报》之所以发展得非常顺利，是因为房地产市场。”

早在20世纪三四十年代，艾德的父母靠着微薄的赢利维持生活，这点利润基本上来自每年一期的烟草货仓专刊；后来一段时期，利润的主要来源为汽车广告；再后来又转向杂货店广告。他们的坚持最终获得了回报，小镇的发展也与报社联系在了一起。“很多年来，南港一直是个昏昏欲睡的小镇。但过去15到20年里，高尔夫（高尔夫球场和退休人员组成的社区）使情况发生了彻底转变。”

最近，轮值美国报业协会主席的艾德告诉社区新闻实习生劳伦•里皮说：“我们要清楚自己的定位，不要去抢大型日报的工作……不过他们也无法像我们一样。实际上每周《州港领航员报》的内容都是紧盯着社区的。‘实际上’也就是几乎百分之百的意思。”正是这条本地化的准则促成了社区报纸的发展。

2. 优秀的员工。艾德说，除了富有才华，他的员工们还有三个共同特点：喜欢彼此，喜欢自己做的事情，也喜欢这个社区。“这就使我们能更容易地留住优秀员工，”他补充说，“团队里的每个人都是赢家。”

艾德还强调要给员工提供“精良的装备和摄影器材”。同样重要的还有工资，《州港领航员报》的记者工资与附近《纽约时报》集团旗下日发行量60615份的日报的员工工资相当，某些情况下甚至更多。

新闻编辑泰里•卡尔霍恩这样解释报纸成功的“配料表”：热点新闻和社区新闻混合成优质、醇厚的面糊，每周的底料都要新鲜，顶端放一小撮肉桂的精选，或者巧克力味的专题特写……

1996年，《州港领航员报》通过一个独立的主页（stateportpilot.com）将网站与当地商会链接起来，而意义最为重大的是，《州港领航员报》成了一家本地内容网络供应商。

3. 制作优质的社区新闻比赚取利润更重要。“我们的动力来源于自尊，而不是一心想着赢利。但我们也相信，只要报纸做得好，读者群和广告也就会给我们带来利润。”艾德非常自信。

4. 努力工作、眼光长远的领导者。“我并不要求任何人的工作时间和我一样长。”艾德说，“但确实有一些员工会长时间工作……”

他自己周一工作到晚上11点，周二整晚，有时一直工作到周三凌晨一两点。“我可以找个人来做这些事，但我不想那样……那太自我放纵了。”

“而且，”他坚决地说，“我还没做出最好的报纸。”

星期三他曾一整天都跟一名新送报人一起骑车沿途递送报纸。“那很棒，我非常喜欢。”他咧嘴一笑，“没有什么比看着人们排队买你自己出版的报纸更棒的了。”

欢迎来到“管弦乐团”

一家报社就像一个管弦乐团，而每个管弦乐团都是不一样的。

出版人、执行编辑甚至总编就是负责对付各个难以驾驭的分部的指挥。精巧的木管看不起自负的高音铜管，高音铜管又看不起低沉的低音铜管，低音铜管又讨厌浮夸的打击乐器，打击乐手又不理解为什么人们会想在弦乐上浪费时间——分歧就这么持续着。

高效的指挥必须解决所有这些潜在的个人和专业方面的摩擦从而创造出乐曲。管弦乐团想要最终成功，为了团队的作品，众多分部都必须把技术和思想上的分歧抛开。

如果你暗中观察大部分报社，你会发现商业部门与新闻部门并不很合得来，也不相似。商业部门会认为新闻版面是浪费空间，最好能都用来放能够挣钱的广告。他们也很不满，名声和荣誉总是被新闻部门所垄断。你见过歌颂报纸广告销售的电视节目或者电影吗？

但即使是在新闻部门内部，长久以来也有很大的分歧。文字编辑与美术编辑不和，新闻作者和社论作者不和，体育版还跟所有人都不和。因为大部分人都倾向于自我选择，也就是说，会被吸引到与自己的性格相适应的岗位上，这也意味着在你的管弦乐团或报社员工里，每个人都处于最适合发挥自己才干的位置上。但搅和到一起，则难免产生摩擦。

老板管理方法101

一家报社要运作顺畅，必须有一样东西来调和不同的小团体，只有让他们和谐、流畅、明确地同心协作，读者才能接收到准确的信息而不被混乱的表达所误导。

这种顺畅，有时候来源于一位杰出的编辑，有时候来源于追求卓越的优良传统，还可以是编辑加上传统再加上一个强大的社区中的读者对质量有很高的要求。但不应弄错的是，最终能使一家报社成功的是拥有远见而不是只盯着财务底线的出版人。睿智的出版人不仅了解而且珍惜管弦乐团固有的差异，还知道如何指导每个乐手、每个分部发挥到最好。

在社区报社里，人员流动特别频繁，新闻编辑室的成员通常大部分是刚开始职业生涯的年轻人，编辑就成了他们在现实世界里的第一位老师。了解到这一点也就要意识到，社区报层面的管理性质完全不同。

作为这样一名编辑，你的角色比起大城市里的同行更重要，对你的要求也更高。对于年轻记者来说，你是榜样也是导师，他们永远不会忘记你。不管是好是坏，你给他们留下的印象是无法抹除的。

但说句公道话，有时间有热情的新手记者确实该经受一下大学里不曾有的严厉责备。“社区报社成了刚从新闻学院毕业的学生们的研究生院，这些能干但初出茅庐的记者们还不懂业界的规矩。”一位久经沙场的图片总编这样说，“所以就要由我们来‘训导’他们。”

有时候这种再教育还需要亲自动手。“孩子们径直冲进突发新闻事件的现场，不经调查也不挖掘重要新闻的核心，就对现场的人抛出一大堆问题。”这位资深社区报编辑如此描述。如果年轻记者挡住了现场应急人员的路，他们会被温和地警告一下。但如果挡了现场一位头发灰白的大摄影师的道，只有上帝能保护他们了。这叫作抢镜，可够你喝一壶的了。

“我会抓着他们的后颈把他们拖回来，”他露出了父亲般的笑容，“然后平静地告诉他们，‘如果你再敢跑到我和我的摄影对象之间，只要有一次，我就宰了你’。”

这位表面易怒，但内心像棉花糖一样柔软的老摄影师所说的话，其实是“严厉的爱”的表达。

社区报社暨草根研究生院

在社区报，大概每年新闻编辑室里都会增添新人，大部分直接来自新闻学院。这些新手肯定会犯错误，这是接受新人时的“附赠品”。实际上，是错误而不是成功才让人快速成长，编辑的水平就在于怎样处理这些过失。其间的差距可能就像地狱和天堂间的距离。

有的出版人和编辑不知如何克制，听说新手犯了错误，就冲进编辑室，当着所有员工的面大声辱骂。这种做法不但不能调动其积极性，而且还会催生糟糕的事情：工作中断，员工重整简历准备另寻他路。如果出版人、编辑经常发表攻击性长篇演讲，事情就会传出去。更糟糕的是，他摧毁了员工的动力和目标。如果员工团结一致，他们就会开始对抗这个神经质的老板。除非意外，否则报纸上不大可能有高质量的作品。员工们艰难地忍受每天的工作，就像在监狱里一样。

这种“来自地狱的报纸”的情节经常上演。员工们离开这样的报社并不是简单的离开，他们完全是一种逃离。此后，当他们在谈笑中提及这件事时，会说自己是难民或者生还者。

还有一个巨大的阴谋：有时候坏人并不是老板。据说在每一个机构里（包括报社）都有一个潜伏在角落的人，像一个巨大的负能量黑洞，偷偷地、狡猾地、奸诈地吸食着未起疑心的新来者们柔软活泼的灵魂。甚至一些容易上当的老前辈也不幸成为吞噬能量的黑洞先生，他就是一头披着羊皮的狼。别说我没有警告过你。

管理风格

每一家报社都有“企业文化”，无论是明文表述还是隐性规则。

规模较小的报社里，通过一两个人突出的个人风格就能一览报社的管理风格。在规模较大的报社里，明确定义管理风格的过程就比较复杂。最成功的报社都主动及时地用清晰明了的信条或者任务条目来表明其管理风格。有效的指导方针必须成文并普及，还要在日常运行过程中作为固定模式得到贯彻。

如果一家报社没有关于管理风格的任务明细，那么它的风格就是没有风格。它蹒跚着，仅靠惯性推动着前行，没有方向，没有指引，也没有任何自我观念、欲望、目标或使命。

管理风格其实很容易归类。之前我们已经提到过神经质老板，你会很自觉地不去招惹他，因为他就是掌权的赫鲁晓夫，你知道会被毁掉。其他类型还有：

● 生人勿近型。高层人士总是关着门，传递出这样的信息："别来烦我；我特别忙，特别重要。"

● 行尸走肉型。基本上不是活物。报社缺乏有效的领导，只是在浑水摸鱼。当然，读者们也意识到他们正在读僵尸编年史。

● 结果至上型。报社的领导人只想要一份报纸成品。于是他们得到了小小的新闻版面、沉闷的新闻编辑室，可想而知以后的新闻产品也毫无创意。

● 你死我活型。每个人都只关心自己的利益，只顾及自己的职业发展。请参考行尸走肉型。

● 圈地为王型。领导不力的报社常常会出现小团体的领导者发起小型的暴动。就像一个管弦乐团没了指挥，结果只能是混乱的噪音。请参考行尸走肉型和你死我活型。

● 爸爸妈妈型。一所家族企业仅由一个家族或一个家长型人物统治。去上班就像与这个家族结亲，如果你和家庭成员互相都喜欢的话这可能就是好事。但是一旦失宠，情况就会急剧恶化。

● 十全十美型。开明的、追求高质量新闻的社区报社，管理风格亲切而有活力，团队有很高的协作精神，每个人都知道并且认同报社的任务、核心价值和责任，并分享所得的回报。能够进入这种报社的年轻记者实在非常幸运。在这里工作就像是进入一所免费的新闻研究生院。

如何让编辑室保持活力

那么，有什么管理策略能够切实有效地处理社区报员工问题尤其是年轻员工的问题呢？做个更好的领导应当考虑以下几点：

● 禅与报社管理的艺术。早在公元6世纪，中国的贤者就已经研究过伟大的领导人应有的品质。老子曰："夫唯不争故无尤。"换句话说，不要当众生气地责备一名年轻的记者。

● 尊重记者。对犯错记者的指导应在私下进行，以保存他的尊严。如果他们搞砸了事情，自己也会非常难过。你的处理方式要严厉而不失启发性，给他时间仔细斟酌你的建设性意见，这样记者们才能学到可以致用的东西。这能加强你的团队对这句社区报箴言的理解："人是最重要的。"

● "不存在的错误"理论。错误是不存在的，它们其实是经验。

● 高科技和人际关系。就算你的工作室已经数字化，到处都装上了各种糖果色的电脑、连成蒲公英一样的网络，也不要因为高科技而无视人的本性，这一直是我们这一行的传统优势。电子邮件无法取代面对面的沟通，也无法替代轻拍后背的小小举动。

● 行胜于言。不要指挥你的员工做事情，“我们行动吧！”始终比“你应该去做这个那个”要好得多。比起在项目中只负责发出乏味指令的编辑，融入团队的活跃的编辑能得到远远超出前者的成果。实际上，只有乐于分担责任的编辑才能赢得员工的敬重和忠诚，反过来这也能鼓励员工做出高质量的成果，这将远超于单纯命令所得。

● 本•富兰克林（Ben Franklin）的格言：“我们必须绑在一条绳上，否则我们各自会被绳子吊死。”这位美国伟大的出版人这样告诉大陆议会的同僚们。这句话对社区报也同样适用，小规模报社里，编辑、记者和摄影师在日常生活中更容易彼此联系，如果同事间缺少交流，新闻编辑室肯定会产生严重的问题。如果事先各部门沟通充分，最后的报道成品质量会大大改观。

● 不用便条，少用电邮。世界上真的有人喜欢便条吗？大型机构采用便条这种缺乏人情味的小纸片来节省时间，便条的潜台词大概是：“像我这样地位高又重要的人，十分繁忙，才没有时间穿过大厅去跟低等渺小的你们交谈。”你要想和下属疏远，便条奏效最快。

如果你的店铺很小，就该用比较令人舒服的面对面方式沟通。

这对电子邮件同样适用。如果你的工作室很小，注意避免过多使用电子邮件。随便一个人都可能遭遇过电子邮件的意思被曲解的情况。只缩在自己的壳里会大大削弱你的创造力。

● 漫步的编辑。事实证明“闲逛着管理”的方法非常有效。如果你是一名编辑，花点时间，走到大厅里，跟你碰到的每个人聊聊天。或者，你要对某人说什么事情的时候，亲自去他的办公室或座位前。先说些别的话题，比如他们的孩子在少年棒球联合会表现如何，再转移到你实际要说的内容。关于领导力的研究显示，最无能的老板正是那些从来不离开办公室，只用电子邮件和便条来传达命令的老板。如果你在社区报工作，请走出办公室，与同事们混熟。在整个社区里，你都应该这样与人面对面交流。沿着主要街道闲逛，去一趟本地的便宜小饭馆，带着清醒的头脑、相机和笔记本回家。你说没时间？挤出时间来。这能延长你的生命，也会让你的报纸更有趣。

招聘和留任

怎么有效地招募到高质量的新闻编辑室成员并留住他们？同样，答案是本地化，本地化，还是本地化。

根据社区报学员克里斯蒂娜•雷克斯罗德的说法，20世纪90年代中期，北卡罗来纳州阿什伯勒市的《阿什伯勒消息论坛》几乎每两年就会换掉一批员工。1994年新编辑雷•克里斯科（Ray Criscoe）上任，他之前在史蒂芬传媒集团其下一份发行量为16300份的日报工作。雷克斯罗德说，克里斯科上任后，就开始雇用来自社区内部的记者。她在报告中写："这个策略奏效了。目前的报社成员，几乎无一例外曾在小镇居住过一段时间，他们中许多人就是在那里长大的。几乎再也没有人跳槽了。"

走出你的安乐窝

待在自己的安乐窝内完全是人的本性。但在新闻编辑室里，这可能导致报道中有潜意识的偏见。

弗兰克•费（Frank Fee）是位于教堂山的北卡罗来纳大学的一位副教授，曾任职于东北部的一份连锁经营的主流大城市日报，该报社的新闻编辑室管理方式被称为"漫游日"或者"走走谈谈"。在长达三四周的时间里，记者们离开编辑室，走进社区，并不是为了新闻故事本身，而只是去感受社区，"走出去了解真正的人们"。最后，员工们聚在一起评估大家的经历。当他们把图钉按在城市地图上以显示所去之处以后，费发现没有一个记者探索过黑人区。

那这间新闻编辑室的种族构成是怎样的呢？当然大部分都是白人。费有些讽刺地写道：新闻编辑室里的几位黑人记者也没有去那片所谓的"危险"区。

新闻编辑室的多样性

我们的行业内有个可悲的事实：新闻编辑室，无论大小，都没有真实反映出他们所报道的社区的人种和民族构成情况。

美国人口普查报告指出，1990年到2000年间，拉丁裔的比例上升了62%，人数从1730万增加到2810万。但是，有多少主流社区报的新闻编辑室里有哪怕只有一位西班牙裔的记者呢？而根据美国西班牙裔出版人联盟2004年的数据，美国的西班牙裔所办的报业正在繁荣发展。从1990年起，日报数量翻了一番，而他们的发行量增加了两倍。这还没算上周报！

从事新闻报业的人大多数还是"自由派、受过高等教育、婴儿潮中出生的白人男性"，印第安纳大学的保罗•S.沃克斯（Paul S. Voakes）在《90年代的报纸记者》（*The Newspaper Journalists of the'90s*）一书中这样写道。根据美国报业编辑协会2005年发布的数据，女性员工在新闻编辑室中仅占37%。少数族裔（黑人、西班牙裔、美籍亚裔以及印度籍美裔）所占比例更少，只有13.42%。然而在全国人口中，少数族裔占31.7%。

倘若新闻编辑室员工的性别、人种和民族分布情况与实际情况差别如此之大，又谈何在报道中准确、公正地反映众多不同群体的真实意见呢？沃克斯的研究显示，42%的报纸只雇用白人记者。这种现象使作家兼ABC新闻通讯员法拉伊•奇德亚（Farai Chideya）在一篇1999年发表于《媒介研究期刊》（*Media Studies Journal*）的文章里总结道："一间全是白人的新闻编辑室不是没有竞争力。但它是不完整的。"举例来说，没有西班牙裔记者的新闻编辑室根本无法深入，更不用提理解一个西班牙人社区。"在新闻业中实现人种多样性并不是为了面子上好看，"奇德亚写道，"这对于记者真正做到新闻所要求的准确公正是非常关键的。"

得克萨斯基督教大学的新闻学教授托米•托马森（Tommy Thomason）近来强烈要求得克萨斯报业联盟（Texas Press Association）的成员们增加本地新闻业的少数族裔，尤其是西班牙裔员工的数量。《艾达卢灯塔报》（*Idalou Beacon*）的帕姆•菲克斯（Pam Fikes）参加了那次研讨会，随即意识到她此前的文化视野一直都被挡住了。"我们小镇上西班牙裔人和白人数量各占一半，但我们发现，除了学校外，在做过的那么多特写报道里，没有一则是关于西班牙人或是天主教派的。"在《艾达卢灯塔报》开始报道本地西班牙裔新闻的第一周里，报纸零售量大幅下跌。报道多元化的新闻对提高收益没有好处，但这是正确的事情。

早在40年代，传奇的大学校长弗兰克•波特（Frank Porter）在北卡罗来纳教堂山给童子军们上了关于文化多元化的重要性的一课。他说："孩子们，永远记住这句话，当你坐下来弹奏国歌《星条旗永不落》时，不仅要用到白键，而且还要用到黑键。"

"'美国是个熔炉'是个虚构的神话。'沙拉碗'才是对其最好的描述。"威斯康星大学密尔沃基分校（University of Wisconsin-Milwaukee）城市研究项目的史蒂芬•拜尔斯（Stephen Byers）说，"当外国人移居到美国时，他们很难融入美国文化之中，相反的，他们会创造拥有自身独特文化的群体。这种现象近年来越发明显。"拜尔斯断言："在这个变幻不定的时代，社区归属感变得格外重要。"只有为社区新闻工作的我们重新评估对地区、利益以及民族的认识，才能最大化地为理论上扩大了的社区服务。

第13章

我们也是生意人

敬爱的中国读者：

我很清楚金钱在中国社会的地位，你可能会纳闷：那为什么关于经营的章节还会被安排在书的后半部分？不是要优先考虑赢利吗？啊哈！这其实不是失误。聪明的你可能已猜到我的暗含之意：你若能将社区报办得出色，赢利自然随之而来；相反，你若一门心思想着赚钱，成功只会对你敬而远之。

——作者

超级马里奥对抗现实

马里奥（Mario）一直希望拥有自己的报纸。8岁时，他为街区出版了一份新闻通讯，高中期间创办了杂志，他从来都克制不住这种冲动。

现在二字头的年纪已经过去了一半，在一家平平常常、发行量达14000份的连锁报团所属的晚报干了几年，马里奥觉得这份工作平淡而缺乏激情，没什么人关心新闻质量或者社区的成长。该做点自己真心想做的事了：去一家更好的报纸找份工作，或者出版自己的报纸。

创办一份自己的报纸的想法让他兴奋得失眠了几个晚上。有一天，他在镇上转悠时有了一个大发现。当地一位商人最近买下了一家生意欣欣向荣的印刷厂，这笔交易还包括一份已有些年头的《太阳报》的所有权。这份报纸由前任所有者的祖父创办，因为某些原因，这份报纸的命运随波逐流，最终成为印刷生意的一部分。

现在，这位新买主不想要这份没用的报纸。他给出了一个在马里奥听起来难以置信的低价。只用不到一辆新车的钱，他就可以拥有自己的报纸了。

但有个问题一直在他心头萦绕不去：昔日的《太阳报》能够在镇上获得成功，到了自己手里之后，还能恢复往日的光辉吗？马里奥不得不承认，虽为媒体人，但他对报纸运营这块仍是新手。回顾大学生活，他从未想过要选修广告、商务或媒体管理之类的课程。现在他有点后悔当初太没远见了。

大学时期校报的指导教师博尔顿（Bolton）教授就曾是一名拥有自己报纸的社区新闻老手，马里奥决定打电话给他。

“我也是在你这个年龄创办了自己的第一份报纸。”博尔顿告诉这个打来电话的年轻人。马里奥先是感觉飘飘然，接着就跌到了谷底，博尔顿警告说：“你必须明白，报纸首先是一门生意。其次，如果区域内没有足够的广告，无论你的报道多棒，报纸都无法经营下去。”

马里奥回答：“但《太阳报》有很多广告，博尔顿教授。”

“没错，但广告是从哪里来的？收入有多少？在报纸收入中占比是多少呢？”教授追问。

马里奥不得不承认他主要关注的一直是那些鲜美多汁的新闻版面，对广告一无所知，直觉告诉他这份报纸的大多数版面看起来都有广告。

博尔顿建议马里奥随机选取四期《太阳报》，然后按照以下方式登记广告：

广告商的名字、广告所占版面大小、广告反复出现的频率。马里奥需要汇总报纸的总栏数（即栏数乘以垂直厘米数），接着计算出广告的栏厘米，然后计算出广告所占的比例。

最终，博尔顿告诉马里奥把广告的栏英寸乘以每英寸广告价格，就能相对准确地计算出每期《太阳报》的广告收入，以此为基准，简单的数学运算就可以知道每月广告收入。

调查显示，平均每份《太阳报》里有24则广告，大小不等，最小的是一栏乘2.5厘米，最大的是三栏乘25厘米，平均面积是两栏乘10厘米。没有整版广告，没有大百货公司的广告，甚至没有镇上任何一家连锁杂货店的广告，广告的比例在20%以下。除此之外，马里奥发现，《太阳报》整版分类广告竟然都是免费刊登。

比较了广告收入和开销预算，马里奥惊呆了，他根本没有多余的收入雇用记者，养活这张报纸，他必须一个人包揽所有的事，此外，还需要再找一份正式的职业才能让它每个月不破产。

无须多言，要不要一头扎进《太阳报》，马里奥已经不需要博尔顿的意见了。难怪这么多年《太阳报》都卖不出去。博尔顿说："如果社区广告基础不太理想，除非你极为富有，否则你的报纸最多只能做成小打小闹的规模。"

虽然有点失望，但马里奥变得更加明智了，他决定继续守住原来的工作，与他的顾问保持联系，等待另一个机会的到来。他知道这只不过是个时间问题。

信不信由你

经验丰富的编辑兼出版人肯•里普利认为，社区报分别有四种不同职能：

1. 社区报首先是一门生意。它必须获取收入，不仅仅是为了生存，也是为了支持其他三个功能。

2. 社区报是一家创意商店。它的产品是新闻、摄影图片和设计。

3. 社区报是一家工厂。报纸是一个循环生产的过程，哪一个环节都不能掉链子。

4. 社区报是一家社区机构。报纸之所以被称为"第四权力"自有其理由所在。

置身事外？

当琼在后车间的剪贴板上瞥见电影广告的一刹那，她觉得血冲到了脑门。《号角报》的资深广告总监布兹，怎么会让这样的垃圾出现在版面上呢？这份宝石剧院的广告画面上是一个跪着的年轻裸女，双手被反绑在身后，等待着被那个站在身后色迷迷的男人施虐。

年轻的主管编辑怒视着庸俗的广告，她不知道该怎么办：布兹本周休假了，报纸马上要付印，看来她只能撤掉这个广告。很显然，好色之徒设计了这个广告用来挑逗，它超出了社区可接受的限度。

没有告诉任何人，琼从剪贴板上移走了这个占了四分之一版面的电影广告，取而代之的是报纸自我促销的广告，督促读者使用《号角报》的分类广告。然后她迅速把这一事件从她的头脑中抹掉，继续工作。

“你怎么能这么做？!”布兹几乎大叫。“做什么？”琼从电脑上抬起头看过来。她全神贯注于即将截稿的复杂的市区规划报道，她很少和经营部门的人打交道。

“你很清楚我在说什么!”布兹激动地说道。广告总监试图遏制住怒气，努力把音调降下来：“琼，我知道你是主编，但我度假回来却发现上周的宝石剧院的广告没有了！你事先问过我吗？有没有人先去提醒一下报社剧院的经理？没有！现在他把广告从我们这里撤掉投到竞争对手那里去了。没有人把我放在眼里吗？”

琼现在完全明白了：“对不起，但那部电影广告是彻头彻尾的软色情。”

“可能是。”布兹理直气壮地答道，“但这是我的范围。如果我走过来一身不吭地把报道从头版拿掉而不告诉你，你也会觉得同样被冒犯了。”

“嗯，你是对的。”她说，“这将点燃我的导火索。”

“不仅如此，”布兹接着说，“宝石剧院经理非常生气，到处和他所有的商业伙伴说这件事，这已经破坏了我和《号角报》在小镇整个广告界的信誉。”

“但这只是一个小广告。”琼不假思索地说。布兹不得不坐下来，深呼吸之后再告诉这个年轻编辑社区报纸广告业务方面的真实情况。

“你还没明白，是吗？琼，整份报纸都要依靠所有这些小广告商，从5厘米的社区小店的水果摊的广告到大型超市以及整版的广告，每一个都是我和店主们精心设计的，对我和报纸来说，都同样重要。”

“也许这听起来像是说教，不过你想想报社靠什么支付所有账单还有大家的工资？新手都有一个毛病，总认为你们是最重要的，看不起广告部的人，总觉得他们一天到晚在算计。我告诉你，没有我们，没有广告，你就没有钱来印刷你的报纸。新闻不赚钱，广告才赚钱。”布兹显然声嘶力竭了。

琼举起双手，笑道："好了，打住，布兹，我开始明白了。我承认我从来没有想过报纸经营方面的事。但是，嘿，订阅呢？卖报箱、超市报架不也在赚钱吗？人们买报纸是为了新闻而不是为了广告。"

布兹又一次深呼吸。"让我来普及一下社区新闻业务入门知识。"他说，"首先，你会惊讶有多少人是为了广告买报纸，而只瞥一眼新闻。其次，是的，发行量确实带来收入，但订阅和街头零售收入只占10%。换句话说，发行量最多只够支付发行员的工资，靠广告——一个一个的本地小广告——报纸才能运转。"

琼坐在那里思考了一分钟，然后说："从某种意义上说，我把那个广告撤掉应事先告知，你是对的，我真不应该那样做。但我认为《号角报》广告不可以这样描绘女性。这种广告令人发指，这是一份家庭报纸。我是认真的。"

"我现在想明白了，确实应该向宝石剧院的经理道歉和解释。你觉得我有必要去剧院和他谈谈吗？让他把广告重新设计得更符合这个社区的接受度，然后再刊登出来。你的意见呢？"琼说完了。

布兹呼出一口气："琼，那太好了。我承认，广告尺度有点过大，当小样交上来的时候，我正急急忙忙为了度假而准备结束工作，甚至没有看它一眼就签发了。"

随即布兹有了一个主意："琼，你、我与出版人应该抽时间坐下来，仔细谈谈，把和广告相关的社区标准定下来，如果我们有一个书面的指导方针，对报社和广告商都会有所裨益。"

关于底线

琼和马里奥的故事并非杜撰，这些每天都发生的事揭示了社区新闻中关键性的事实。

"我爱广告。"任教于华盛顿州立大学（Washington State University）的前编辑兼出版人鲍勃•福莱（Bob Hillard）如是说，"因为我从未见过报道能直接带来收入。"

无论具有多么利他的价值观，我们也无法逃避这一现实：报纸实际上是一门生意，自始至终都是一门生意。没有广告，报纸关门就意味着失败。当一份报纸成功时，虽然首先想到要归功于新闻报道，但也不能不说这是一种商业上的成功。广告——本地广告使新闻成为可能。想要在这一竞技场上生存，就要学会尊重和支持当地商家。

记住《南松镇领航员报》墙上的标语："广告成就自由的新闻界。"

如果报纸的财务状况如履薄冰，创造性和新闻热情不可能维持。成功的、发行量达4800份的《爱索新闻》（*Azle News*）的编辑兼出版人鲍勃•伯克勒（Bob Buckel）曾在20世纪80年代关闭了自己的一份报纸，他从中学到的教训是："当银行账户没有钱的时候，面对一个威胁要撤掉广告的广告商，你很难做到无所畏惧。"

一家社区报必须生意兴隆，才能成为对社区发展起积极有效作用的一份子。成功的甘尼特产业链的创始人弗兰克•E.甘尼特（Frank E. Gannett）1948年就已经意识到这一点："独立的社区报有两种动力，一是促进公共福利，二是赚钱。就好似医生，比挣钱更重要的是做对他人有好处的事。"

金钱是诚实的资本吗？

马克，一名专注的新闻系学生，困惑地听着社区新闻教授肯•拜尔利说："你必须足够富有才能足够诚实。"

两年之后，马克发现自己被冠以《军号报》——一家发行量达5000份、苦苦生存的周刊的新闻编辑的名头。不久之后他便发现自己对拜尔利教授的话产生了共鸣。布莱克百货公司经理的儿子因为涉嫌酒后驾车和藏匿大麻被捕,那位父亲走进报社办公室时，很担心报纸会在头版的醒目位置报道他儿子的坏消息。编辑平静地解释了《军号报》将如何处理这样的报道：它会被放在报纸的内页，和其他"警方提示"之类的小豆腐块放在一起，不会特别显眼。马克告诉这个抓狂的父亲，《军号报》有义务提供公正、完整、准确的报道。

这位父亲威胁说："如果你们报道我儿子的事，我就撤回广告——你懂的，我是你们最大的广告主。"

马克现在意识到老教授是多么正确。但砍掉这篇报道，保住广告会被千夫所指。他不得不礼貌而又坚定地抵抗住经理的威胁："如果我的儿子犯事了，我也必须报道，这都是一样的。"

布莱克百货公司经理没有善罢甘休。离开报社后，他兑现了他的威胁，将整版广告从当周的《军号报》上撤下。

《军号报》必须足够有钱，才能保住马克的诚实，报纸才能安然地渡过这场广告损失的风暴，这可能会影响到报社每个人的收入。但屈服于大广告主则意味着要牺牲报纸的公信力。

整整一个月过去了，事情还不见转机。广告主管在公开场合勇气十足地支持马克的决定，但私下他也会为事态的发展担心，每当他面如死灰地在办公室走来走去时，马克总是屏着一口气。

然而奇迹发生了，布莱克百货公司的广告又回来了，一起归来的还有总经理的附函。这位父亲写道，“我被两件事所震惊，许多人告诉我他们敬重《军号报》恪守职责的行为，而且‘我们想念你在《军号报》上的那些广告了’。”

马克暗中感恩他的老教授。

当广告多到不能再多

如果一位出版人的兴趣点只在于赚钱，他可以去出版广告纸，这类东西到处都是。上面除了广告什么都没有，要说有新闻的话，要么是通稿，要么就是那些只是用来填充版面的无聊内容。这类报纸存在的唯一理由就是赚钱。通常，你可以在超市货架上免费获取。这样的出版物称不上真正的报纸。

有的广告纸伪装成社区报。他们用高企的发行量声称“完全覆盖市场”，向当地广告商显示他们的市场渗透率。这本身没有什么伦理问题。然而为了省钱，他们或者从其他报纸扒拉一些新闻，或者直接用通稿，这会造成不明就里的读者的误会，让他们认为社区新闻没什么看头，给社区报行业造成极大伤害。无奈之下，许多高质量的社区报以毒攻毒，通过创建自己的全市场覆盖产品和这些伪装的广告纸竞争。

什么最重要

报纸顾问比尔•富勒（Bill Fuller）认为，对一份报纸来说，成功的重要因素是不可或缺性。他不仅仅指报纸作为社区消息的来源，也指报纸的业务。

一份社区报应该是读者必不可少的信息来源：商业信息、销售、售后服务、企业信息——换句话说，就是广告。富勒强调报纸必须对广告商有不可或缺性，通过及时的报道、大量的发行和高度市场渗透为他们搭建和读者沟通的平台。

《迪克森电讯报》的出版商威廉•肖这样理解广告商和报纸之间的互惠关系：“读者是报纸真正的主人……我们说服人们购买报纸，还不够，还要让他们产生主人翁意识。只有这样，我们与读者才是健康的合作关系。从出版人到读者，贯穿始终的使命就是《迪克森电讯报》必须是一份给读者提供全面服务的报纸，有了这份报纸，他们的生活才更有意义，更有价值，更有趣。”

《迪克森电讯报》六个广告销售全部是本地人，可见“我们就是所报道社区的一部分”，在《迪克森电讯报》上刊登广告的理由何在？广告价格手册上算了这样一笔账：“如果你邮寄7.6 × 12.5厘米的明信片给《迪克森电讯报》的11000

个订户，它将花掉你2090美元。但是，如果在《迪克森电讯报》上登一个整版广告，就可以达到同样多的读者，花费却只要737美元。毫无疑问，一个整版广告比明信片有更大的冲击力，而且还省钱！！！”

读者如何用广告

报纸广告自有其作用。人们阅读社区报获取本地信息，民意调查已经显示出报纸广告内容对读者的价值。

根据北卡罗来纳州记者协会在2000年进行的全州范围读者调查，2/3的成年人表示，相对于电视、广播和互联网来说，报纸上能够获取最佳的购物信息。

其他数据表明：3/4的受访者表示，报纸是获取特别折扣信息的最佳选择；60%的人表示报纸提供的广告最有帮助；60%的人表示他们在报纸上寻找超市商品广告；还有70%的人表示他们在购买全新或二手的车与房时依赖于报纸上的信息。

互惠关系

鲍勃和佩格•艾伦夫妇花了将近50年的时间来打造高质量的、家族所有的报纸《维克周刊》。多年以来，四个儿子也不时为报纸工作。艾伦夫妇1998年把报纸卖给了儿子。现在他们仍旧运营着这份报纸，同时也在反思如何做社区新闻这门生意。

广告已成为一门科学。仅仅告诉广告商高质量报纸的读者忠诚度很高还不够，广告商想要的是具体的人口统计数据，比如什么人在看报、年龄、性别、职业等等。他们想要的是硬邦邦的事实。

佩格解释，所有的社区报要和直邮还有那些准备收复社区失地的大日报竞争，他们通过出版免费报纸挤进原本为社区报所占据的领地。

“也许最大的竞争是那些大报上的插页广告，在美国，连锁商业觉得不需要在地方性报纸上投放广告，尽管社区报的当地家庭渗透率远超入侵的周边城市大报。”

为了和大报竞争，鲍勃要求广告销售必须和当地广告商走得很近，他们自己以身作则，多多消费当地产品。当草莓季来临，农场主主动来电说要做广告，鲍勃周末赶紧去了趟农场，拍了照片以备未来的特写所需，然后买了一堆草莓回家，这些草莓都分给了报社的员工。

鲍勃也许不需要那些草莓，但是在这个行业，如果我们不购买本地产品，怎么能指望当地广告商在当地报纸上投放广告呢？支撑社区运转的基础理念是互惠关系。只有相互扶持，才能走得更远，发展得更好。

出版人面临的难题

《号角报》面临一份新出的广告纸《商家》的竞争，后者没有新闻内容，只有分类和展示广告。《号角报》的编辑马克说：

> 通常，各类地方组织会联系《号角报》报道他们组织的活动，有时他们会投来一张照片，有时我们只做一小篇报道。但我们拿起这周的《商家》，一个社区组织居然做了一整版广告！他们可从没在《号角报》上登这样的广告！我的出版人想那些组织既然给《商家》那么多钱，他们就应该给《号角报》同样的广告。所以出版人不愿意再报道这些组织的活动，除非他们也买我们的广告版面。比如说，一家高尔夫球场给我们寄来一份新闻稿，说他们即将召开一场招聘会，他们在《商家》上做了整版的广告，却从没给我们投广告，出版人决定《号角报》不报道任何关于这场招聘会的事。

你认为《号角报》应该什么做？他们应该把在对手报纸上登广告的商家屏蔽掉吗？报纸是否有更崇高的使命？报纸是否有责任保证读者的知情权？如果你是马克，换位思考，你会怎么做？

论教会与国家的分离

虽然广告可以增加报社收入，但新闻内容（无论是特写版、体育版、生活版还是社论版）都必须独立于财务影响之外，不为广告商的游说所影响。内容一旦与金钱挂钩，则意味着新闻是可以被收买的。

对我们来说，仿佛神圣的教会与国家必须分离一样，广告与新闻内容之间绝对应该是井水不犯河水的关系。只有道德堪忧的出版人才会脱口暗示：“如果你做广告，我就给你写个报道。”

请记住，广告依赖影响力，以及他们所谓的“落在页面上的眼球”。而新闻所要确保的是公信力。一旦失去信誉，新闻就会贬值。如果你的读者开始认为，他们在报纸上所读到的内容只不过是由不同的企业所购买的广告，那么你的报纸已经面临严重的问题。

得克萨斯州发行量达到5000份的《山区朝阳》周刊在报社大厅中放置了两个牌子，上面用英文大写着“他们”和“我们”，分别画着两个指向相反的箭头，一个指向广告部，另一个则指向编辑室。

第14章

社交媒体和《桑福德先驱报》

敬爱的中国读者:

灾难降临，你的城镇位于风暴眼，这时郡、州和国家级媒体突然涌入，你该做何应对？在你的社区报道“工具箱”中，社交媒体应是至关重要的一枚棋子。接下来要讲述的便是一份社区报被推到风口浪尖上的故事。《桑福德先驱报》面对社区危机事件的报道应对举措被许多媒体观察员视为灾难报道的一把标尺。一份小报如何凭借自身的开创性行为获得举国认可？发行人比尔·霍纳三世将细说有关龙卷风报道的前前后后以及当自家后院发生“大事”时从中学到的经验。

——作者

背景：《桑福德先驱报》（以下简称《先驱报》）是位于北卡罗来纳州中部、发行量8000份的社区小型日报，周二至周日发行。2011年4月的一个周六下午，一场龙卷风给桑德福带来重创，造成2人死亡以及数百万美元损失的后果。比尔•霍纳三世——《先驱报》创始人W.E.老霍纳的孙子，《先驱报》1998年后的发行人——是这场风暴余波的见证者。

坏风暴，坏时机

对于《先驱报》而言，龙卷风可以说是在最不理想的时间到来——星期六午后3点左右。这个时间周日版大部分版面已经付印，记者和其他员工已经完成（或即将完成）周末工作，周二报纸也基本完成90%以上的工作量。

和竞争对手相比，我们在新闻生产周期方面处于劣势，风暴这个时候来临意味着报纸将失去一些潜在机会，因为此时距每周定版的截止时间实在太近了。报道前景一片灰暗。如果不进行大规模报道，报纸在读者心中的信誉和价值就会受到永久性伤害，难以弥补。因为其他媒体，如地方电视台以及一些对本社区虎视眈眈的大型日报会“趁机下手”，为那些受风暴影响的民众提供信息。

作为社区第一信源，服务读者和社区是社区报的天职，我们别无选择，在紧迫的时间内报道各种与龙卷风相关的高质量新闻，我们便可向社区成员（特别是非报纸订户）展示报纸非凡的价值，而这种机会只有在类似大事件来临时才会出现，而且稍纵即逝。

另一场风暴，另一份报纸

当龙卷风呼啸而来时，我记起十多年前的一场对话。当时因为报纸前任编辑离任，我正为报纸招聘一位新编辑。我曾通过电话和俄亥俄州的一位应聘者谈过几次，正准备让他前来就职。某个傍晚，我给他的办公室打了个电话。当电话接通时，我从他的声音中判断发生了些不好的事。

“我现在不能和您谈话，”他说，“我们的小镇刚受到龙卷风袭击。”

我明白了，报道新闻要紧，工作录取事宜暂且不谈。

但听起来有些疯狂的是，当时我却抑制不住地嫉妒，作为一名新闻人，我的想法是："报道这样的事情该多让人激动啊……"

作为一名记者，你会时刻想象自己会报道什么"重要新闻"，思考自己该如何报道。你会观察其他报纸对重大事件的报道，并对他们的成就赞叹不已。至少站在我的角度，我会想："如果大事件发生在这里，我们会怎么办？"

只有当风暴横扫小镇，才能明白灾难的真切之殇。但是毋庸讳言，对新闻人来说，当坏事就发生在自家后院时，这是必须抓住的机会。

家园被毁，个人损失

新闻的性质要求我们尽可能进行及时全面的报道。但我必须重申一点：这不仅是因为作为一份报纸"理应如此"，也不单是由于我们想成为人们了解这场风暴及其余波状况的"唯一"新闻来源，而是因为，当社区在灾难过后恢复重建时，我们希望让大家看清一个事实：社区报是人们了解这场风暴的最佳信息源。

在桑福德，我们还面临着一个颇为独特的额外挑战：两位员工家庭，包括编辑部副编辑在内，都是龙卷风的直接受害者。

我和妻子李•安（Lee Ann）庆幸能从周六这场风暴中幸存下来。但看到电视上报道圣安德鲁斯（Saint Andrews）地区受袭时，我们的情绪由宽慰变成恐慌。住在该地区附近的R.V.海特（R. V. Hight）是《先驱报》的终身荣誉员工，我立即往他家里打电话，希望能听到一些安好的消息，希望他告诉我电视上的报道是不真实的。但从他妻子那几近惊狂"你能听见我说话吗"的叫喊中我听出，事情可能很糟糕。"比尔，我们的房子没有了。"她绝望地尖叫。海特、夫人以及同在《先驱报》工作的女儿躲在大壁橱里才奇迹般地生存下来，但住宅几乎毁坏殆尽。

《先驱报》的工作人员在彼此不知情的情况下，好像有心灵感应似的，借助救援人员的帮助，穿过混乱的街巷交通不约而同来到圣安德鲁斯地区。为避开众多紧急救援人员造成的拥堵，我抄近道直接穿过海特邻居的后院到达他那废墟满地的家，见到彼此，我们眼含泪光拥抱在一起，就像全郡人周六所做的那样。

龙卷风带来的惊恐显而易见。圣安德鲁斯地区的许多房屋千疮百孔，不少屋顶坍塌。在海特家里，一块碎木头干净利落地穿过一辆家庭轿车的保险杠；一块原本不知用途的木板残片四分五裂，也被卷到墙壁上；房间的一面墙倒塌了，但房里的书橱未遭损坏，书架上的书都完好无损；他家附近的房子都遭到不同程度的毁坏，倒下或被连根拔起的树木随处可见。目之所及，玻璃碎片遍地都是。望着被毁坏的一切，我们说了同样的话："从没见过这样的状况。"

接着有消息传来，靠近桑福德市区的劳氏家装店（Lowe' s Home Improvement）

和拖拉机供应配件公司（Tractor Supply Co.）遭到摧毁，有不少人员受伤，可能还有人遇难。感觉一切都坏到那么不真实，让人难以相信。整个小镇陷入绝望。然而，当我们行动时，当我们拾起碎片时，当我们试着帮助、安慰他人时，我们开始思考：这场灾难究竟坏到什么程度？它的影响范围有多广？怎么报道？我们该如何将周围正在发生的事情告诉读者和社区居民？我们该如何拆分周日版版面并重新整合内容以便能及时报道这场风暴的最新消息？幸存者中有不少引人入胜的故事，我们该如何加入这些元素？按照惯例，周一不出报，但我们是否该多做些什么？

新闻人的本能

在这次风暴中，没有什么现成的指导手册能告诉我们下一步该如何行事。作为新闻人，只有本能在驱动。

编辑比利•里格特（Billy Liggett）的住所离市中心的办公室只有两条街道之隔，那是大家都想到的最安全的地方。他说："风暴来临时，我带上夫人、一岁的孩子以及小狗去了报社。"他在那儿遇到了其他员工，包括摄影师韦斯利•贝森（Wesley Beeson）、记者比利•鲍尔（Billy Ball）和詹妮弗•金泰尔（Jennifer Gentile）。

当通过警方广播听到"劳氏家装店受袭"的消息时，大家站着发抖了好一阵子，随后传来必乐透（Big Lots）和拖拉机供应配件公司被毁的消息，那些被摧毁的店铺就在距办公室东南方1.6千米之外。

里格特和一些员工挤进一辆轿车，快速驶向重灾区。他之后承认，为到达劳氏家装店，他们"做了一些你可能不想做的事……"，并"从邻居家里迂回前行，穿过一个露天片场和一块草地……"

据里格特描述，当他们到达劳氏家装店时，眼前一切已被完全摧毁，救援人员尚未到达。他拿起手持摄像机拍些原始素材，没有报道，也没进行采访。只是摇动镜头拍摄现场，猛烈的风声和来自远处的警报声不时传来。稍后他们将录像上传到报纸网站，录像中的画面引人关注，令人恐怖，让人难忘。这便是新闻，我们将从这里开始报道。

社交媒体第一，网站紧跟其后

当里格特将这些录像上传到Facebook时，我也在拍些关于圣安德鲁斯地区受灾情况的照片，并将它们上传到推特上。不久，里格特和其他人开始在官方推特上发布照片。一切都是依靠直觉行事，不过效果很好。《先驱报》已然成为使用社交媒体发布新闻的先行者。在本州，我们是第一份拥有Facebook网页的社区报。我们还不是推特的“大V”，但这身份不久后将会改变。在风暴来临的几个小时内，推特粉丝数量翻倍：从225涨到500多。

这还仅仅是开始。

出于服务公众的目的，我决定暂时取消《先驱报》付费墙。此时此刻金钱已然无关紧要，服务民众才是核心追求。风暴之前，网站平均每天访问量接近2000次。现在短短几日，访问量增长6倍，达到12000多次。我们也拍摄整理了一些视频，并将它们分享到YouTube上；员工自制的一些视频获得了5000次的点击量；有位居民在劳氏家装店停车场拍了段风暴来临时的视频，并上传到我们的YouTube网页上——这段视频最终获得了10万多次点击量。

报纸发行

但在这些数字开始上涨之前，我们仍得做好报纸的发行工作。尽管已利用社交媒体抢先报道，也发布了一些独家新闻，保证明天报纸的发行在技术和体能上仍是主要挑战。

我们先做了以下这些事儿：在清理海特家房屋废墟的间隙，我给在《达勒姆太阳先驱报》（*Durham Herald-Sun*，帕克斯顿公司旗下《先驱报》的姊妹报纸）的发行团队打了个电话，请他们推迟周六晚的截稿时间，好让我们有时间重新编排周日版面。

利用争取来的六小时，我们几乎重新编排了要闻部分。最终，周日早晨的报纸标题变成“毁灭之路”，下面是由摄影师韦斯利•贝森拍摄的照片，展现劳氏家装店被摧毁得支离破碎的场面——照片不仅占据这期《先驱报》几乎整个头版，也被美联社、《纽约时报》、《华盛顿邮报》、天气频道等多家媒体广泛采用，最后流传到世界各地，据说也被中国大报转载。

第一天的报道非常棒，报纸用了6版内页报道这场风暴，其中包括一篇关于劳氏家装店近100名顾客和雇员如何奇迹般存活下来的深度报道。整个报社忙活到凌晨1时，这已是风暴到来后的第十个钟头了，个个精疲力竭。

按惯例，周一休刊，因此下一期报纸得在周二才能跟大家见面。按理说，我们可以休息一天。但我突发奇想：在周一推出一期号外，怎样？这在《先驱报》历史上是创纪录的举动。

虽然记者们体力都已透支，但依靠新闻人使命感的激励，我们仍共同努力编辑出八个版的龙卷风特刊，我们将风暴来临时发生的故事与幸存者的神奇经历结合在一起，并附上这场风暴中令人难忘的照片。头版上有一张韦斯利•贝森拍的照片，一位妇女正捡起风暴过后的残碎物品，其下是标题："拾起碎片（意即重建）。"此外提供实用信息，比如幸存者救助站的地址、电话，等等。这期特刊被一业内行家评为"风暴报道的杰作"。若有读者前来《先驱报》办公室，我们免费提供这期特刊；若从超市报架上购买，则需75美分。

接下来的日子里，关于风暴的报道总是占据头版。我们采访了这场风暴中的遇难者家属，谨慎地报道这些可怕的死讯；采访马场主，他的马场被完全摧毁，至少12匹宝马在这场风暴中死去；采访需面对灾后重建的生意人；采访一位尽管业务全无也向员工承诺付薪的雇主；采访紧急救援人员、医疗人员；采访从全国各地赶来与我们共渡难关的志愿者；采访前来组织救援工作的联邦政府官员；采访这场风暴的见证者；采访死里逃生的幸存者。我们讲述他们的故事，分担他们的悲伤，为陷入绝望的小镇带来希望。

此外，我们在报纸上汇总灾民需要的物品和援助信息，回答一些常被问及的问题，比如如何处理风暴废墟、有关保险、食品、交通等事宜。我们不停地环顾四周问自己：今天要告诉社区（不仅仅是我们的读者）哪些最重要的事？我们向两个遭受重创的社区的所有居民免费提供报纸，还把报纸送到救济机构和志愿者聚集场所。

我们一直在坚持。一周后才有一条非龙卷风新闻登上头版，而一个月后与龙卷风相关的新闻才从头版消失。总之，我们在做分内的事，无论做什么，怎么做，总应该把社区利益置首。

随着时间推移，桑福德慢慢恢复过来。风暴过后的痕迹（如被折断的树木、几栋还未重建的房屋，以及一些仍未重新开张的店面）依旧存在。但是，也出现了众多新事物，其中就包括《先驱报》的同仁们内心对工作平添了几分新的敬畏。

众多人表达了对报社工作的感激和赞赏。读者来信不吝赞美，"感谢来自《先驱报》的伟大报道""向《先驱报》致敬"是对报纸的最高奖赏。

一位在社交媒体上拥有众多粉丝的媒体观察员曾在多个场合推介我们的头版报道。风暴过后，他在推特上用简短的几个字给予了我们最大的肯定："小报做大事！"

当我们重新审视风暴期间所做的工作时，编辑比利•里格特还记得我见到记者时经常说的话："比尔常说报道要与民众生活息息相关，风暴过后，许多人都知道我们做到了。这事也让我明白，报纸的存在仍有重要意义。当类似事件再次发生时，报纸依然是人们可以依赖的信息来源。"

完成了一次"大"事件报道后，即使风暴已远去成为一份回忆，即使阳光明媚，天空蔚蓝，我们仍要绷紧那根弦。是的，我们团结一致，并在几乎无法想象的疲劳状态下完成这场风暴的报道。不变的是，风暴过后三年，与社区“息息相关”的新闻依然是最大的新闻。我们一生可能只会经历一次类似风暴，然而，我们并不总是需要依赖一场龙卷风来成就英雄壮举。每天持续不断地告诉读者发生在他们身边的新闻，这是社区报对平凡生活、对英雄的另一种诠释。

第15章

优秀的社区报

敬爱的中国读者：

在美国走过无数州、郡，我见识到众多社区报办得普通、平庸，有些甚至可有可无。但可能在这些报纸附近的另一个城镇，我会发现一份极为出色的社区报——我不得不好奇：这份报纸为何出色？它是如何办成的？它的成功之道有何秘诀？于是我开始寻找答案，最终所得就写在本章中。在这一章，美国的一些极为成功的编辑和发行人分享了经营之道，介绍了人事和小媒体的管理经验。我希望这些能对你的工作有所帮助。

——作者

社会学家雷•奥登伯格（Ray Oldenburg）钟情于使用“第三空间”概念，它不是你居住的地方（第一空间），也不是你工作的地方（第二空间），而是指其他一些日常生活中的社交区域，即你平时闲逛、放松、养精蓄锐的地方，比如说：小餐馆、酒馆、酒吧、书店、保龄球馆或是隔壁的咖啡店。当第三空间成为一个包容的、热情的、不断提供养分的重要社区中心时，奥登伯格就称这个社区为“一个绝好的地方”，而不仅仅是“一个不错的地方”。

我认为奥登伯格不但会原谅我们“挪用”了他的重要概念，甚至还会为这种活学巧用鼓掌。我在研究和游历过程中，发现了很多不错的社区报，但我只选取了其中一些绝好的进行研究。

优秀社区报的特点

我经常思考以下这些问题：一份真正优秀的报纸应该有什么特性？他们是如何变得优秀的？他们又是如何保持这种高水准并不断进步？有什么样的事例能把优秀报纸与平庸报纸区分开来？以下共性可供分享：

● 给读者交流渠道：与读者的互动既要体现在版面上，又要开门欢迎读者来访。

● 拥有灵活性：灵活的思考、具有弹性的工作时间安排和良性的上下级关系。

● 高明的领导层：让记者及时了解你对报道的看法，源源不断的灵感得以让报纸不断进步，要像员工隐晦地传达严父表象下的慈爱。

● 尊重：不要像对待民工一样对待你的读者。

● 采用的语言和决策要以读者为本：不要把报纸当作产品，更不要把社区当作一个出卖产品的市场。

● 把报纸当作一种公共设施：明确地告诉员工报纸的核心价值所在，并严肃地传达报纸所负的使命。比如像《密西西比麦库布进取报》一样简单明了——一份最关注麦库布的报纸。

● 成为一个快乐的工作坊：从上到下都要共享一个工作信条，即“努力地工作，也要玩得尽兴”。

● 让员工成为报纸的利益攸关者：无论他们的想法多么疯狂，要保证所有的想法都能被听到并且受到尊重。

● 较高的职业满足感：分享报纸所得，不论是有形（奖金）的还是无形的（正面的精神鼓励），是内部的（投资于新设备）还是外部的（资助社区活动），并降低人员流动率。

这些在我看来都可以促进报纸内部形成健康的、有创意的、滋养人的文化氛围，当然你也可以自己列一份出来。曾任报纸编辑、现任"威斯康星大学—密尔沃基城市调研项目"（University of Wisconsin-Milwaukee Urban Studies Program）的讲师史蒂芬•拜尔提供了以下这些用于生活和工作的准则：

● 了解读者在关心什么。

● 坚持从不同角度持续报道重大社区问题直至解决。

● 选择立场。

● 为能做一张不同于城市大报的社区报而自豪。

● 本地化。

● 了解你所在的社区是如何沟通的。

● 不要忘记社区报的教育职能。

● 学会当一个领导。报社要在社区主动制造新闻事件，报纸不仅反映社区，更重要的是领导并引领社区变化。记住，报纸提供了一个团结公众的平台。

● 把你的读者摆在首位。有了读者，广告就会送上门来。

● 不改变就有消失的危险。

现任康涅狄格州《诺维奇公告报》[*Norwich (C.T.) Bulletin*]的执行编辑吉姆•凯弗林创立了一句响彻新闻编辑室的口号："当地人才是我们的特权阶级"。

好想法源自好报纸

一份社区报要真正繁荣下去，决不能仅靠把报道刊登出来，除社区报外，没有其他媒介可以去报道这些真实的、持续的、综合的东西，包括当地发生的新闻、比赛、特色活动、生活方式、言论思潮以及视角。但是，如何区分一份真正优秀的社区报和一份还不错的社区报呢？下面是一些优秀社区报与社区共生共荣的例子。

怀特威尔（Whiteville）的奇迹

2001年7月4日[①]的早晨，大概有1500人在北卡罗来纳州怀特威尔的主街上振

①每年7月4日为美国国庆日。

Thursday, July 5, 2001

50 cents

The News Reporter

Record-setting Fourth in Whiteville

Team members and supporters surround the copy of the Declaration of Independence, believed to be the world's largest, written in less than three minutes.

Staff photos by Bill White

From left, above, team members get ready to write a gigantic copy of the Declaration. The writing is fast and furious. Teams hurry to the sidewalk to show they are finished. Below, gunfire signals the start and participants work on the document.

Re-creating Declaration unites residents

By LEE HINNANT and LES HIGH

Roughly 1,500 people put their "John Hancocks" or eyes on what is believed to be the longest, largest copy of the Declaration of Independence on July 4 in Whiteville.

Scores of volunteers scurried in the predawn hours of Independence Day to unfurl a 1.25-mile-long roll of paper along Madison Street from the courthouse to downtown. Shortly after 9 a.m., re-enactors in period dress fired antique weapons, signaling men, women and children, who furiously scribbled a copy of the document in two minutes, 29 seconds.

About 80 teams worked on lines from the Declaration or on reproducing the names of the document's 56 signers. The teams then cut the paper into 127-foot sections, assembled pieces in a downtown parking lot and added personal touches with paint and brushes.

"We all want to be a part of this great event, this historical event," said Jessie Davidson, whose team from the Seventh Day Adventist church had 10 members ranging in ages from 3 to 64.

"I actually heard about this and came up," said Brandon Clark of Charleston, S.C., who painted stars and flags on the top of the document. Marty Bell came from High Point to work on one line of the Declaration, the one that speaks of separation from Great Britain. "I had to go to the dictionary to look up 'consanguinity,'" said her teammate Emily Owens.

Many area businesses and service organizations sponsored teams, while other teams were composed of extended family or groups of friends. Participants came from as far as Indiana, Ohio, Pennsylvania, California, and Delaware and from N.C. towns that included Currie, Richlands, Wadesboro, Supply and Lumberton.

Organizer Mark Gilchrist

Elaborate, detailed preparation by sponsors paid off as the event stuck to a strict time schedule and wrapped up at noon, just as participants and spectators finished eating free ice cream sandwiches.

"This is what the Fourth is all about," said Whiteville Mayor Anne Jones. "It shows that patriotism is still alive and well in America ... It's so exciting to see all these people who have come out."

Conner Brooks, 5, of Charlotte, sat on the front steps of his grandmother's Madison Street home, watching the proceedings.

"He got up at 6 o'clock to the see the truck with the paper come by while he was still in his pajamas," said grandmother Deloris Harrison. "He just thinks this is the greatest thing."

The event took on special meaning for Thomas V. Barden, 80, of Whiteville. His grandmother was a Hooper and a distant relative of Declaration signer William Hooper of

See Declaration, page 2-A

County deaths

- Vanlece Mott, Bolton
- Willie McCoy, Whiteville
- Ralph Prince, Tabor City
- Joseph G. White Jr., Whiteville

Sports

Jerrod Mustaf has teamed with service organizations to bring the Street Basketball Association (SBA) to Whiteville High School on Friday, July 6.

The public is invited, beginning with a pre-game presentation at 6 p.m. Mustaf, a native of Columbus County, played with the N.Y. Knicks and is a standout in the European league.

SBA play here benefits the Governor's One-On-One program and the county YMCA. City and county parks and recreation departments are also sponsors. Admission is $5.

Briefly

"First Saturday," an arts and crafts show and sale, will be held in Tabor City July 7 from 10 a.m. until 5 p.m. in the air-conditioned former Heilig Myers store off Fifth Street. Barbecue will be sold on site, beach music will be played outside, and a classic car show will be held. Artists and craftsmen are invited to participate at no charge. Call Steve Lynch, (910) 653-4141. Town officials plan to make this a monthly event.

臂高呼,创造了一次被认为是持续时间最长、也是最大型的《独立宣言》复制运动。大家一齐动手花了2分29秒，在一张当地报社提供的1.25米新闻用纸上写下《独立宣言》，并将其铺在了小镇的中心。

这次“独立宣言”复制活动是一名记者头脑风暴的产物。

“我一定是疯了。”马克•基尔克瑞斯特（Mark Gilchrist）在活动后这么写道，许多人都认为这次国庆日是有史以来最棒的一次。“任何一个有理智的人都说，不可能组织1500个人排队，并在几分钟之内手抄出一份1500字的文献”。

但他们真的做到了。结果是，活动之后，《怀特威尔新闻记者报》（*Whiteville News Reporter*）头版半个版面都被这张欢呼的人们在一座停车场内举着巨型《独立宣言》的照片占据。《怀特威尔新闻记者报》是一份销量在10200份的一周两刊的报纸。

基尔克瑞斯特回忆：“当我在五月末第一次走进发行人吉姆的办公室并提出这个想法时，我确实以为他们会把我开除（我还隐隐希望他们这么做），但他们却充满激情地按我的想法去实施了。”

在同一期的社论中，报纸为基尔克瑞斯特竖起了大拇指：“向历经无数个不眠之夜、花了大把时间来组织独立日庆典的马克•基尔克瑞斯特致敬，同时也向怀特威尔致敬！这次里程碑式的事件表明，当人们看清一个事件背后更深远的意义时，齐心协力之下能够成就多大的奇迹。”

优秀的新闻

赶在圣诞前出版了一期厚厚的广告分量很足的报纸，疲惫的员工想尽早回家，可报纸还要持续出版，是否有一种简单有趣并且可以赚钱的方法解决这个问题呢？不妨看看下面这个例子。

田纳西州《阿力多社区新闻报》[*Aledo (T.N.) Community News*]的出版人兼编辑兰迪•凯克（Randy Keck）说，他收购这份报纸之后，花了将近一年的时间在想怎么解决这个问题。“这主要是由读者需求决定的，我知道一些报纸甚至不出版年终刊，但我做不到。我经常开玩笑说，我不发行报纸的那个周一定是因为有不明飞行物降落到市政厅里。”

似乎人们的生活中从不缺乏坏新闻，如果把一年以来社区里的好新闻汇集成册会是个好主意。“那些关于市政委员会的报道、新闻、观点都可以先放在一边。现在，所有的一切都只专注于那些生活在当地的人们。这个时候，我们发现周围确实发生着很多事情。”

随着每一年年末的到来，发布“年度好新闻特辑”的想法逐渐成型。曾经被报道的内容包括：当地的长期志愿者被小镇授予荣誉；在韩国服役的夫妻回国探望一岁多的双胞胎儿子；当地男孩斯科特（Scout）得到了童子军鹰徽；当地老师获得国家顶级荣誉；一个蹒跚学步的小孩使用一个高科技助听器；两个牧师坠入爱河，结婚后各自作为传教士服务于当地两个不同的教派。

凯克告诉他的读者："虽然从下周开始我们又要回归到'真实世界'这种说法听上去很诱人，但你们本周读到的这些新闻和那些'坏消息'同样真实。我们希望随着时间流逝，人们能逐渐意识到这些报道的价值。"

他们一般从9月开始策划《年度好新闻特辑》。"这个想法要在一个较早的广告截止日期内开始着手，并在年末之后尽快发布。"他说，"这样也能让我多给员工放几天假。"

这才是真正的好消息。

当地报道指南

每个地方都是不同的，每份报纸也各有特色。那些新记者、摄影师、编辑究竟如何了解那些复杂的细节，使他们在报道和写作的时候好像知道所有重要的事情一样？

编撰一本当地报道指南就是答案之一，北卡罗来纳大学教堂山分校副教授弗兰克•斐说："虽然这样会花很多时间，但的确很值得。"

除了拼写习惯、标点符号、当地缩写用语之外，指南还要为保持一致性设立一些规范，诸如用于政治报道的当地术语、社会与法律执行机构等，比如教堂山警长把他的名字拼写为"Gregg"，在词尾用了两个g，但是在当地的电话簿中被拼错，以后报道应以"Gregg"为准。

让社区报融入社区

北卡罗来纳州《阿什伯勒消息论坛》每年都会组织一个当地专栏作家小组，包括一名商学教授、一个退休的郡级选举董事，还有一个当地政府官员。社区报还有一个由当地商界领袖轮流主持的经济类专栏。前任编辑及专栏作家鲍勃•威廉姆斯说这个一周两次由读者主持的专栏可以帮助他的员工更好地了解读者的想法。

帮助年轻人成为安全驾驶员

优秀的社区记者在各自服务的小镇上都是很显眼的人物。伊利诺伊州的《杰纳西奥共和周报》[*Geneseo (I.L.) Republic*]的前任出版编辑汤姆•特里（Tom Terry）全身心地投入到当地镇中学关于驾驶教育的项目当中。

特里回忆："我拿出讣告表格，然后发给那些十五六岁的青少年，我让他们把空格填出来，比如教育、成就、后代，等等。'这张表上没有太多东西可填，对吗？当然，因为你还没开始真正的人生。'说完之后，他们很安静，房间里甚至可以听到针落地的声音，接着我使出了杀手锏：'我希望你们能想象，当由于你们或开快车，或开车发短信，或酗酒，或吸毒而出车祸去世时，父母脸上的表情。当他们把你们用作讣告最好的照片递给我时，他们好像一下子苍老了20岁。'听到我这样说，一些女孩开始掉眼泪。"

"学校的老师一般都是我相处多年的人，有些甚至是曾经教过我开车的人。我们之后会花几分钟，当着学生的面谈一谈我们都认识的那些小孩以及他们去世时候的情景：那些在十字路口企图超车的人；那个在距离学校两个街区的地方错过转弯路口，结果撞在大树上的人；那个在丁字路口开车太快，由于没有系安全带而发生意外的学生；还有在上坡时把车开到路中间而发生车祸致死的双胞胎，等等。说实话，这样做显得冷酷无情，但如果可以救人一命……"特里的声音慢慢弱去。

你能听到吗？

你可能会遇到一些老年读者，眼力不济，但他们仍然是你的读者，不是吗？怎么才能让他们得到渴望的新闻？明尼苏达州发行量在3000份的周报《蒙蒂塞洛时代》[*Monticello (M.N.) Times*]的出版人唐纳德•Q.史密斯（Donald Q. Smith）和他的员工参加了当地公民协会的一个公共服务项目，活动的名字叫"磁带里的《时代》"。志愿者朗读《蒙蒂塞洛时代》的内容并录音，然后送给那些有视觉障碍的读者。

有旧，有新

每份报纸都需要一些能让读者惊呼"嘿，妈呀，你看看这个"的内容。密苏里州发行量达到5000份的独立日报《黎巴嫩每日纪实报》[*Lebanon*（*Mo.*）*Daily*

Record]的经典页面就是这样的。阅读时你无法将视线从报纸上移开：夫妻庆祝结婚25周年、50周年的照片。自从20世纪50年代订婚到现在，他们被岁月改变了什么，又有什么是持久不变的坚守。

那些年代久远的家庭快照很能吸引读者兴趣。得克萨斯州的《阿瑟港新闻》（*Port Arthur News*）发行量在17200份，“历史上的一天”是报纸长期以来极受欢迎的特写专栏，每天在第二版上半部刊登一张由读者提供的老照片。根据规定，提供者要写一张关于照片故事的简介，并标注照片里出现的人名、电话号码，然后装在一个贴上邮票写好收信人回信地址的信封中，方便被报纸采用后寄回。

最好的实用工具包

按字母排序，以下八名优秀的社区报领导者回答了作者提出的几个问题。他们是：

鲍勃•布克尔（Bob Buckel），得克萨斯州《埃诺新闻》[*Azle (T.X.) News*]的出版人。《埃诺新闻》是一份非报团拥有的周报，发行量为4880份。

林达•吉尔摩（Linda Gilmore），堪萨斯州《章克申城每日联合报》[*Junction City (K.S.)*]的前任编辑，报纸发行量为5500份。

安德鲁•赫莉，密苏里州《玛莎斯维尔记录报》[*Marthasiville (M.O.) Record*]的编辑，报纸是一份发行量为2500份的周报。

约翰•格雷•蒙哥马利（John Grey Montgomery），堪萨斯州《章克申城每日联合报》的现任主编。

唐•Q. 史密斯，明尼苏达州《蒙蒂塞洛时代》（发行量为3000份的非报团拥有的周报）的出版人。

帕特希•斯贝茨（Patsy Speights），密西西比州《伦培提斯前灯报》[*Prentiss (M.S.)Headlight*，发行量为2803份的周报]的现任主编蒂姆•L.沃特纳（Tim L. Waltner），南达科他州《弗里曼通讯报》[*Freeman (S.D.)Courier*，发行量为2000份的非报团拥有的周报]的出版人。

大卫•沃伦诺夫，北卡罗来纳州《南松镇领航员报》（发行量为15000份的非报团拥有的周报）的主编。

问：一份相对较好的社区报与一份真正好的社区报的区别在哪里？

沃特纳: 真正好的社区报无论是新闻还是摄影，都会超出那些流于表面的内容。关注本社区的多样性，对社论版负责，希望从各个角度激发社区思考如何能取得更好的发展。

史密斯："人的目标应该超越他的能力。"也就是说，一份好的报纸应该追求在新闻、排版、文笔、社论、专栏以及特色板块上做得更好，不能仅仅满足于现状。

沃伦诺夫：优秀的报纸都很乐于冒险，无论是在报纸之外的新产品还是报纸本身的内容创新，他们都愿意花时间精力进行新的尝试。这会激发读者阅读和参与的主动性，让报纸更具活力和吸引力。我始终坚信优秀社区报的使命应该是服务社区。以《南派恩斯领航员报》为例，我们的工作重心按照重要性排序是这样的：1. 社区和读者；2. 广告商；3. 所有人。很不幸的是，最近大部分的报纸都被一些大公司收购，他们对报纸重心的优先顺序与我们的正好相反：所有人，所有人，还是所有人。

蒙哥马利：创造力。

布克尔：好的社区报可以涵盖所有的热点议题，做得很好看。伟大的社区报日复一日把利润的很大部分再投资于报纸，我认为这是出版人对读者承诺的体现。你是持续投资让报纸日益变得更好，还是把钱装进私人口袋做一份平庸的报纸，过自己悠闲的生活？这就是本质的区别。

赫莉：走进社区！与当地居民和社区负责人称兄道弟，拉近关系。把当地报道做到极致，比如校园报道、有关本地话题的社论版、丰富的体育版以及充分考虑读者阅读习惯的设计。通稿类报道就留给城市大报吧。当然还要注意这个关键词：图片，图片，更多的图片。每个人都喜欢拿起一份印满了真正有趣图片的报纸。所以《玛莎斯维尔记录报》每个月推出三个整版的图片集。

吉尔摩：无论哪种规模的优秀报纸，都要挖掘令人惊奇的故事并努力把这些故事讲好。一份优秀的报纸会一直努力尽可能完整地展现所在社区的情况，勇于承认报道的失误并采取措施去避免再犯，尊重读者并将与读者的关系视为社区交流的重要部分。

问：为社区报工作的记者与那些大报的记者有什么区别呢？

沃特纳：小规模社区让较小的报纸有先天优势，社区报新闻往往给人更亲密的感觉。在小型社区中，这些故事普遍能以更私人的形式引起读者共鸣。周刊有更充裕的时间挖掘事件背景和新视角，挖独家报道大报更有优势，但周报有时间给读者提供更多的事件相关信息，帮助他们更好地理解新闻的意义。

斯贝茨：你每天都能够与你的读者接触，银行、百货商场、服装店、教堂和俱乐部，读者无所不在。

史密斯：与读者的亲密接触，让你得到更快的信息反馈，对社区和居民的关心程度甚至超过社区领袖和读者对报纸的关心。

布克尔：我们每天都应该用眼睛观察周围的人。我们和他们生活在一起，他们就像家人一样毫无保留地爱着我们。同样的，我们不能仅仅把他们当作一则故事或一条新闻，他们更是一群鲜活的人。在我刚开始工作的时候我就意识到了这个道理。一次我在安德鲁斯拍摄一组醉酒驾车事故的照片作为头版，我最终选取了“一个年轻人躺在丢满破碎的啤酒瓶的血泊中，一条毯子下露出一双腿”的照片。这张图让人震撼，照片发表后，那个男孩的母亲来到报社坐在我的对面泪流满面，那个煎熬的15分钟让我愧疚地意识到，把这样的图片登出来无异于在这个母亲伤口上撒盐，这个男孩不仅仅是毯子下露出的那双腿，他是一个优秀的学生，一个足球运动员，一个秋天就即将开始大学生活的孩子，还是一个好儿子。你必须把这部分故事也展现给读者。

蒙哥马利：关联性。你可以在社区报里看到你生活的世界。有时你可能不喜欢，但是它确实就是你所在的世界。

赫莉：个人化。我们就生活在社区中，我们与社区的未来有着密切关联，我们与那些报道中描述的人物一起行走在同样的街区里，并在超市与他们一起排队，在牙医的等待室里并肩而坐。正因如此，我们才知道要如何去理解这些故事；当报道有偏颇时，我们才能及时发现并改正。这些生活在社区里的人们其实就是我们的试金石。

吉尔摩：社区报的记者认为读者不仅仅是读者调查报告里的那些数字。读者是那些走近你并和你交谈的人，并且你也乐意他们这么做，即使有时对某些观点存在争执。社区记者认为那些也许看上去很不起眼的故事对某些人来说是很重要的。你不能迎合每一个人，但是你可以努力把尽可能多的社区事件写进报纸里。

问：你如何塑造社区报中的人物？

赫莉：我们不仅是社区的一个组成部分，更是其中一个很重要的部分。在这个框架之内，我们的角色就是向读者提供那些主流都市报不能提供的东西，比如：本地新闻、本地社评以及本地专栏作家的文章。我们努力向读者提供那些关乎“他们生活的地方”并且有必要了解的事件。我们很看重“无以复加的本地化”。

斯贝茨：我们是居民很重要的信息获取源。镇上没有电视，只有一个直播几个小时流行音乐的电台。

史密斯：我们是新闻的报道者、地方历史的记录者以及反映公共意见的平台。

沃特纳：通过提供新闻报道、广告服务和可以针对社区事件进行讨论的公共论坛，《弗里曼通讯报》给不同的组织提供了“每周对话”的机会。作为社区的一个机构我们要超越那些天生的隔离因素，比如年龄、性别、种族、地位、宗教的差异把社区整合到一起，没有什么比社区报更能提供这样的联结。

吉尔摩：报纸努力展示出社区的复杂性和完整性。有时候我们确实比别人做得好，如努力报道好消息和坏消息；努力帮助社区理解我们如何决定哪些是他们生活中真正需要知道的新闻；通过当地的专栏作家，报道不同的组织，努力让不同的人群都能发声，如那些最近才组建起来支持男女同性恋、变性人群以及他们的朋友和家人的组织。

沃伦诺夫：我们对社区的关心并不是偶然的。社区由那些热心公益事业的群体慢慢扶植发展而来，每周三大版面报道他们在公益事业领域的探索。我们不满足于坐在办公室里冷眼看社区。这是我们的家，我们住在这里，如果幸运的话，也将在这里告别人世。比起出生的时候，我们下决心要让这个我们幸福地称之为家的地方在我们离开时变得更好。这些使社区变得更美好的自愿活动，无论是否有报社记者的参与，都值得被报道。

布克尔：我们是社区公告平台，是唯一一个严谨的沟通渠道，也是使那些我们希望实现的好事发生的催化剂。我觉得，很大程度上我们是把整个社区结合得更紧密的胶水。

问：你所在社区面临的三大挑战是什么？

斯贝茨：经济，无情的连锁超市——沃尔玛已经抢占了整个镇；种族主义的遗留；年轻人的搬离。

蒙哥马利：1. 很少有年轻人愿意留在社区；2. 经济不景气；3. 我们并没有一个连续的计划来推动社区发展。

布克尔：经济增长，领导层，在郊区缓慢发展的情况下保持社区特色。

赫莉：增长——沃伦郡的发展速度很快，我们要尽力跟上其发展速度；犯罪——贩毒窝点真的是一个问题，特别是在我们这样的乡村；选民热情低下——低投票率，特别是在市级选举中，一个市甚至推选不出一个市长候选人。

沃伦诺夫：1. 制订合理的增长计划；2. 创建和谐社区；3. 保持地区特色。

吉尔摩：经济、住房、对未来的规划。

沃特纳：人口减少、零售业数量下降、缺乏发展眼光。

史密斯：1. 合适的增长率；2. 非本地拥有的商业不关心社区发展，对家族店造成毁灭性打击；3. 找到能替代老一辈的年轻一代领导者。

问：你怎么形容报纸和所在社区的关系？

赫莉：非常亲密并且个人化。我们报道的地区（整个密苏里州沃伦郡）包括3个城市，是这个州增长速度最快的六个地区之一。即使如此，我们努力让所有的报道都能被当地人100%接受。因为我们尽可能地独立于事物之外，地方政府和居民了解我们并确信能依靠我们。

沃伦诺夫：这是一个互相参与的过程。引以为豪的是，社区报是个开放的场所，也就是说“专栏对读者是切实可用的，并且员工会倾听读者的建议和意见”。观点鲜明的社论使我们成为社区不可或缺的角色。

吉尔摩：我认为是充满了互动。读者可以来报社和记者交谈；我们邀请公众参与每天出版结束之后召开的新闻选题会；读者经常给报纸打电话咨询各种信息，他们希望报纸成为他们的信息源。

沃特纳：《弗里曼通讯报》在一个有1300人的小镇里发行将近2000份报纸，这么高的入户率，到处都有社区报的身影。居民习惯了有社区报陪伴的生活，觉得一切都是天经地义的。

布克尔：相当好。过去的两年里我们做了很多改变。不幸的是，我觉得这使很多读者不太高兴，当然其他人还是逐渐习惯了《章克申城每日联合报》直白坦率的风格。

布克尔：就像大部分报纸与报道地的关系一样，爱恨交织。我们常常惹恼人们，因为我们发表的东西往往是他们不希望我们报道的。比如：当醉驾被捕时他们的真实姓名被曝光。很像一家人，我们会小题大做，我们会吵架，但是我们深爱着彼此和生活的社区。很多年前，当一名地方议员去世，我写了一篇社评介绍她是一个如何优秀的女人，但有时又有些喜怒无常。就在最后一次我见她的时候，她还严厉地批评过我，当时我们谈了很多关于各自家庭的话题，之后离开时我们还互相拥抱。文章见报之后的那个周末，在主街上，我遇到另一位地方议员，他紧绷着下巴，眼里泛着泪光看着我，然后紧紧抓住我的手臂（当时我还以为他疯了），颤抖着对我说：“我真的爱我们的社区报。”那样的时刻让人感觉所有的付出都是值得的。

问：你的报纸面临的三大挑战是什么？

布克尔：1. 继续卖广告，大型零售商已占据社区，并且威胁到那些我们可以走进门去讨价还价的家庭经营小店。我们必须学会适应这些大企业的游戏规则。2. 保证报纸能够获利，保证我们负担得起这份报纸的发行成本。3. 当社区不断扩张报纸要增加发行量。对新住户，可能存在这样的情况：他们根本不知道社区报的存在；或是他们之前住的地方没有这样的社区报，因此他们还不会珍惜也没有意识到这份报纸的意义；或者是他们压根就没有读报习惯。这是美国“报纸参与教育”项目的重要性所在。我们要努力培养新的读者，并且使年轻人养成读报的习惯。如果他们没有明确意识到自己拥有怎样的财富，那么当我们消失时他们也不会珍惜。我们必须成为他们生活的一部分。

斯贝茨：订阅量下降以及想办法吸引年轻读者，并吸引那些想在报社工作的年轻人。找到那些优质的大学毕业生，培训他们并使其留下来。

蒙哥马利：1. 过去一年来发行量的减少。2. 在线读者数量的上升。我们需要对在线读者收费，希望这样能反过来解决纸质版发行量减少的问题，但前提是我们要好好修改电子版。3. 零售商业的衰退。长期来看这会减少社区报的广告收入。

赫莉：1. 人手不够——雇员减少，社区扩展，如何解决这个矛盾。2. 收入减少——靠广告赚钱越来越难，特别对免费报纸困难更大，我们的竞争对手是报团拥有的郊区报纸，他们能给广告商一些我们给不了的东西，比如极低的价格等。3. 地理位置——我们处在郡的偏南部，是三个社区中最乡村化的。还有一座山像天然屏障挡在我们和其他郡之间，曲折的盘山公路使我们与最近的郡还相距21英里之遥。

沃伦诺夫：1. 继续超越社区对我们的期望。2. 合理增长并保持报纸特色。3. 雇用有能力的人来担任领导，三个最高领导职位现任者都已超过60岁了。

吉尔摩：员工，员工，员工。要知道频繁换员工很难保持报纸的质量。

沃特纳：人口减少——导致读者数量降低。零售业数量的减少——导致报纸收益的减少。在新技术背景下如何保持现状。

史密斯：1. 非本地拥有的商业和连锁经营业务的发展使得当地广告萎缩。2. 看看那些外来竞争者售卖广告的水平如何，特别是那些都市报。3. 在一个还在成长的社区中，随着互联网的普及，人们对当地事物的兴趣逐渐减少，因此人们不买也不读报纸。

问：如何创造或维持一个“愉快的工作坊”？对于实现一个“具有创造力、愉快、高产的”新闻编辑室有些什么建议？

史密斯：持续强调团队合作的重要性。

沃伦诺夫：报纸应该是有趣的。实际上，做“有趣的报纸”是我们的核心价值之一。我想要听到走廊里有更多的笑声，各个办公室之间有来回反复的玩笑话。我们希望通过内部的装饰来培养出这种氛围。我们弄了很多自然的灯光，像流动的河流一样打在大楼里的墙壁上。我们还使办公室成为开放的区域，如此一来大家可以在任何地方看到各自每日的工作。我们努力向员工灌输每个人都是相互依赖的观点。在员工来上班的第一天我就说，你们要么是在编辑室为了报道而工作，要么是在广告或者发行部为赚钱而工作。对报社而言，我们必须把两者都做好，别无选择。

赫莉：这要从员工的雇佣过程开始算起。我们有一个“愉快的工作坊”，并且我真心觉得是因为我们很好地融合了每个人的性格特点。这永远不是简单的工作，特别是对于像我们这样的小办公室而言，正规员工只有四个，我们享受彼此的陪伴，并且为一个共同的目标努力着——让《玛莎斯维尔记录报》成为一份最优秀的报纸。我们之间的关系远远不止合作伙伴那么简单，我们之间更像是朋友。

斯贝茨：多和大家一起交流。要知道什么时候该玩，什么时候该工作。

吉尔摩：我们常常一起吃午饭。报纸主编邀请新员工在圣诞节之后到他家去吃一顿“迟到的假期大餐”，以此感谢大家在困难条件下的坚持：一名编辑离开了，其他员工也跟着离开了，甚至有段时间新员工人数下降到6个。我们缺少那些精壮而有耐力的员工。体育记者的桌上总放着一碟饼干，一群人只要有空就一起谈笑。

沃特纳：营造一个放松舒服的氛围；关注于美好和愉悦的工作环境；商量而不是命令，多说“谢谢”；敢于承认你犯的错；处事灵活，特别是在涉及有关家庭的事情上；真正关心员工的生活，一起出去玩；允许员工自己做决定；向你的员工寻求帮助；公开分享有关报社的情况；培养记者的主人翁意识。

问：如何在报纸中培养、维持一种“社区文化”？

布克尔：我相信要找到那些不仅有工作技能，而且能真正融入报社文化的人。我们的文化虽然是闲适的，但工作是高效的。当新人加入时，他们都还没有意识到进了一个高速运转的工作环境中。我们平时玩得开心，但一旦工作起来，干劲十足。新员工很容易找到在报社受人尊敬并真正融入进去的方法，那就是主动分担一部分工作量。所有这些无法要求每个人都做到，当然我也与其他人一样努力工作。这些年来，我很庆幸手下总有受到前辈激励而勤奋进取的员工。在报社的17年里，从没有人见过我发脾气，我也没有斥责或大声吼过任何一个员工。我很尊重他们，所以我可以要求他们也这样对待我、对待其他人。如果你问他们，我相信员工可以告诉你，成为这个团队中的一员，和这些优秀的人一起工作，并且参与创造一份值得他们骄傲的报纸是一件很让人骄傲的事。

斯贝茨：融入当地。去教堂做礼拜，成为当地商会的一员，出席葬礼并且在小镇购物。

赫莉：投入社区事务。作为一份社区报，我们努力成为积极参与社区事务的一分子。我们每年资助全郡集市上的老年日活动并承担活动的印刷资料费用；今年，我们赞助了皇后集市的一项比赛，并参与了家畜的拍卖，然后拍得的钱全捐给当地慈善机构；在过去两年里我们参与当地的花车游行。我们尽可能多地参与社区活动，并且坚持开放的工作原则——欢迎每个人到报社访问，并告诉我们他们对报纸的看法。

问：对于怎样启发整个编辑室，你有什么建议？

布克尔：带员工们参加一些高质量的专业会议，他们需要了解所做之事的重要性，并且意识到他们不是一个人在奋斗。编辑室里的那些“老人”必须设立一个标准，激励新人向它靠近并超越它。

赫莉：年初的时候我们坐下来制定了一个目标，今年要成为社区不可缺少的一个部分。

沃伦诺夫：我们希望员工就像詹姆斯•米切纳（James Michener）说的那样，“掌握生活艺术的大师往往是不把生活和工作分开的人”。我们努力在报社营造一种愉快上进的氛围，这是因为我们相信创造一份报纸的核心其实就是一种极富创意的努力。如果不能享受你所创造出来的东西，创意就会枯竭。我们雇用那些精力充沛、近乎狂热的人；我们努力给员工尽可能的自由和决定权，告诉他们要像一个领导者那样去协调自己的工作；之后我们向员工强调要热爱自己的工作，如果不爱，那这份工作就不值得你坚守，因为员工在工作上花的时间比在家还要多，人生太短不值得活得那么痛苦。没人愿意和一群一天到晚满腹牢骚的人一起工作。

史密斯：无论用何种方法，让员工意识到他们与报纸有着利害关系。他们与新增设的专栏有密切的联系，通过让他们定期主持专栏使他们在社区中更有地位和存在感。

问：你是如何看待自己的领导风格的？在做管理决策时哪些准则起了作用？

斯贝茨：以身作则、常识和基督教信仰，并了解对错的区别。

赫莉：以身作则，但能退就退。我是那种不到最后一刻不做决定的人，之后承担有必要的谴责。我的指导准则是：傻瓜，让事情变得简单就好。

沃伦诺夫：一位老农告诉我，其实最好的肥料就是你在田地里走来走去留下的脚印，这就是为什么我通过在办公室闲逛来加强对报社的管理。我每天做的第一件事就是去每个办公室闲逛一圈，与每个人交谈，有时谈工作，有时谈体育，每次我都可以学到点新东西。我很关心员工，也希望他们感觉到对我可以有除了尊敬之外的坦率直白。这种参与的方法帮助营造了更紧密的工作关系，使得员工每天早晨工作都能保有热情。我对报社的传统持有一份尊敬，但不会被这些束缚。我努力想办法做一些改变以迎接每天都要面对的挑战。我要做的就是考虑哪些是竞争对手做不了或不能做的，之后再想办法去办成这些事。

布克尔：我的风格就是坚持大家都是工作伙伴。在报社里，我没有必要是最好的作家、最好的广告销售者、最好的广告商或是最好的页面编辑，但是这些工作我都擅长。我希望那些为我工作的人看到我在工作，看到我工作上的优秀，并为成为我团队的一员而感到骄傲。我不是一个喜欢责骂别人的人，也不是一个喜欢大声叫好的人，但是，我一直在寻找机会与员工一个个探讨“我们在做什么”，并努力把灵感和信息传递下去。我的指导准则就是以商量的态度去让人们做事，而不是命令他们该做什么事。为员工树立一个好榜样，与员工打交道时表现出足够的尊敬和友善，并在需要的时候果断和敢于冒险。如别人能做的事就让他们去做好了，我只专注于只有我可以做的事情上，因为这才是他们希望我扮演的角色。

沃特纳：以身作则；领导而不是命令，鼓励而不是要求；反复思考，不要害怕接受别人的想法；己所不欲，勿施于人，也不要忘记倾听。

史密斯：民主、参与、开放性思考。每年每位员工都会得到一个我的“10条准则”的小册子，上面写了：要诚实，有职业素养，支持广告商，对社区积极地建言献策，参与志愿活动，读《蒙蒂塞洛时代》，永远不要说“这不是我的工作”，支持整个团队。

问：如何成为一名高效的社区报出版人？

沃伦诺夫：一个高效的出版人必须常常学习关于报纸运作各个方面的知识。出版人要关心广告的售卖、报纸是否按时出版、雇员啥时有了新宝宝等所有事件。首先，出版报纸是在做生意。如果作为一项生意不能成功，那么报纸也不能成为一个社区机构。所以，出版人必须懂得如何使企业利润增长以及如何提高发行量。我们相信实现这些的办法就是发行一份一流的报纸。一份好的报纸也是一个好的生意。对我来说，一个报纸出版人必须是勤奋、充满热情并且精力充沛的。

布克尔：这需要花很多时间。需要保持一颗平常心，有一个理解你的妻子，保持积极的态度并在对现状评估时保持客观真实的判断力。我觉得应该像骡子那样干活——年复一年承受所有的起伏，承受那些鼓励或者让我们沮丧的事，并努力使社区变得更好。最重要的是，你要真的爱这个社区，真的希望这个社区变成一个可以更好地生活、工作、哺育下一代、养老、过日子的地方。没有这份爱，其他的都没什么价值。而且，你还需要有足够的头脑使报纸在商业上取得成功，因为你需要维持商业运作，支付员工工资，为股东赢利，否则从责任感上来说你就是亏欠这个社区的。一旦面临利益冲突，你的大广告主威胁要撤掉大幅广告，如果没有足够的资金，你就会双脚发软，不可能成为无惧的真相揭露者。

沃特纳：与你所在的社区、你的员工以及整个行业保持联系。尽量做到真实、公平并拥有领导力。认真倾听，关注报纸的商业运作。不要把自己太当回事。

问：你认为一份好的社区报的编辑应该具备什么样的特点、个性和能力？

沃伦诺夫：一位编辑之前供职于一份大日报。我常开玩笑要通过他打败大日报，我希望他能花更多时间找到一个方法对读者说“YES”。一个好的编辑应该是平易近人、精力充沛、充满热情、独立思考的，同时还要有能与人们用心用文字沟通的能力。

吉尔摩：我认为一个好的编辑需要知道不用什么事都重起炉灶，从头开始。员工有自己做事的方法，一个新主编应该努力去了解报社的工作流程，自己去试一试，然后再决定是否要做改变。如果原先的方法没有错，就不要去改变它。如果一个编辑能主动表现得愿意向大家学习，员工会更愿意在需要变动时相应做出配合。我认为一个好的编辑还会利用这些问题去发现员工的长处，并和他们一起更好地工作。

史密斯：你必须热爱你的报纸，想要得到额外的进步，就需要更关心报纸，并且厚脸皮。

布克尔：要有高涨的激情和燃烧的欲望去挖掘故事。在一份社区报中，他或她还需要有一种能与周围人迅速打成一片的个人魅力。记者与采访对象不是一次性的接触关系，以后还有很多机会在生活中、采访中再次相遇，性格不招人喜欢的记者很难在社区报干下去。记者还要勤奋工作，多与人建立联系，尽可能多地让人们愿意以非匿名方式出现在报道中。他们还会被希望去做一些对社区有用但对“报纸报道新闻无用”的好事，比如火灾发生时，冲上去灭火要紧还是任其蔓延，先跑过去为报纸抢拍照片重要？

问：对那些刚从事第一份社区报的年轻主编或新主编有什么样的建议？

布克尔：世界是属于你的，每张面孔背后都有一个故事。对我来说，这是世界上最刺激的工作。不要畏惧，去了解真实的故事，准确地去理解，并用一种自己也有欲望去阅读的风格把故事写下来。当然再拍一些好照片。

赫莉：从办公桌后面走出来，到街上看看；在咖啡店的角落里喝杯咖啡；去看足球训练，与父母们交往；到校园里散步，去看看这些年来校园发生了怎样的变化。成为这个社区的其中一员，而不仅仅是为其工作。

蒙哥马利：有节制地工作，健康是最重要的，保持耐心，并且脸皮要厚。

沃伦诺夫：保持主动，平易近人，让大家看到你的身影。关心你的社区和报纸。

沃特纳：到社区去接触不同的人；花时间和当地的历史学者交谈；读读过去三年的报纸；永远不要害怕问那些你不了解的问题；学会依赖身边人。

吉尔摩：了解你的社区；参与社区活动，比如垒球比赛、学校运动会、教堂聚餐、社区节日；保持好奇心并且平易近人；不要想通过一件事来改变世界；小型社区是在很长一段时间内慢慢发生改变的，改变不可能一蹴而就。

问：你最看重新员工的哪些特征？

蒙哥马利：创造力、理解力、热情、精力、技术。

赫莉：道德修养、精力、热情以及同情心。如果这些品格都已经具备了，其他的就不用担心了。低劣的拼写和糟糕的语法都是可以逐步改进的，但你永远无法教会一个人拥有同情心和热情。

沃特纳：理解力、诚实、强烈的学习和工作欲望。

布克尔：首要考虑的是写作能力。社区报新手必须对小镇发生的事情感兴趣，他们每天要多打几个额外的电话，建立各种联系，说服采访对象发表各种看法，拍出好照片，积极乐观并且愿意主动学习，这些都做到了的话，两年内他们就能成为优秀记者。

斯贝茨：诚实、主动、独立、写作天赋，还有工作的欲望。

沃伦诺夫：精力、热情、好奇心。

吉尔摩：我认为好奇心和想要去学习的意愿是最重要的。对基本语法的掌握和故事结构的把握固然有用，但这些都是随着时间的增长可以后天培养的。

问：对于应聘者的招募和留住人才有什么建议？

蒙哥马利：通过州立大学我们雇用到了很多优秀的年轻人，他们带来很多活力、热情、创造力，并拥有无畏的态度。把他们留住确实比较困难，因为我们只是他们成功路上的垫脚石，但我很理解。我相信可以通过“善待员工、营造愉快的工作氛围、为进取心且表现出众的员工加薪”等方法留住人才。

斯贝茨：雇用当地人，并优待他们。

沃特纳：当人们在薪酬和福利方面需要得到补偿的时候，留住人才的关键就是为他们建立一个“可以实现自我价值并值得为社区报付出”的环境。允许他们做更多的事，让他们接受更多挑战，承担更多责任，培养员工的主人翁意识。

赫莉：“招募应聘者”只是嘴上说说而已，这里只是一个小地方，我几乎认识所有人。我至今做过最有价值的一次招聘是雇用了一名与我同在另外一份报纸工作过的记者。我知道他是目前报社空余职位的最佳人选。至于“留住人才”——我发现除非你不停地给员工挑战，否则他们会感到疲倦。而一旦他们对工作产生疲倦，就意味着你要失去他们了。另外我发现现有员工也有奇才，我的办公室经理原先只是做接电话和打字的工作，偶然的机会让我发现她其实是个对历史有着强烈热情且极具天赋的艺术家。现在她已成为一个有个性的作家和优秀的摄影记者。更棒的是，她对处理一些突发性的新闻极具热情。

布克尔：雇用社区里的人。报社社会版女编辑就是从暗房冲洗照片开始做起的，之后辞职离开报社后又回来做图片编辑，之后又再次离职再次回来，她说其实更想当一名作家，事实证明她确实做得很好。而我们优秀的体育版记者直到去年退休之前一直是附近城市的一名全职消防员，报纸出版围绕他的工作时间做了些调整，因为他值得我们这么做。我能给的另外一个建议就是尽量保留一些实习职位。我有两名记者都是通过实习阶段考核被留下来的。幸运的是，离我们48千米远的北田纳西大学要求毕业生在毕业前拥有一段实习经历，并有自己的作品出版（这就是编辑最初加入我们的原因）。这提高了报纸的质量，并且给了我们一个机会去认识那些将来有可能会回来竞聘职位的人。无论何时，雇用一个你了解的人还是雇用一个不太了解的人，前者都是一个巨大的优势。

沃伦诺夫：努力与大学生们交流，使我们能成为他们的一个训练基地。我告诉他们如果能在社区报工作几年并且表现优异的话，在时机成熟时我们会帮助他们跳槽到更大的报社去工作。多年以来，我们为遵守之前的诺言收获了名誉和口碑，这使得我们对大学毕业生来说更具吸引力。

问：谈谈报纸的辅导制是什么——这种辅导有多重要？实践起来怎么样？

赫莉：这很重要，但不复杂。辅导制本身其实就是关怀——关心你的员工和报纸。因为报社只有很少几个员工，辅导制度就显得自然天成。我尝试提出一些准则和建议，但我发现，他们在关于“我能带来什么”方面的思考其实比我还要明确。

蒙哥马利：辅导制度很重要。因为来报社工作其实是很多新员工的第一份工作，辅导制度就是授予全部的经验。年轻的雇员在第一份工作中往往得到很多新的体验。真实的世界与大学是不同的，而在编辑室之外所需要做出的调整也许比适应报社文化还要困难。而有这种认识非常关键。编辑们必须多在办公室走动，了解记者的各方面情况。问问他们周末都干了什么，过得怎么样。愉快轻松的沟通，从中你可以了解到很多东西。

史密斯：作为一个出版人，我常常定期与新编辑见面。我热衷于用留便利贴的方式感激或表扬员工。

沃特纳：当员工人数很少的时候，我就会找机会和年轻记者一起工作。听取他们的意见，用一种积极、建设性的方式和他们讨论工作，也给他们一个机会对我的工作发表意见，等等。帮助他们在那些得心应手的工作与略感吃力的任务之间寻求一个平衡。对他们来说，给一个在真正的新闻行业里锻炼的机会是很重要的。从中，我也可以学到很多。

问：社区报都会报道社区年度活动，比如节庆、交易会、当地庆典，你的报纸会用什么新的视角来使这些报道每年都有新意？

赫莉：在我的建议下，体育编辑在今年的乡村交易会上参加了撞车大赛，之后再亲自报道这个活动。读者很喜欢这个内容，我们希望他明年继续去参加杂技表演活动。主动参与到这些可以制造新闻的事件中，我们不仅可以为自己的版面拍很多不错的照片，而且还可以为特写增加很多亮点。

史密斯：今年“大河节”之后的评论版上是每个记者拍摄的3到4张以“最美的大河节瞬间”为题的照片。我们会采用类似这样的活动来增添新意。

沃特纳：当举办这样的活动时，我们会邀请一些外地的记者和摄影师来采访，使得报道有一些新意。我们试图找到一些“还没有被发现”的视角和观点。我们试着去挖掘每年节日中那些独特的点。

吉尔摩：每年从6月4日开始持续一周的“致礼太阳节”是报纸的重点报道项目——刊印每日行程表，并重点介绍每天最有特色的项目。去年我们征集当地人拍摄的爱国主义题材照片，并挑选出最好的印在报纸的彩页上。

蒙哥马利：我们不断为之绞尽脑汁。我想出的最好的一个办法就是以一问一答的形式做了一个本郡年度集市指南。

问：所有做过的成功专题报道中，在你心中最特别的那个报道是什么？

史密斯：报纸参与了社区与“9·11”受害者家庭的结对子活动，主编劳拉去了纽约和华盛顿做采访。

布克尔：每年春季报纸推出艺术节特刊，读者不断高涨的热情使得报道从最初的两个版发展到目前几十版的定期专刊。我们为每位初中音乐老师拍照片并配发简短的介绍报道，采访了社区4到5个居民发表关于“艺术对于生活的意义”的看法。同时我们在页面底部售卖广告。几年后麦克（现任得克萨斯州报业协会执行主管）举办了一个广告研讨班，他提议说可以在版面里设立一个专区让孩子们来画广告。我们决定吸纳这个主意。我们先把版面出售给广告商，邀请广告商到社区学校中找五六年级的学生，邀请所有的孩子给他们的产品画广告，然后让他们挑选中意的作品。孩子们的画作和之前那些简单的人物介绍一起搭配成广告刊登出来，于是很多这样的活动开始和教室挂钩。我把这些投稿的画作（包括那些没有采用的）全年挂在墙上。

为了推广这个理念，我去每个学校和每个年级的学生谈媒体、报纸的运营、广告的作用、新闻报道和广告的区别、宪法第一修正案以及如何做出好的广告，对于新闻内容，我们在音乐、戏剧、舞蹈以及其他与艺术节相关的校园项目上挖报道，并且挖掘社区里那些歌手、雕刻家、画家的故事。每年，我们都被社区里丰富多彩的艺术文化震惊。但最大的收益是，我们让社区的孩子们开始主动看报纸，并提供机会让他们稚嫩的艺术作品能够见报。上周我去参加一个婚礼，其中一个来宾得知我的身份后兴奋地告诉我，六年级的时候他的作品曾被当作广告在我们的报纸上刊登。

沃特纳：为庆祝《弗里曼通讯报》成立100周年，我们筹划了13个主题、每部分40页的专刊，回顾从1901年以来的新闻事件。每月发行一个主题，每个主题都有一条时间线，按照10年间我们所能收集到的出版物和挑选出的文章、照片、艺术品等排列。头10个月专注于介绍几个特殊的时间段（如1901—1910、1911—1920等）及期间发生的故事。第十一期重点是“世纪之交的照片”。第十二期则是总概性介绍，重印一些20世纪已经出版过的特写和照片。第十三期突出了与未来展望有关的一些“进步事件”。社区以及广告商的反应都非常积极，对《弗里曼通讯报》的美好祝愿源源不断，专刊创造了很强的社区归属感，帮助人们重燃对社区历史的兴趣。

赫莉：《玛莎斯维尔记录报》每周都包含一些需要读者互动的专栏，比如《这是谁》栏目，通过发表一些存档的老照片，来让读者猜测这是发生在多少年以前的故事。我们每周都发表一次，并让读者猜测照片里的人是谁。读者们可以打电话或发邮件来猜答案，我们在下一期公布答案。这个专栏很受欢迎。报纸每周四早上8：00出版，中午11：00一般就有电话打来了。《每周热点》是另外一个读者参与的专栏。每周选一个主题，比如：建筑、日出日落、奇怪的角度、动物某个有趣的动作，等等，从读者寄来的照片中选出合适的刊登在副刊上。年终再从每个月的入选照片中选出12张，印成社区日历，这些读者会得到社区商业赞助的餐券、洗车券，等等。

问：请举例说明除了正常出版之外，报纸还有哪些创造性做法？

赫莉：我们资助了“书虫项目”——向那些愿意写读书报告的孩子们提供免费读物的阅读计划。

布克尔：我们为高中毕业生设立奖学金，为高中免费提供报纸，我们卖广告，学生们负责撰写新闻和评论，他们获了很多奖。这只是我们所做的事情之一。我们努力让社区更紧密，努力让社区纳税人了解学校和学生，了解社区的运作。

沃特纳：我们通过多门学科与同学们交流，包括新闻学、摄影、写作，当然还有社区历史学，我们常常被当作社区历史研究者。

蒙哥马利：我们为社区做得最好的事是即将与威奇塔州立大学（Wichita State University）合作“公民新闻意识项目”，研究接下来的5年、10年、20年里居民对章克申城的发展愿景，希望居民能比过去更进一步参与到城市规划和建设中来。

第16章

我的三份社区报

敬爱的中国读者：

如果说经验是最好的老师，那么这一章会是整本书最有价值的部分。我会详述三份社区报案例，成功也好，失败也罢，我在其中都起了主要作用。

2009年创办《声音》时，我以大学教授身份参与管理报纸的日常运营工作。我们为市内处境艰难的少数族裔少年提供独特的就业机会，教导这些孩子采写、摄影、摄像和电脑使用等专业技巧。这份社区报是在与贫穷、犯罪以及美国城市平民区中典型的无助感和疏离感做斗争。时至今日，这些工作开始渐显成效！

——作者

你要非常想得到它

很多年来，罗宾斯维尔（Robinsville）高中黑骑士队是一只强大的橄榄球队。一个位于山区的小社区为何能不断产生出优秀的队伍，这让我百思不得其解。确实，教练的功劳毋庸置疑，但也有其他东西在起作用。

刚刚结束跟主要竞争对手常规赛季末的一场大战后，一个看起来不怎么起眼的边锋在跟记者聊起为什么他觉得自己能赢：“我觉得我们比他们更想得到这场胜利。”

在美国每个大城市数不清的新闻编辑室里都会有少部分编辑、记者、摄影师、商业和广告从业者，怀揣着“某天能有自己的小周报”的秘密梦想。他们有充足的理由这么想，有自己的报纸对新闻工作者的召唤就像跑马拉松对于跑步者一样，都是最终梦想。

那么，你准备怎么来做自己的报纸？需要一个经纪人吗？要卖掉牧场来买一份报纸吗？还是应该跟疯狂的哥们儿一起白手起家办一张报纸？从哪里开始呢？怎么找到合伙人？难道不觉得这样太冒险了吗？或许还是坚持当前每月拿固定薪水的工作最保稳。

不管做什么，记住罗宾斯维尔的黑骑士队。

你必须非常想得到它，是的，必须比“他们”更想。

“他们”是谁？“他们”是竞争对手，你一定会遇到他们的。

双城记

单单这一章的价值就足以抵上你买这整本书的钱了。它可能让你完成自我救赎，省下一大笔钱。它也可能让你心潮澎湃以致无法入眠，或者改变你摇摆不定的态度。

下面要讲述的是我亲身参与的两家社区报的案例，故事是这样的。

我一直知道，我想要自己的报纸。幸运的是，1967年我大三时，在北卡大学教堂山分校上肯•拜尔利的社区新闻课程时受到了启发：我要做社区报。

我在《教堂山周报》（*Chapel Hill Weekly*）做过所有的工种。大学学费就是靠在《教堂山周报》做兼职拼版、设计布局等工作赚的。早在我上高中的时候，《教堂山周报》的主编吉姆•舒美克（Jim Shumaker）就告诉我：“你先去大学学完新闻学，然后回到我这里工作。”

大三那年，我在北卡罗来纳州布瑞尔一周两刊的《特兰西瓦尼亚时代》实习。我被北卡罗来纳州西部的山峰给深深吸引，感觉找到了归属。大学期间，我爱上了一个来自山区的女孩，她和我一样都有一个在家乡办报的梦想。

毕业后我在《教堂山周报》工作了一年，然后在北卡州西部斯巴达镇找到一个在一份社区周报工作的机会，《阿勒格尼新闻》（*Alleghany News*）的出版人不在镇上生活，我一个人支撑这份8个版的报纸，却没有自由，我在《教堂山周报》时总是尽量把照片做得大一点，可出版人不允许我登大照片，我们之间发生了多次无意义的争吵。三个月后，我辞职了，开始计划在这里办自己的报纸。

在弗罗斯特市出版人的圣诞晚宴上，我坐在了《弗罗斯特通讯报》（*Forest Courier*）的工作团队中。当我告诉他们我的想法时，有人直截了当地对我说：“不，你不应该在斯巴达镇办报，你应该到这里来，我们一起干。”

我看到了此事的可行性。弗罗斯特市是一个有潜力的报业市场，值得赌一把；这些人都是有经验的能手，比尔来自卢瑟福郡（Rutherford），他是《弗罗斯特通讯报》当时的商业和广告经理，主编罗恩已经在当地工作了两年。换种方式说，他们已经深入当地并做过调研，我只是去给本已经很棒的团队再加上一朵小花而已。

在当地一名投资者的帮助下，我们凑够了约1万美元，尽管这在今天的标准下看起来少得可怜，但是可以起步了。

接下来三个月发生的事是营销奇迹。罗恩堪称新闻奇才，比尔商业敏感性很强，他俩离开了《弗罗斯特通讯报》，就在街对面创立了自己的报社。他俩买了便宜的二手设备，添置了必需的新设备，比如手工制作的排版桌子等。总之当我3月1日到那里时，除了暗室之外，所有都已经准备好了，暗室就由我来监督完成。我拿来了相机、放大机和暗室设备，添置了一台立式复照仪和一台自动扫描的照片处理器。

我们把一家美容院改成报社办公室，没有足够大的空间，一间办公室三人共用，好多年里，我都在使用一台史密斯科罗娜公司的便携打字机。在那又脏又小的新闻编辑室里，还有一台古老的森泽牌子的邮件地址印刷机，虽然已经很老旧，但依然经用，只要我们不介意排版时发出的巨大的穿孔带的声音。刚开始阶段，除了暗室，其他地方没有安空调，狭小的印刷室里有一张自制的拷贝台、一架我从家里带来的涂蜡机，还有一张两面的排版桌，不久后，买了一张看版台。

每个家庭都为报纸的第一期投入了全力。凑巧的是，罗恩的妻子贾妮斯（Janice）和我的妻子玛姬（Maggie）都怀孕了，她们的肚子大到要伸直手臂才能打字的地步。

该怎么推广发行呢？我不记得是谁想出的妙计：邀请本地在全美享有盛名的东部高中军乐队推销报纸，给他们一定比例的回扣。

报纸因此获得了巨大的成功。这大部分归功于一流的学生队员、指挥、音乐，他们标准的行进步伐吸引了小镇居民还有成批粉丝，关心乐队的孩子父母们也都痛快地订报。谁会对这些“行进的骑士”说“不”呢？我们出版第一张报纸之前，他们就已经卖出了上百份。

1969年3月17日，第一期报纸问世了。

接下来，毫不夸张地说，订阅量潮水般增长。小镇太需要一份好的报纸了，居民们张开双臂欢迎我们的来到。这是我们得意的时刻。

罗恩把报纸命名为《本周谈》，并在报头下冠之以“卢瑟福郡的现代周报”几个字，好像在说：“我们跟对手报纸不一样，不走寻常路。”又好像在说：“对报纸来说，《本周谈》是个奇怪的名字，但是，对你来说，它是份现代的报纸。”

比尔处理了商业方面的所有事务：卖广告位、排版广告、记账、报纸订购、还账，等等，总之是让我们能边还债边经营下去。加上从《弗罗斯特通讯报》跳槽过来的弗吉尼亚•洛克（Virginia Rucker），她给报纸带来了一种成熟的气质。

我和罗恩自称联合编辑，但是这个称谓会让人误解。罗恩年纪更长，经验更多，在本地更出名，他负责新闻，是事实上的总编辑，而我负责特写兼摄影。但是作为联合编辑，我们坚守一个规矩：他不告诉我该做什么，我也不告诉他该做什么。绝大多数情况下工作进展顺利。我们这样分配版面：

卢瑟福郡有三个镇（包括斯宾戴尔镇、郡政府所在地卢瑟福顿镇和弗瑞斯特镇）和三所高中，以现有能力，报道不可能覆盖所有区域。我们在地图上画了一条直线，右边的地区，也就是位于卢瑟福郡东半部的弗瑞斯特镇以及两所高中是我的报道范围。过些日子报纸壮大了，就可以把报道范围扩大至全郡。尽管目前卢瑟福顿镇基本不在报道范围之内，但罗恩还得定期去采访郡政府会议，当地的《弗罗斯特通讯报》周刊是直接的竞争对手，好多年以来我们都觉得，去卢瑟福顿镇进行报道的时候，总感觉像是在做越境报道。

社论版

我们每周都用本地文章把社论版填满，不掺杂一点通稿类内容。我们甚至会尽量找本地漫画，做这些并不容易。两位编辑各自负责一个专栏，主旨是幽默、轻松、反映现实的评论。有时我和罗恩对同一个事件观点不一致，各自写的社论都要署名，清楚地表明这是个人观点而不代表报纸。同时，报纸上也从不缺少读者来信。

体育报道

我们决定全力以赴报道高中橄榄球赛事，给每个高中每场比赛每周一整版。对创业阶段的报纸，配专职体育版编辑太奢侈了，我们都自己干，我负责东卢瑟福高中，罗恩负责蔡斯高中（Chase High School）。每周赛后每人写一篇详尽的比赛报道并摄影，做赛后教练采访以及预测下周比赛的报道。当东卢瑟福高中对阵蔡斯高中时，我俩就合力办一个两页的关于这次横贯全郡的对决报道。

为了激起读者的兴趣，我一般会尽快冲回暗室，处理并印出周五比赛的照片，然后周六上午10时前把它们张贴在主街史密斯杂货店的橱窗上。一旦这个消息传出，整个球队都会在周六上午到杂货店门口来看正式出版前的小样。这不是CNN新闻，但是对于1969年的小镇来说，第二天就能看到重大比赛的照片是件值得一提的事情。另外，对周报来说，这是抢在一周两刊的《弗罗斯特通讯报》之前报道新闻的一个巧妙办法，否则《弗罗斯特通讯报》就会在周一报纸上抢先做橄榄球报道。

我和罗恩很快发现东卢瑟福高中和蔡斯高中的新闻课都想拥有自己的版面，这样可以节省报纸人力，是个双赢的局面，于是我们创造性地提出给每个学校每周一个整版，同时还帮助他们拍摄照片。随着时间的推移，我们的体育报道渐渐发展成对学校的报道。

社区通讯员

利用罗恩在《弗罗斯特通讯报》工作时积累的社区网络，我们联系了一批能够提供消息的社区舆论领袖。他们主要报道社区的参观活动、教堂新闻等内容。大部分人长期给报纸提供消息，其中最受欢迎的查理斯•赛尔富夫人（Mrs. Charles Self），来自金色阳光山谷社区，她的作品活色生香。我们很快意识到，使用她的作品——还有其他人的作品——的最好方式就是不加任何修改直接发表，这样可以保留作品的美妙个性。

报纸生产流程

每到周二出样稿的时候，比尔做完广告拼版后，罗恩和我就分别拿走自己的版面。罗恩负责做头版、硬新闻、本地新闻和政府类报道，需要的时候他也拍照。我负责第二叠的头版，然后用特写把版面填满，那一页上不允许打广告，我还负责与摄影有关的工作。

《本周谈》一炮走红。从此以后，没有人再抱怨周二要加班赶制报纸。这让我想到一句老话："胜利的那天，没有人感到疲惫。"

第一期报纸出来时，我像只斑点狗一样乐得直跳，可罗恩却站在一旁骂骂咧咧，如果我没有记错的话，他是因为排版机打出来的断字而感到不满。"该死！"他冲着报纸咆哮道。

个性相反的人如何向一个共同目标携手并进，我和罗恩的合作是个很好的案例。罗恩是个现实、理性，对产品质量绝不感情用事的管理者，而我却是个痴狂、凭直觉做事、感情用事的人。这种类似阴阳互补的合作在某种程度上却使对方完整起来。我们一起做了份出色的报纸。

初出茅庐的《本周谈》第一年就在北卡州报业协会评比中赢得了10个奖项。我们不仅是本州最棒的周报，而且还很有可能是本州最棒的非日报类报纸、最棒的社区报。人们开始关注我们的动态，那的确是最得意的时刻。从那时起，我们这些"从弗罗斯特来的家伙"就出名了。

放任自流的发展

报纸在迅速生长。两年内，我们租了旁边的屋子，把墙凿通，修缮了前台，让办公室看起来像个真正的报社工作室，而不是以前那样，看着像不靠谱的人在原先美容店的前台迎宾。我们买了空调，把得到的奖状挂在墙上。尽管还是三人共享一个空间，但是把印刷间和办公室隔离开来了。空间扩大了一倍，感觉自己像皇帝一样。报纸欣欣向荣，马路对面的另一家竞争对手的编辑却走马灯似的换了一个又一个。

《弗罗斯特通讯报》顽强地坚持出版。就像有人说的那样："那张报纸就像李施德林漱口水一样，虽然都讨厌它，但还要用它。"

《弗罗斯特通讯报》每周一和周四发行，他们在周一会抢我们的新闻，我们会在周三抢他们的新闻，两家报纸最大的不同在于版面。一张充满活力，一张墨守成规。主要是我们的照片质量和平板印刷技术远远超出他们，尤其有了对比，这种差距所有的读者都能注意到。

到了1974年，石油输出国组织（OPEC）实施了限油令，所有的印刷和印刷品价格都翻番，我们却足以在这场风波中存活，并且化解了财务方面的冲击。新闻版面变小，我们勒紧裤腰带就挺过去了。而对手却遭受了损失，他们不得不联合小周报《斯平代尔太阳报》（*Spindale Sun*）组成一个《太阳通讯报》（*Courier-Sun*）。

次年，我们遇到了转折点。1975年4月，我们在主街买下一所大房子，这让每个人都拥有了自己的办公室。这所房子最好的一点是有很多水泥地下室，简直像是为报纸的印刷设备量身定做的。我们在千里之外的路易斯安那州找到一台二手印刷设备并从银行获得了一大笔贷款，即将对报社设备进行大投资。

竞争对手方律师给我们传话希望出售，在得到另一笔银行贷款的情况下，1975年8月27日，我们买下了《太阳通讯报》。

下一周，我们定好了如何合并两家报纸员工，谁留下谁离开，这些都完成以后，我们新买的二手印刷设备也到了。

罗恩在社论中写道："这周发生的事对我们来说是个里程碑式的事件。"

1975年秋末，报纸欣欣向荣，我们已经可以顺利地在地下室印报纸了。接下来的三年里，因为有了自己的设备和更多的员工，而且没有竞争对手，《本周谈》进入了鼎盛时期。

到此，我们已有能力招聘一位体育版编辑、一位副主编，原先《弗罗斯特通讯报》妇女版的编辑现在负责订婚和结婚的消息发布，还有两名女性员工各自负责排版和广告拼版，两位员工负责印刷，挺让人感觉有面子的是终于有了一位接待员，之前都是自己接电话并与来报社的读者直接见面。

20世纪60年代中期建起的社区大学不断成长，并得到社区的支持，我们的报纸为之铺路，做了所有我们能帮的事情。结果，社区大学、社区和《本周谈》形成了一种共赢共生的关系。可以说报纸和整个郡的发展是同步的。

社区文化处于一个未开垦期待复兴的阶段。一个充满活力的社区艺术委员会在《本周谈》出刊那一年成立了，报纸搭上了顺风车。完全由社区剧院演出的剧目被大量报道。我们像卖热销品一样卖报纸。

同时，一条从谢尔比到卢瑟福顿的四车道公路终于完工了。在路开通前，社区商会激动地宣称“这里的发展将借这条路大踏步而来”。社区商业现在有了发展空间，这可能是种掠夺性的发展，但不可否认它是发展。对我们而言，这就意味着更多的广告收入。我们曾经短期尝试过做一周两刊，但很快就恢复到一周一刊的原样。

1978年夏天，一座购物广场拔地而起，报纸版面达到60至72版，而我们必须手工分拣所有版面和广告，完全没有个人休息时间，这是我们需要付出的代价。

那年秋天，新购物广场的商人告诉我们和《卢瑟福郡新闻》（*Rutherford County News*）：“谁能吸引到最多的顾客，谁就赢得所有广告。”《卢瑟福郡新闻》是一家南卡州连锁报业旗下的报纸，他们得到消息后就开始出版一份全市场覆盖的免费广告纸——《进取报》，用一些便宜的通稿让它看起来像份报纸。

我们该怎么办？没错，现在“发展”已经接着公路冲我们来了，而且都到眼前了，如果我们不跟上社区的发展潮流，不管报纸有多好，曾经拿了多少奖项，新购物广场的商人们都会走掉。

除非我们也改为免费期刊，否则不可能赶上《进取报》的发行量。为了应对竞争，我们回击的唯一方式就是提高发行频率，那就意味着要把周报改为日报。

比尔支持这个做法，罗恩也看到了这样做的现实需要，而我是一百个不同意。但最终，我意识到周报的老模式要被淘汰了，或许是郡里的经济增长要淘汰周报。在这种挑战面前，如果不改为日报，可能就没法生存下去。尽管很不情愿，我也对转型投了赞成票。从1978年的11月开始，我们改为每周发行五刊。

从经营和新闻层面，这样做都是正确的，但我的内心从那以后就没有进入正轨。我们把新日报命名为《每日通讯》（*Daily Courier*）。两年里，我尽我所能想燃起热情，但《本周谈》始终盘踞在我心中，无法超越。

《博斯科公报》：奋力一击，结果是牺牲高飞球

作者提示：为了公正和保护隐私，下面的段落中名字会使用化名。就像是任何办报失败的经历一样，当事人心中总会有些不好受。但是，比起成功，人们可以从失败中学到更多。

1979年末，不管多么不现实，我无法抑制新的梦想——无论如何也要再办一份周报。放眼一望，我立马就被临近的博斯科镇显现出的可能性吸引了。这个郡政府所在地有一份根基很深，但质量很烂的一周两刊报纸——《博斯科时代》（*Bosco Times*），它由一个小报团拥有，除了赚钱什么都不在乎。很多和我交流

过的博斯科镇的居民，不管是商人、政府人员、教育家、公民、教堂领袖，都对《博斯科时代》的主编表示担心和厌恶。这对我来说是个棒极了的事，我的想法越看越可行。如果去的话，可以立马得到支持。

我颇为乐观地认为《博斯科时代》简直不堪一击，为什么不去做呢？如果《本周谈》可以打败根基深厚的《弗罗斯特通讯报》，我怎么就不能在《博斯科公报》（*Bosco Gazette*）那里重演奇迹呢？我要做的仅仅是复制《本周谈》的成功模式，但有一点不同，这次我们可以做一份全市场覆盖（total market coverage，缩写为TMC）的周报。

这种想法当时是全新的。本州没有一家报纸曾经通过邮寄把报纸免费发送到郡里的各家各户。我们将借用免费广告纸的概念，但事实上，依然办的是一份有着大量独家文章和图片的社区新闻纸。我的合伙人认为我这么大胆出格的行为有些疯狂，因为没有一家报纸这么做过。他们好心地与我迅速商量好公道的价格，买下了我手中的股权。我毫无怨言地离开了《每日通讯》。

现在我要做的就是找到罗恩和比尔的替身。我从认识的人名单中寻找起来，把目标锁定在吉姆身上。他年纪不轻（那时接近40岁），没有太多干新闻的经验，但是他有很棒的天赋、干劲和幽默感。做了11年联合出版人和联合编辑这样的创始人、舵手的位置，我感觉同这样一个尽管年龄不小却未经大考验的人平起平坐有些不舒服。因为我拥有报纸60%的所有权，我就把自己提为总编辑，安排吉姆为新闻编辑，他的年轻夫人会以兼职的形式来记账或者做前台。吉姆接受了这样的安排。

为了找到商业主管兼广告营销员，我给附近一所大学的新闻学院打电话，询问商学教授是否能给我推荐人选。他很看好临近大城市一家日报的广告营销员。两天之内，我就安排了一次和这位叫鲍勃的年轻人的会面。他刚刚大学毕业几年，让我印象深刻的是他的干劲和经商的敏感度。除此之外，他也想要有自己的报纸。尽管鲍勃来自加利福尼亚州，我希望南方小镇博斯科可以接纳他。除此之外，鲍勃的妻子也想做广告而她又是本地人。看起来，鲍勃是个合适的人选。

除此之外，鉴于我的妻子在做女性版面、吉姆的妻子做前台，我们有个很大的家庭团队在处理事务。如果三对夫妻能够融洽相处，我相信《博斯科公报》会一炮走红。

但首先，我要组建好工作室。我在主街找到了一家以前是律师所的空房子，价格适中。我买些必备的二手设备，并把办公室、排版桌和暗室做了隔断。

三人共同负责发行，从郡税务办公室拿到了所有大约一万户住户的姓名和地址，单单把地址打出来就是一项浩大的工程。在第一份《博斯科公报》出来之前，三对夫妻花了三个星期才完成打字工作。接着，听从邮政局所长的建议，我们按邮编和邮路分好邮件。我们现在成了镇上邮政局的最大客户。因为邮资负担太大，所以必须尽早实现赢利。

我从《每日通讯》得到的部分酬劳支撑了从3月到9月的“免费印刷”。

1980年3月19日，那是一个星期三，我们出版了第一期《博斯科公报》。那是一份24页的宽幅报纸，里面全都是本地新闻、专栏、社论还有图片，广告版面只占17%，没有一家是超市广告。为了成功，我们知道必须搞到当地四个超市广告大户的整版广告。

不到三个月，我们得到了其中的三个。

那是春风得意的时期。社区迫不及待地接纳了《博斯科公报》。经常听人说：“你们的到来是博斯科50年来发生的最好事情。”在经营方面，我们也取得了胜利，广告比例从17%上升到可观的48%。

直到那时为止，对手才开始重视我们。就像在弗罗斯特市一样，开始时，对手不管不问，自以为是，想看着我们栽跟头。两个案例中，在我们最脆弱的开始阶段，对手都没有做出反应。而等他们反应过来，我们已经把他们甩开了一大截。

《博斯科时代》已无路可退。对手做了我们没有能力做的事：降低广告费来拉拢广告商。在一些重要的竞争中，他们免费赠送广告位和“礼品”。我们不愿意玩这种游戏，于是开始失去广告合同。

因为巨大的发行量和邮寄费用，我们必须比对手在广告费上定价高。这样的发行手段对于一家新报来说是危险的尝试。现在《博斯科时代》又开始在广告费上和我们来硬的，到处抢生意，相比起来，我们就成了一份昂贵的报纸。

9个月后，我们被迫改变发行方式，大幅调整经营策略：从一周一刊改为一周两刊，并从免费改为收费发行。这样好像奏效了，但是我们无力再出版24页满是社区新闻的宽幅报纸，代之以稀释了的通稿内容。一年之后，鲍勃告诉我和吉姆说他不喜欢广告销售。我俩震惊了，我们同意鲍勃快速出手自己的股权。幸运的是，我们找到了一位新的商业伙伴泰德。泰德人缘很好，是个受人尊敬的商业领袖和社区领袖，他刚刚被一家大工厂解雇。尽管他在财务和销售广告方面很有才能，但1981至1983年美国遭遇经济衰退，广告跟着一落千丈，谁都无能为力，我们感觉像被一种巨大而又凶狠的东西叼住了一样。

我记得有天晚上坐在打字机旁，想写点有创意的东西，但内心充满忧虑，因为我们刚刚在最后一家超市广告的竞争中败给了《博斯科时代》。我所有的创意灵感全都冻结了，是我遇到了写作瓶颈，还是江郎才尽，抑或是出版人的夜惊？不管是什么，我都写不出来了，最后我只好敷衍了事。

绝望之下，我们试图买下竞争对手。南卡的报团有时看起来似乎愿意把报纸卖给我们。但其实这是他们的拖延战术，我们亏损越来越大。最后才意识到，不是我们买不了《博斯科时代》，而是他们太骄傲不愿意卖给我们，就像我们骄傲到不愿意卖给他们一样。我们就像主街上两个鲜血淋漓的斗士，誓死斗争到底，谁也不肯倒下认输。

最后，吉姆经过斡旋巧妙达成了一个三方协议，一家非本州的“帕克传媒连锁公司”来收购两份报纸。我们得救了，吉姆在新公司里被聘为中层编辑，泰德也很快有了着落，他被一家本地企业抢去做执行官。《博斯科时代》被改造为一周五刊的日报，而我们的《博斯科公报》被降低为一张免费广告赠刊。

我感到辛酸，感情上受到重创，离开了小镇，这里用“被遣散”或许更合适。两年半的辛苦好像竹篮打水一场空，我再也不想见到那个地方。我在那一带地区不同报社换了无数工作。直到1983年，我出乎意料地得到了在大学教书的工作。

反思：哪里出了问题？

第一，错误的人，错误的地点，错误的时间。

经济大萧条的背景下，三个外乡人并没有做好办一份出色报纸的准备。

从一开始，就没有深入调查。在那个比较排外的社区里，我们完全是三个外来户。这个郡和小镇的人有一种不好的习惯，如果有人真正决定搬到这里，本地居民的第一反应是“你是不是在逃避某个人或者组织？为什么会有人搬到这里来？你搬来的理由后面肯定有些黑暗的邪恶的原因”。尽管我和吉姆来自那片区域，但对于博斯科人来说，我们跟火星人没什么两样。为了在博斯科证明报纸存在的合理性，我们浪费了很多精力。尽管报纸确实给博斯科带来了一次新闻革命、一场有创造力的复兴，也的确赢得了一些支持，但是我们没有真正赢得民心，大广告商们在压力下向《博斯科时代》做出了让步。

第二，在初期找合作伙伴的时候，永远去找那些你能雇得起的最有经验的人。

我把《每日通讯》的部分收益作为《博斯科公报》前六个月的投入。一开始这听起来是个好主意，但当交税的时候，才发现所得税高得惊人，这完全怪我没有进行很好的财务咨询。以我的头脑我本该弄清这些重要的细节，可是我没有。最后一点也是最重要的：资金不足。办《博斯科公报》的起始资金是35000美元（我的前期投入有21000美元），剩下的钱不够支撑太长时间，特别是前六个月过于乐观和高估的损益报表，加上高昂的邮寄费用，由此而来的伤害十分严重。

第三，低估了对手。

情感上错误估计了它的决心，财务上错误估计了它能坚持的时间。如果我们有更多财务上的储备，《博斯科公报》有可能度过经济不景气的那段时期，接着可能会变得更强大或者能够买下《博斯科时代》。

对比和不同

启动资金。两家报纸一开始的时候都没有那么多钱，但区别不仅在于收费或免费发行模式，还在于时间。70年代初，不多的资金也能撑一段时间。当胶卷、纸、墨水等价格都因限油令而飞速飙升，竞争的情形就不同了。对于这个时代起步的报纸，最明智的做法是至少能有撑足六个月的资金储备。

发行。尽管两家报纸都是周报，但发行方式却不同。弗罗斯特市报纸的发行方式是付费，因此可以享受便宜的二等邮费。而博斯科镇的发行方式是通过邮件覆盖各家各户，美国邮局对这种免费报纸的收费非常贵。两种方式都有风险，付费方式意味着一开始没有可观发行量，无法给潜在广告商看“数字”。但另一方面，这是开办一份报纸最经济保稳的方式，你基本上是手把手地经营报纸，一开始体量小并慢慢成长，在某些案例里，这是正确的方式。当你用全市场覆盖的方式发行时，你可以立马获得读者数据，把广告卖出去，没有几个广告商可以对一家几乎覆盖全郡各家各户的报纸说“不”。但是，你的投递费用开支巨大，这个赌注就在于广告的收益是否能够抵上发行方面的巨额投入。如果你是在跟一个墨守成规的对手竞争，而且你有强大的资金支持，这种办报方式或许是一条出路。但是要提前警告你：如果这样做的话，你就处于邮政局的摆布下了。他们可以并且最终会提高收费，并随意改变邮件分类和投递时间，根本不会考虑报纸的死活。

研究调查社区的背景情况。创立或者购买一份报纸就像买房。要根据一句老话：当你要买一套房，你要看好三个重要的因素——地址，地址，还是地址。在弗罗斯特市，比尔和罗恩已经做了功课，进行样本调研、收集信息、摸准社区脉搏、了解社区商业对一份新报纸出现的想法，等等，简直是无懈可击。在博斯科，我是按照“另一个弗罗斯特市”的模式来复制，每一个社区都有自己的特点，简单复制行不通。

时间选择。两家报纸都是在春天开始发行。这正是广告商成群出现的周期性时节。但是另一个重要的因素是：你有多少时间用在规划和调研上了？在弗罗斯特市，我们的团队进行了长时间研究而且静等最佳时机。在博斯科镇，我们直接冲入赛场，充满活力和热情，同时也很稚嫩。或许更深入地对对手、市场、经济走向的调查会警示我们远离博斯科。

对手。不管如何运营——是自己办报还是买下别的报纸，你肯定会在某处遇到竞争对手。你需要对它进行客观的评估。它是家族拥有并运营的吗？那么它可能会比较脆弱。它是连锁公司旗下的吗？如果是的话是哪所公司的？公司有多大？总部在哪里？这家连锁公司应对竞争的典型策略是什么？是被动挨打型还是主动出击型？比如说，一家小型的、由一个年长的首席执行官运营的家族报纸会比一家较大的、有野心的连锁公司运营的报纸脆弱一些。当你要创办一家报纸时，需制订一套最坏情况预案。如果针对你的进入，对手也开始做全市场覆盖产品，你会怎么办？

伙伴。在弗罗斯特市，比尔和罗恩了解当地社区，社区也了解他们。在社区卖广告的人一定要有广泛的人脉资源，只有人人都认识你的脸才行。不管我们这些做新闻的报人多么有意识地偏爱社论，商业方面的成功是推动报纸起步的力量。在弗罗斯特市，广告销售不仅是本地人，还在本地工作了一辈子。再怎么强调这点因素也不过分。另一方面，我们在博斯科的广告销售不是本地人，这只会更加凸显团队每一个人都不是本地人的现实，非本地拥有的报纸从情感上很难被当地人接受。

我如果能早一点预料到博斯科人对外来者的抗拒态度，或许早就该放弃在这里出版报纸的整个计划。

更新和后续报道

当这本书在中国出版的时候，上述那些报纸的演变也在继续。

《博斯科时代》和《博斯科公报》的新东家帕克传媒有限公司在1997年把两份报纸卖给了将军媒体有限公司（Media General）。《博斯科时代》现在是一份发行量在5155份的日报，而《博斯科公报》仍然是免费的广告周报，发行量约在8000张。2013年，两份报纸被巴菲特的伯克希尔公司所购买。

回到卢瑟福郡，仍然独立运营的《每日通讯》继续发展壮大。90年代我曾经的合伙人买下了主要竞争对手《卢瑟福郡新闻》和《卢瑟福进取报》。1998年他们把《每日通讯》卖给了肯塔基州的帕克斯顿传媒集团有限公司（Paxton Media Group），这家连锁公司在肯塔基州、北卡罗来纳州、乔治亚州、阿肯色州、印第安纳州、路易斯安那州和田纳西州拥有30多份日报和几十份周报。在他们接手的第一年，公司的新管理层完全重新设计了报纸，把《每日通讯》的单份售价提高了一倍，并且把报纸改为早上出版。

《本周谈》和《每日通讯》的联合创始人都在享受他们提前退休所带来的快乐：比尔比任何时候都喜欢他的高尔夫；罗恩于2008年去世，生前他是各种社区公益活动的参与者。

2001年，我在北卡大学教堂山分校的新闻和大众传媒学院创立了“卡罗来纳社区媒体计划（Carolina Community Media Project）”时，我请罗恩来当董事会顾问。

我依然会不时去第二故乡卢瑟福郡的一个小木屋小住一阵，所以我经常找机会和罗恩在当地的小餐馆小聚一番。通常情况下，当地人看到我俩坐在一起吃三明治的时候，都会盯着我们看，并悄悄地说：“他们不是那谁谁谁吗？他们现在又准备做些什么？”

听到这个，我们会冲着对方咧嘴一笑。

赋予沉默者的《声音》：通过社区报构建桥梁

两份报纸已让我耗尽心血，满是伤痛不忍回望，本以为这辈子不会再有机会做报纸，但奇怪的是似乎总有一根隐形的线连接在我和报纸之间，在合适的时机，它就会现身挑弄我身上那根报人的敏感神经。命运兜兜转转，我再一次义无反顾地从零开始打造一份社区报。

我们的故事

故事以悲剧开场。2008年春天，深受大家喜爱的北卡大学教堂山分校（以下简称UNC）学生会主席伊夫•卡森（Eve Carson）被两个来自达勒姆中心城区的少年残忍地绑架并杀害。之后那些悲伤的日子里，许多老师和学生都在求索着这桩可憎罪行所遗留的教训。不出所料，大多数可传授的经验都是些态度消极的老生常谈：别在晚上一个人外出；教堂山不再如你所认为的那样是个玻璃球中的安乐窝；不要相信来自达勒姆的人……

我们在求索着什么——我们在求索着伊夫•卡森之死的回响，但在此时此刻，似乎注定没有什么积极向上的东西能从这一悲剧中浮现，真的如此吗?

灰烬中重生

也许是命中注定，同年春天，我受邀与另外7位教授组成一个特别小组，研究如何帮助三角地周边的高危社区走向良性发展，我们来自不同科系：医学、人类学、传播与新闻学、城市与区域规划学、社会学、计算机科学、公共卫生学等。也许是巧合，所有研究最终都指向达勒姆，尤其是犯罪猖獗的达勒姆东北部街区（以下简称NECD）。警察们称这里为“公牛之眼”，因为当在地图上标注那些枪击案件、卖淫、毒品交易、已知帮派成员的家时，那些地点形成了一个同心圆，如同放置在地图上的一个箭靶。

城市与区域规划系的助理教授阮梅带着学生走访过达勒姆旧城区，她了解到我创办过报纸，便通过电子邮件告诉我，她的一个博士生提议NECD社区应该拥有一份自己的社区报，想知道我对这个主意有什么看法。

这就是我对伊夫•卡森之死的回应：借助一份社区报挽救问题青年，建设社区，加强公民参与。

我该怎么做?

开创一份商业性报纸，背靠银行就可以了。但开创一家非营利、以志愿者为主、试验性的报纸和网站可需要各型各色的资本。如何建立、与谁建立战略伙伴关系都是亟需明确的事项。

通过阮教授，我联系上了厄尔•菲利普斯（Earl Philips），他是达勒姆街区改进服务部部门助理主任，“大厄尔”是联结非裔美国人社区领袖群和达勒姆市政治力量的重要环节。

下一个同样重要的合作伙伴是当地传统非裔大学（HBCU）和北卡罗来纳中心大学。我获得了来自校园顾问助教德派斯勒（Pyssler）和新闻系助教丽莎•保兰（Lisa Paulin）的热情帮助，他们都意识到这个项目的重要性和改变社区的潜力。

2008年的整个夏天，某种意义上的运作委员会（厄尔、厄尔的助手梅尔瓦、派斯勒、丽莎和我）开始碰头喝咖啡、开会，进行头脑风暴。

在一次起步会议中，我意识到无论是达勒姆城，还是任何个人都无法提供真金白银来支持出版计划。如果得有人去弄到资金的话，那肯定是我。命中注定的好运再次降临，新闻和大众传播学院刚刚雇用了詹妮弗•嘎琳娜（Jennifer Galina）为学院的第一位专职资金申请写手。福星高照，她的专业判断及技巧果然不同凡响，我们顺利地申请到了来自史密斯•雷诺兹基金会（Z. Smith Reynolds Foundation）5万美元的资金。三个月之后，资金缺口就填满了一半。现在所缺的只有我们梦寐以求的新闻编辑室了。

进入课堂

2008年秋季学期开始了。派斯勒、丽莎和我发起了一系列的学生交流活动。我那来自不同学科、不同专业的14个学生（大多数是白人）不时去达勒姆拜访中心大学的学生。同样，那边的学生（全是黑人）也来教堂山拜访我们。这是之前从未有过的团队合作。

但仅那么做还远远不够。

每当聚在一起，学生们却各自独立成两派，导致“交流”的成效寥寥无几，以至于我的学生事后打趣说这是“奥利奥饼干体验”。

我们因此意识到，如果要进行有效交流，教师应安排两组学生互相融合在自然的氛围下交流，因此，车览NECD之旅诞生了。

车览之旅

从2009年1月开始，每个学期之始，我承担起车览之旅的组织工作：两辆大篷货车，特意把两个学校的学生混杂在一起。厄尔坐在一辆上，梅尔瓦坐在另一辆上，在我们乘车穿行NECD的旅程中，他们介绍本地人口数据、历史以及与“公牛之眼”的相关问题。这样的一天在野餐会中结束，来自两所学校的学生记者很自然地有了交流的机会。

招募NECD的青少年：没那么简单

可以肯定地说，唤起本地学校和教会的兴趣可没那么轻而易举。很遗憾，NECD没有自己的高中，孩子们得乘坐公共汽车到6个不同的偏远高中去上学。我没有得到老师——更不用说孩子们——对这个项目兴致勃勃的支持。

同样的事发生在教堂里。当厄尔呼吁地区牧师召开公益会议时，只有一人现身。

我们做错了什么？也许太远离现实，太高高在上了，我被难住了。那真是一个令人愤懑的冬天。九个月过去了，虽然得到了一定的资金，但仍然止步不前。

这个学期，来自UNC的学生们和我一起得到的经验是：社区组织是一项耗时又常常令人沮丧的事业，原来通称的“黑人社区”并不是某种意义上同质化的人群，而更多的是一些高度政治化、容易被激怒、充满妒忌和竞争的“社群”。

来自《沥青脚板日报》（*Daily Tar Heel*）的帮助

很快一切都开始好转。校园报《沥青脚板日报》有意向帮助我们的报纸，随后，董事会通过决议承担一年大约7000美元的印刷费用。

北部威廉•施拉德尔高中（William Schrader of Northern High School）建议我们的报纸向本地青少年开放，而不仅仅局限于NECD的孩子。不久之后，阮教授明智地建议大部分内容应由来自NCCU新闻系的学生提供——与此同时，丽莎、派斯勒和我分别将这个以体验性项目为基础的教学模式引入各自的课堂。

突破

看吧！我们起步了。2009年夏天，我们决定出版五期网络版双周刊。接下来的秋季学期中，为了激发这个教室/新闻编辑室的创新活力，我们三人重设了教学大纲：一周的教学和报道准备，接着是一周的《声音》制作，接着是一周的教学和反思，以及筹划更多的报道……如此循环往复。

为《声音》命名

但我在订制时间表的过程中遇到了另一个关键问题：给这份报纸起什么名字？“公牛之眼新闻”这样的名字肯定是行不通的——我一直自然而然地这样称呼，直至一位非裔城市领袖尖锐地指出，“公牛之眼”是个谁都不喜欢的负面词语。我深为自己的愚钝脸红。

每一对父母都知道起名这件事十分重要。我原本认为NECD的社区报应该由本地青少年来命名，以此唤起他们的自主权和荣誉感。但我们连个青少年都找不到。

如果仍将这份报纸叫作“东北达勒姆社区报”就过于无聊和冗长了。这个项目和这份报纸应该得到——也需要得到——一个能够体现出个性、使命与实质的生动报名。

在与NECD社区合作伙伴们会面和讨论的整整一年时间里，我们总是听到有人如是说：“我希望我们的声音能够被听见……”，还有“我们希望在洽商中有一个声音”，以及那句史上著名的非裔口号“赋予沉默者一个声音”，于是这个报名——《声音》——像是有自己的生命般地冒了出来，在我们眼前绽放。

在一次头脑风暴中，我和学生卡莉•布兰特梅耶（Carly Brantmeyer）想到了与报名相关的口号：“我们的社区。我们的时代。我们的声音。”

报名和口号紧密结合，被社区欣然接受。

谁教会了谁?

我也在一点点进步。2009年那个令人不愉快的冬天里，新闻摄影专业的卡莉带来一个社区新闻课毕业设计的新点子。她要给内城区的救世军男孩女孩俱乐部青少年们上摄影课。她还告诉我，她想用《声音》的新相机。

我的回应可没有那么热情。

“你是说，我的相机？你要带着我用项目资金买的相机到内城区去？”

卡莉不动声色地劝说：“你已经有相机了，而且你又不用新相机。”

“它们可是为了报纸买的。”我回嘴。

“但你的报纸现在还没出呢。”她温柔地提醒我。

卡莉•布兰特梅耶用她与生俱来的说服力战胜了我。但我仍然不会让那些相机在去内城区的旅途中脱离我的监护。

另一个灵感时刻

卡莉的首堂摄影课让我当即意识到我的偏见。她站在那里，一个惹人讨厌的陌生人，面对着满满一教室乖戾的、眼神沉重的非裔和拉丁裔学生——却在几分钟内使他们都投入到关于构图、取景、光圈等的激烈讨论中。当孩子们把他们的手放到相机上并开始把玩、拍摄和体验的时候，我似乎能感觉到他们身上发生的细微变化。

被改变的不仅是孩子，还有我自己：如果我想接触内城区的孩子们，我就得给出他们需要的东西。就那么简单。

接下来的十周内，卡莉和我，还有与我们同来的UNC学生，目睹着这些原本冷漠的孩子成长为摄影师，在课程的最后几天举办了自己的摄影展。

学期结束了，卡莉也离开了，去完成她的夏季摄影之旅。但她已经给我指明了方向。通过一系列佛教称之为“吉祥因缘”的事件，我为另外两组NECD的大学生安排了相似的摄影课程，一组在跷跷板工作室，另一组在位于SEEDS的达勒姆中心花园。

罗恩•帕里斯基金会

为了让孩子们能看到自己的学习成果，最好的办法就是给他们办影展，但我们如何支付得起三个摄影展（每一个都价格不菲）的费用？

与我一同出版社区报的前合作伙伴罗恩•帕里斯于2008年8月逝世，我曾为他设立一个纪念基金会。我们并没有募集到太多资金，但数目足以为摄影展的印刷和布展提供充分支持，罗恩•帕里斯的遗孀贾妮丝，终生致力于为卢瑟福郡有特殊需求的孩子提供服务，因此我认为使用罗恩的基金帮助那些处于危机之中的年轻人是纪念他的最好方式。还要赘上一笔：当大学城商场的沃尔夫相机店获悉达勒姆项目后，慷慨地减免了印刷照片的大笔费用。

夏天结束之前，我已经给老城区的另外20个孩子开设了摄影课，并组织了另两场摄影展。更重要的是，摄影课为我们正在孕育中的《声音》编辑部补充了少年记者：编辑泽耐泽勒•巴尼斯（Zenezele Barnes）、美术合作编辑罗萨利亚•普莱斯（Rosalia Preiss）和普雷西奥•威尔逊-盖（Praycious Wilson-Gay）表现抢眼而逐步成为骨干。

和妈妈们有关

这是我一路走来学到的另一件事：想接触到孩子们？最好先接触妈妈们。近两年里，不止一次，某个不苟言笑、不眨眼的非裔妈妈直接质问我：“你要在这里泡多久啊？”寥寥三言两语似乎在告诉我：你最好不要成为另一个抱着不实际改良主义过来施恩于黑人的白人教授，利用达勒姆来为自己赚取支票和学术名声！

我明白。一清二楚。

找到突破口

说的已经足够，是做事的时候了。第一步是将发行日定在2009年9月24日，之后“三管齐下”地协调内容供应者：丽莎在NCCU的高端报道班、我的社区新闻班，还有三位青少年作者/编辑。同时，新闻学院的IT专家佛瑞德•汤姆森（Fred Thomsen）和杰•阿尔莫斯（Jay Almers）用博客软件Wordpress设计了《声音》网站。

在秋季学期的课程中，我的学生艾米莉（Emily）和考特尼（Courtney）带领大家出版了《声音》的5期双周版本。艾米莉甚至为《声音》工作人员们设计了彩色T恤，在毕业设计中，《声音》的同仁们在工作手册编辑朱利安•马驰（Julian March）的指导下，创作出了第一本《〈声音〉编辑手册和设计指南》。

星球大战

地点。地点。地点。

在拥有一个安全、便利、免租的空间用来“罩住我们”之前，我不相信这个项目将会真正地在本地青少年中流行开来。即使有人提供免费印刷，那又怎样？我们连新闻编辑室都无法落到实处，一切都是纸上谈兵。

2009年“大厄尔”的街区改进服务部办公室迁到了由曾经的纺织厂改造的艺术街区。这可是NECD的黄金地段！

当看到这个新办公区时，我告诉厄尔，能否在这里为《声音》找一个办公室。我们在焦虑中等待了几个月，对方没有一点动静。2009年8月12日，在没有先兆的情况下，厄尔突然打来电话说产权所有人已表态可以为《声音》提供六个月的免费租期（可续租）。原来，一切又归功于阮教授，她的学生史蒂芬•费边（Stephen Fabian）在厄尔办公室做暑期实习，利用这个机会，他再次替《声音》提出免费租用办公室的请求，有关各方经过五个月的法律细节磋商，终获通过。2010年1月的第一周，我们搬进了自己的新闻编辑室，那里办公设备齐全，桌子、文件柜和墙壁上都装饰着夏季摄影课中拍摄的照片。

“数字鸿沟”与不会消亡的报纸

近几年来，菲尔•梅耶对这个行业的末日审判书——“消失的报纸”正在话题的风口浪尖之上。大报已死。

但我认为，社区报会生存下来并且蒸蒸日上地发展。它存在的时间，将远远超过那些专业葬礼承办人所预言的死亡时间。

看吧：从2009年的9月份到2010年的3月份，我们发行了七期《声音》的线上版本，只收获了边缘性的公众反应。而当发行量达2000份、16版的纸质版被分发到50个学校、教堂、企业、政府机关的周边地点后，却引发了大量的评论、媒体报道、电子邮件、电话和Facebook上的“赞”。

在达勒姆的出版开始之前，我听说过“数字鸿沟”，但我一直都没有意识到这个鸿沟已经如此之深。NECD的许多居民要么没有电脑，要么只有一台系统崩溃的电脑，要么无法承担奢侈的上网费用。因此，我的学生和我所直接领悟到的是：《声音》在线网站应是一种“衍生媒体”，是那份对开的、用纸和油墨印刷的《声音》的增强版。

致谢一

出于各种目的或直觉或推理，唱衰报业的声音越来越响亮，一片鼓噪声中，这本书像荒腔走板的调门踩不上点，但她历经几年才终得面世证明实在不是冲动的产物。

多年前，在图书馆书架上不经意抽出英文版《社区新闻——无以复加的当地化》一书时，乍一接触激情喷射的笔触，美国新闻人的职业追求和饱满的成就感让已接受了客观冷静是新闻标签说法的我甚至有点恍惚。“社区新闻到底是什么令人着迷的东西？”的好奇从此埋在心底，只要有机会我就想去一探究竟。不曾料想这种邂逅可以如此丰厚地改变我的学术乃至生命体验。一路走来，要感谢的人实在太多，在此仅就与此书有直接关联的人略表真诚的谢意。

这个世界表面浮华纷扰，借助社区报这个媒介，我得以走出书斋感受真实的行业脉动，并遇到了坚守职业理想的同道中人。理想是精神层面的奢侈品，尤其在功利氛围过于浓厚的社会，注定属于极小众的追求。无论国内还是国外，真正能享受社区报出版的人共享某种不变的特质：低调、平和，多多少少带有柏拉图气质。因为如果你想赚大钱，社区报则无法满足欲望，尽管单份报纸利润高，但受制于不能做大的特性，总量并不大；如果你想追求呼风唤雨的影响力，一言九鼎，社区报同样会让你失望，因为你服务的对象是生活在聚光灯之外、普通如尘埃的邻家读者和小广告商，尽管他们会给你零距离的情感回报，分贝却不足以撼动世界。从事社区报出版的满足感可能只有自己冷暖自知。

《珠江时报》系列社区报在我心目中是个标杆。它从2009年单薄的一份发展到2013年底的7份，发行量达到35万份，而且扩张趋势还在继续，其蜕变最难能可贵之处在于摸索出一套具有中国特色的办报模式：以服务社会为首要责任，最终实现媒体、政府与民众诉求的共赢。在媒体经济属性被过分强调而社会属性不断弱化的时代，《珠江时报》的一系列社区报偏安一隅不急于赢利的淡定与坚守，确属异类，弥足珍贵。

李国臣总编是个勤于学习的媒体人，2009年在准备出版社区报的初始阶段，可供研究的资料非常有限，他尽可能把所有国内外资料都找来，其中包括这本书的原版，在网上半懂不懂费力翻译了十几页后知难而退，但他实际上并没死心，后来还盘算着找几个英语过硬的记者把一些重要章节翻译出来，当然难度也是超出想象。几年前听闻我将着手翻译时，他非常支持："需要帮助的话，我会尽力。"感谢报社的支持让所有参与翻译的学生终有一种劳动获得认可的满足感。

当翻译终成，回头看，我是一步步被周遭怀揣新闻理想的朋友们推着走完这个过程的。南方日报出版社向以出版高品质传媒书籍而得到业界高度认可，编辑阮清钰主动提议我把此书引介进来时，我至今仍很清楚地记得他说的一句话：为了社会效益，值得去做这事。尽管当时手头要完成的东西很多，但我内心清楚这是一个充满诱惑而无法拒绝的邀请。

从另外一个角度，出版的欲望是崇高的欲望，对任何一位国外学者，著作有机会在中国面世，仅仅想到庞大的读者基数就是令人激动不已的期盼，为了把当初点燃我探究激情的薪火传导给更多有相近追求的人，某种程度上也算是礼尚往来，这是我能送给Jock最好的礼物。

为了降低出版成本，在征得作者同意的情况下，我们小心翼翼地向美国出版方提出：考虑到中国高度异质的文化特性，如果直接翻译，可能传播效果会大打折扣，能否以此书为蓝本进行改写从而免交版权费？视知识产权为圣物的美国人居然破天荒地亮起了绿灯，同样，他们说了一句似曾耳熟的话：希望社区报能让中国社会受益。

接下来最现实的问题是谁来做初稿翻译，既没有科研经费，也没有带研究生，一穷二白的我只能动员所教公共英语课的本科生。很多人刚一开始很兴奋，不敢相信自己的文字居然有望某一天变成白纸黑字，但这种热情很快消退，专有名词、特定时代的社会现象、俚语比比皆是，每一个陌生的表述都需要查阅大量的资料最后浓缩成几个字，才能看明白作者的意图。而且鲜活的美式英语与我们在国内课堂上学到的英语差距之大不经过这种实操很难想象，比如kids at risk，按照字面理解是处于险境的孩子，但与作者核实后，结合上下文，他所指的是问题青少年；graphs，查遍所有字典依然无果，最后才知道居然是paragraphs的缩写。结果参与者名单被拉得很长，不断有学生退出，接着不明就里的学生又被忽悠进来，再退出。周而复始，所有人都期盼这个过程早点结束吧。

让我欣慰的是从头到尾坚持下来的段宜飞同学经过这一过程的历练，像凤凰涅槃般脱胎换骨，展现了完全不同于同龄学生的能力、视野及抱负，感谢他的成长减轻了我把重担强加于稚嫩肩膀的负疚感，让我明白任何事都可以导向完全不同的结局，关键在于是否有足够坚强的内心去接受挑战，重压不是每个人都能承受的，但是颤颤巍巍能站起来，坚实的第一步迈出之后，心有多大，天就可以被撑得有多大。

说句实话，读翻译过来的外文书总给我一种隔靴搔痒的不爽，翻译不到位，或者太忠实于原著使得表述不符合中文规范等障碍都降低了阅读的流畅与快感。为了尽可能擦掉翻译的痕迹，拿着学生翻译的初稿，2013年暑假，我在美国开始和作者面对面一一推敲，或者删掉过于美国化的案例，或者改写增加具有普遍意义能产生共鸣的细节。不过障碍其实依然存在，社区报散落于美国各个角落，很多地名中国人闻所未闻；作者每引用一句短短的话或者介绍一个简单的事件，他都习惯性地一一注明“谁”“来自哪里”，这些在译者看来可有可无的信息却是美国尊重个体文化的惯性表达，而且与社区报核心理念高度重合，尽管翻起来看起来都很吃力，思量再三，最终尽可能保留以体现原汁原味。

世界像个高速旋转的离心机，在不明就里的情况下，甩掉了应该或不应该保留的东西，其实不管未来如何变幻，社会正常运转总需要类似于一些压舱石的东西。

感谢每一个花时间和金钱买书并看完此书的读者，社会需要一部分耐得住寂寞的人静下心来，踏踏实实做点事，让我们为保留这些原本可以让世界显得更温情的东西一起努力吧。

陈凯

2014年3月

致谢二

我有幸在三年前走进陈老师的大学英语课堂，其时她刚从美国访学归来，忙于把社区报的研究成果集结成书，很多英语资料的翻译急需人手，从此我断断续续地介入与社区报相关的编译事务。作为非新闻专业的学生，社区报于我的意义很少涉及报业模式或者新闻理想——然而社区报赠予我的是观察周边世界的一种视角，并在我的大学课外生活中贯穿始终，最终为我打开了一扇与大部分同学不同的门。

重新发现社区

刚入大学校门，我和两位同学很快就开始在打工子弟爱心会担任志愿者，每周倒两趟班车，穿过正在大拆大建、繁华与贫穷并存的京郊，到东五环外的社区中心，为附近几所打工子弟的孩子们提供课后作业辅导。刚刚走出高中校园的我们震惊于这里巨大的贫富差距和机会差距，对“实现社区参与与赋权（empowerment）”有着幼稚的热情，却不知如何思考并付诸行动。

这时社区报研究令我有幸接触并协助翻译了许多第一手资料。其中一份介绍北卡罗来纳大学教堂山分校新闻学院创办社区报《声音》的故事令我惊喜：这份社区报由大学师生发起，为生活在黑人聚居区的青少年们提供成为编辑或记者的培训，通过对本地新闻的报道，为居民们创造出凝聚社区的力量——这个故事的背景与我在志愿服务中接触到的流动人口社区有诸多相似之处。原来翻译中纸面上“社区建设”“社区归属感”“参与型社区”等词汇中的“社区”，与我在漫天沙尘的京郊建筑工地间接触到的社区，是同样一个概念！“社区”对我而言，不再是地理上的人口聚集地，而是共享社会意义的社会关系组成的网络。一年之后，我转任“生活职业技能培训”项目的教师，这个项目所面向的是16至22岁的贫困打工青少年，为他们提供为期4个月的生活与职业技能培训。这一次，我的学生多数都与我同龄，在他们的帮助和社区报的启发下，我得以用全新的眼光开始“重新发现社区”：社区中心的教育项目将原本互不相识的外来居民联系起来，资源和信息自发地在这个逐步建立起来的社区关系网络中开始流动，居民们甚至主动贡献出时间和精力来探讨公共场所的轮流维护问题；孩子们对社区中心的喜爱，带来了居民对社区中心的认同，这又进一步增加了居民对整个社区的归属感。孩子们点滴积累的成就维系着居民之间的情感纽带——社区报教会我“重新发现社区”，教会我重视人与人之间联结的力量。真正能永久搏动社区心跳的，是社会资本的构建，是居民自治与参与的力量。

社区即田野，生活即田野

公益组织的实习结束后，我创建了一个独立的公益主题播客“重述”。“重述”每期在苹果的音乐商店中发布，访问一位在公益、社会创新等领域有独特想法的同龄人：由环境工程转到NGO管理方向的研究生、几度回访支教地的学姐、渴望颠覆刻板印象的工科女孩、创办独立杂志关注城市中人的哲学系学生……每人来讲一个自己的故事。“讲故事”的想法也是我从社区报中学来的——在传播的过程中，故事这一形式更能唤起人们的共鸣，具有打动人心的力量。更难得的是，社区报的“讲故事”能把每个人物和现象都描述得栩栩如生，记录下外界看来静止不变的人和社区，将他们融入社会结构的具体投影之中。

社区报教会我通过对个体的关注，从而达成理解，以小见大，最终为自己身处的社区和陌生的社区，带去一些帮助和改变，哪怕十分渺小微弱，而与之相关的公益经历则让我在现实生活中接触到不同的群体和他们的文化。这些经历最终引导我选择了人类学作为自己的研究生方向，并得以被该领域一流的机构录取。我在申请中这样解释自己的背景：“我学习社会人类学的动机和愿望，缘于我在社区志愿服务期间的经验，以及我所阅读的与社区相关的书——我阅读这些书是为了了解一些对我而言陌生的文化群体。对个体人的思想和行为的好奇，对理解不同群体生活方式，阐述共性和多样性的渴望，构成了我申请人类学系的理由。”

人类学有一个重要的研究方法与研究传统：“做田野（调查）。”与社区报息息相关的这三年，就好像是做了一场边界模糊的“田野”——混杂各式各样的人类学关键词：城市化对传统社区的冲击、文化与社会的变迁、社会分层、移民、大众媒体、跨文化比较、参与观察、结构性与非结构性的访谈……社区报给予我发现它们的视野。在这种视野中，社区即田野，生活即田野。

感谢与我一起经历这场田野的师弟师妹们，尤其是段宜飞师弟，在编译的过程中我有许多力所不能及之处，他的坚韧与鼓励是编译的最大动力。

也感谢陈老师以及社区报人们，陈老师对工作的热情、对学生的真诚，都令我受益良多，他们乐于与初出茅庐的学生们分享宝贵的经验与知识，并宽容我们在工作中的稚嫩和业余。感谢你们带我走进这场生活的田野。

江舟忆

中国传媒大学文化产业管理2014届